Growth with Equity

Growth with Equity

Economic Policymaking for the Next Century

MARTIN NEIL BAILY
GARY BURTLESS
ROBERT E. LITAN

The Brookings Institution
Washington, D.C.

Copyright © 1993 by
THE BROOKINGS INSTITUTION
1775 Massachusetts Ave., N.W., Washington, D.C. 20036

Library of Congress Cataloging-in-Publication Data

Baily, Martin Neil.
    Growth with equity : economic policymaking for the next century /
Martin N. Baily, Gary T. Burtless, and Robert E. Litan.
        p.   cm.
    Includes bibliographical references and index.
    ISBN 0-8157-0766-5 (alk. paper). — ISBN 0-8157-0765-7 (pbk. : alk.
paper)
    1. United States—Economic policy—1981–   2. United States—
Economic conditions—1981–   3. Income distribution—United
States.   4. Technological innovations—Economic aspects—United
States.   5. Labor supply—United States.   6. Investments—
United States.   I. Burtless, Gary T., 1950–   II. Litan, Robert E.
III. Title.
HC106.8.B345   1993
338.973—dc20   92-44225
                                                                                CIP

9 8 7 6 5 4 3 2 1

1000247992

Foreword

THE 1992 presidential campaign was fought and decided on the issue of improving the U.S. economy. After the long expansion of the 1980s, the painful recession of the early 1990s seemed to awaken Americans to the fact that the economic pie was growing very slowly and was being divided up into increasingly unequal slices. Living standards of middle-class families have grown slowly for two decades; living standards of the poor have fallen.

The crucial factor that determines whether living standards will rise or fall is worker productivity. Since the early 1970s, American productivity growth has been sluggish, leading to slow growth in wages and family incomes. The staff and trustees of Brookings considered this problem so important that in 1987 the institution established a Center on Economic Progress and Employment, whose mission has been to encourage, support, and publish research on the main causes of the productivity slowdown and the poor performance of the U.S. labor market. The center's first book, published in 1988, was *American Living Standards: Threats and Challenges*, which described the nature and scope of the nation's main economic problems. Since 1988 the center has supported research projects that produced eight more books and five annual issues of *Brookings Papers on Economic Activity, Microeconomics* (see the appendix to this volume).

This book represents the final volume to be published by the center. Martin Neil Baily, Gary Burtless, and Robert E. Litan analyze the problems that have been the focus of the center's research, and they suggest policies that address these long-term problems. The two issues they concentrate on are highlighted by the title of the book: slow productivity growth and increasing income inequality. Some of their recommended solutions will not come as a surprise to readers of earlier

Brookings volumes. For example, they argue that better economic performance can be achieved through an increase in U.S. investment, which in turn can be accomplished through sustained and systematic deficit reduction. As voters demonstrated in the 1980s, this suggestion involves great political pain and is likely to be the topic of heated debate for many years.

Baily, Burtless, and Litan do not suggest that the large deficit is the sole policy issue facing the government, however. They provide a range of policy proposals to spur innovation, improve corporate decisionmaking, expand international trade, and increase the amount of investment in worker training, especially of the less skilled. Many of these policies could be adopted even if the government fails to eliminate its deficit. Each of the suggested policies is aimed at boosting growth, improving the equity of the American income distribution, or accomplishing both goals at the same time. The authors caution that slow growth and rising inequality are deep-seated problems that will not be eliminated soon, even if sensible policies are adopted immediately.

Martin Neil Baily is a professor of economics at the University of Maryland and a special guest scholar in the Economic Studies program at Brookings. Gary Burtless and Robert E. Litan are senior fellows in the same program. Litan also directed the Center for Economic Progress and Employment and currently directs the Brookings Center for Economics, Law, and Politics.

The authors are grateful to the many persons who provided valuable comments and suggestions on an early draft, including Henry J. Aaron, Margaret M. Blair, Barry P. Bosworth, Edward F. Denison, Paul R. Krugman, William D. Nordhaus, Timothy Taylor, Charles L. Schultze, Clifford M. Winston, and an anonymous referee. The authors are particularly grateful for the insightful suggestions of Edward Denison, who provided extensive comments on the manuscript shortly before his death on October 23, 1992.

James Schneider edited the manuscript, Laura Kelly and David Bearce verified its factual content, and Susan Woollen prepared it for typesetting. Kathleen M. Bucholz, E. Carole Hingleton, Susanne E. Lane, Valerie M. Owens, Anita G. Whitlock, and Kathleen Elliott Yinug provided secretarial assistance. Brian Friedman, Maya MacGuineas, Karen McClure, Suzanne Smith, and Kirsten Wallenstein provided valuable research assistance.

Funding for this project was provided by the Center for Economic Progress and Employment, whose supporters comprise Donald S. Perkins; Aetna Life and Casualty Company; American Express Philanthropic program; AT&T Foundation; The Chase Manhattan Bank, N.A.; Cummins Engine Foundation; The Ford Foundation; Ford Motor Company Fund; General Electric Foundation; Hewlett-Packard Company; Institute for International Economic Studies; Morgan Stanley & Company, Inc.; Motorola Foundation; The Prudential Foundation; Alfred P. Sloan Foundation; Springs Industries, Inc.; Union Carbide Corporation; Alex C. Walker Foundation and Charitable Trust; Warner-Lambert Company; and Xerox Corporation.

The views expressed here are those of the authors and should not be attributed to the trustees, officers, or other staff members of the Brookings Institution.

BRUCE K. MACLAURY
President

February 1993
Washington, D.C.

This book is dedicated to the memory of

Edward F. Denison

*a pioneering contributor to the literature on economic growth
and a deeply cherished colleague*

Contents

Tables

Figures

One

Introduction and Summary

FOR NEARLY TWO DECADES the U.S. economy has been plagued by two disturbing economic trends: anemic productivity improvement and growing inequality in the distribution of income.

In the quarter century after 1948, during what now appears to have been a golden age of economic growth, output per person grew faster than 2.5 percent a year, a rate high enough to double the living standard of an average American in less than thirty years. But since 1973 output has grown just 1.2 percent a year. Americans must now wait twice as long—sixty years—to see their incomes double.

At the same time, fewer people now feel that their incomes are close to average because U.S. incomes have been growing less equal. In the twenty-five years ending in 1973, families at both ends of the income spectrum as well as those in the middle enjoyed income gains of 2 percent a year. Since 1973, however, the income distribution has grown markedly less equal. The most affluent U.S. households have continued to enjoy moderate gains, but families near the bottom of the income distribution have seen hardly any income growth at all. Many have suffered losses in inflation-adjusted, or real, income.

The American economic pie has been getting larger far more slowly than it did during most of the postwar era. And the pie has been sliced more unevenly. In the next decade and beyond, the nation faces no more urgent economic challenge than reversing these two trends.

On the surface it would appear that the 1992 presidential election served as a referendum on how best to meet this challenge. Getting the economy moving again was, after all, the central issue in the campaign. Bill Clinton largely owed his success in the election to the fact that under George Bush the economy grew at a slower pace—less than 1 percent a year—than during any four-year presidential term since Herbert Hoover's.

In fact, however, the economic concerns that prompted many Americans to vote an incumbent president out of office were focused on short-run problems. The rise in the unemployment rate during the last two years of the Bush presidency made millions of Americans nervous about the security of their own jobs. The slow pace of recovery from the 1990–91 recession did little to allay those fears.

The economy will eventually recover. Unemployment will fall to something approaching its full-employment level, between 5 and 6 percent. This is the lowest rate of unemployment that does not generate accelerating inflation. The recovery may be slow and disappointing, but if the economy follows the postwar pattern, a recovery will eventually occur.

We are not concerned in this book with short-run fluctuations in the business cycle, however. We take a much longer view. What happens when the economy does recover? How fast can it expand after the nation reaches full employment? What steps can America take now and in the next decade to boost the rate of long-run growth? How can income disparities be narrowed? Income inequality can be reduced through rearranging tax burdens and offering more generous government benefits, but can it also be reduced through improvements in the distribution of earnings and other market incomes?

These are the questions addressed in this book. Our answers are based largely on research sponsored by the Center for Economic Progress and Employment at Brookings.[1] But many other economists working in universities, private research organizations, and government have also explored these questions, and our analysis draws on their research as well. This book represents an attempt to derive the pertinent lessons from a growing body of evidence on the determinants of long-term economic performance.

Readers seeking a quick, simple cure for the nation's economic woes will be disappointed by this book. The twin problems of slow growth and increasing inequality have been with us too long to be solved overnight or even in one or two presidential terms. The problems cannot be slain with a magic bullet. The nation was promised a miracle cure for its economic ills in the early 1980s. Enthusiasts in the Reagan administration claimed that lower income tax rates across the board would release a surge of saving, investment, work effort, and entrepreneurial enterprise, the combination of which would permanently raise the rate of economic growth. In the short run the tax cut of 1981 did help the economy recover from the deepest recession since the Great Depression. But it did so primarily by stimulating business and consumer demand for goods and services. We see little evidence that the tax cuts had their intended long-run supply-side effects. The underlying growth rate of the economy rose little if at all after 1981. Meanwhile, the inequality among family incomes, whether measured before or after taxes, increased throughout the 1980s. The tax and transfer policies enacted during the Reagan presidency contributed to the widening inequality.

A variety of other remedies has been suggested to improve the long-run performance of the economy. Some analysts have urged the United States to adopt Japanese-style industrial policy, in which the federal government would encourage investment in specific industries and lines of production, both through subsidies and, if need be, through trade protection. Others have argued for unprecedented new investment in public infrastructure. For reasons we discuss later in this book, these approaches and others have been oversold. Some would even slow the economy further.

We take a more eclectic and cautious approach to increasing long-run growth and improving distributional equity. We do not believe that any single policy reform can miraculously revitalize the U.S. economy. There are no magic bullets. Policymakers and economists should face this truth squarely.

Instead of magic bullets we suggest policies that offer a plausible prospect for increasing long-term growth and improving the distribution of incomes. The benefits of these policies may not be visible immediately, but we are not primarily interested in boosting short-term economic performance. Some of our recommendations are politically painful: like many other economists, for example, we recommend a purposeful, long-range policy to reduce the government's deficit. But other proposals, such as permanent tax incentives for investment and for research and development, are much more politically attractive. We did not, however, use political criteria in choosing our proposals. Instead, we chose actions we believe are most likely, given the available evidence, to improve both growth and equity over the long run.

Growth and Equity: Compatible Objectives

In the next two chapters we outline in some detail the evidence documenting the slowdown in growth and the widening of income inequality. We also explain why we believe encouraging growth and ensuring equity rank as the two most important economic objectives for the foreseeable future.

Before turning to those topics and to our recommendations, we digress briefly to consider the idea that faster economic growth and greater income equality are inconsistent objectives. Our late Brookings colleague and mentor, Arthur Okun, appeared to suggest such an inconsistency in his celebrated book on the "big trade-off" between equality and economic efficiency.[2] The economic agendas of both political parties over the past decade also seem to have accepted the idea of an inevitable trade-off between economic equity and growth. With its emphasis on tax cuts, especially for the wealthy, the Republican party certainly placed far more emphasis on economic growth than on equity. Conversely, Democrats have tended to oppose Republican-proposed business and capital gains tax cuts largely on the grounds that such reforms would be inequitable. More broadly, the Democratic party has for years been associated in the public mind with favoring changes in the tax code to redistribute income. Many Democrats have placed far less emphasis on designing tax policy to enhance long-term growth.

It is time for both parties to move beyond this sterile debate. In fact, there is no reason why growth and equity need always be inconsistent. Recent economic history provides abundant evidence that progress toward both can be achieved at the same time. In the 1960s, for example, the nation enjoyed rapid growth—indeed the fastest economic growth of the postwar era—and a sizable reduction in income inequality. Conversely, the 1980s stands as a decade of both disappointing growth and rising inequality.

Indeed, there are good reasons to believe that appropriate policies for raising economic growth and improving the distribution of economic rewards are inextricably intertwined. The connections are both economic and political. The U.S. economy can grow faster if workers with the fewest skills—and the lowest incomes—are helped to learn more skills. (We define a more skilled labor force as one that can produce more goods or services per hour worked than the current labor force and that can turn out goods and services of higher quality.) Workers with more skills have greater flexibility and mobility than workers with fewer skills. This advantage means they can move from declining to expanding industries and will suffer shorter spells of unemployment when they lose their jobs. If job loss does not result in lengthy spells of unemployment, policymakers can push the economy to lower levels of unemployment without igniting extra inflation. The result can be faster growth *and* greater equality of income.

In addition, the economy can grow faster if extra resources are devoted to addressing the serious problems—crime, drug abuse, limited educational opportunities, lack of access to medical care—faced by the least fortunate in our society. As a practical matter, these problems now act as a drag on our economy.[3] The prevalence of serious crime not only requires heavy public expenditure to capture, try, and imprison lawbreakers, it also encourages wasteful private spending to protect American homes and businesses. In a society in which people are more respectful of laws, these precautions would not be needed. If schools do not teach children the skills they need to succeed in the labor market, society eventually pays for that failure when children grow up and cannot support themselves and their dependents. The results show up in larger public budgets for welfare, remedial education, training programs for adults, and the criminal justice system.

The nation also needs to grow faster to address the problems posed by growing income inequality. It is no accident that antipoverty programs were more popular in the high-growth 1960s than in the slow-growth 1970s and 1980s. Middle-class taxpayers find generosity more affordable when their own incomes are growing strongly. Slow growth in recent years has prompted concern among many Americans about their future welfare and that of their children. When the middle class is uncertain about its own economic prospects, it feels less obligation and willingness to help fellow citizens who are further down the economic ladder.

Our interest in promoting economic growth does not rest on a desire to restore Great Society programs, however. Simple redistribution from the rich to the poor can decrease poverty and improve the income distribution statistics, but this improvement does not change the basic conditions that lead to poverty in the first place. We are mainly interested in changing the conditions that lead to low earned income among the least skilled. But it is important to recognize that there is no free lunch in addressing social problems. Successful social programs usually require money. The faster the economy grows, the easier—and more politically palatable—it will be to fund these programs.

We admit, of course, that some policies that would speed long-run growth are inconsistent with equity. Similarly, policies that improve distributional equity, at least in the short run, may be inconsistent with growth. As we will discuss in chapter 7, for example, freer trade induces domestic firms and workers to raise their productivity to remain competitive. This almost certainly boosts long-term economic performance. But free trade also exposes some American workers to international competition that can reduce their earnings and cost them their jobs. Less skilled American workers come into direct competition with workers in other countries who have similar skills, but are often paid much less. Trade protection can reduce the harm inflicted on less skilled American workers, but it can also stunt U.S. economic performance. We recommend policies that can help preserve free trade while protecting or improving the job prospects of workers harmed by freer international competition.

We also acknowledge some short-term considerations that affect equity. Policies designed to accelerate growth also accelerate change, forcing many workers to learn new skills and seek new jobs. Indeed, productivity growth and improvements in living standards cannot occur unless some workers are continually displaced. To an important degree, unemployment can be minimized, and inflation kept stable, using a combination of suitable macroeconomic policies. But even the best macroeconomic policies will have unsatisfying results if workers lack the skills that give them the flexibility to move to new jobs. Unless the nation finds better ways to ease the disruptions caused by economic change, those most at risk from change will seek to block it. The policies that offer the best opportunity to improve the nation's long-term economic performance may never be adopted.

What we advance in the pages that follow is a comprehensive program for encouraging long-run growth that, at the same time, does not damage equity. Several suggested policies would significantly improve distributional equity. By adopting an appropriate mix of policies, the United States does not need to sacrifice progress toward greater equality to achieve faster economic growth.

A Framework for Enhancing Growth and Equity

In constructing a program to address deep-seated economic problems, it is natural to begin by looking at the recent past to diagnose what went wrong. If the underlying causes of slow growth and increased inequality can be identified, suitable remedial policies can be devised and the problems solved.

A cottage industry has developed within the economics profession that focuses on explaining the disappointing slowdown in productivity growth. This slowdown has not been restricted to the United States; it has occurred in nearly all industrialized countries. Various suspected causes have been identified, including the aftereffects of oil price shocks of the past two decades, a slowdown in innovation, an increase in regulatory burdens, deteriorating educational performance, and so on.[4] A similar search for an explanation has focused on identifying the villain behind the deepening income inequality in the United States. Some have pinned the blame on tougher foreign competition, which they say has caused the loss of high-paying manufacturing jobs. Others see fading unionization or a stagnant minimum wage as the culprit.

In the next two chapters, we briefly review the research on these issues. We summarize what economists have been able to learn about the main questions, but we do not pretend to resolve all the difficult issues that still divide scholars. The inability to resolve issues does not mean, however, that policymakers should wait until analysts fully understand why growth has slowed or incomes have become less equal before doing something to reverse the trends. Citizens and politicians will not wait for answers. Still, if policies are to be adopted to improve productivity and distributional equity, people should be offered a reasonable interpretation of the information we already have and the uncertainties that remain. Otherwise, enthusiasts for implausible and potentially harmful magic-bullet theories will charge in. (Many already have.)

The economist's challenge is to develop policies that have a reasonable chance to improve both growth and equity, based on the evidence available, without raising unrealistic expectations about the magnitude of improvement. Several kinds of evidence are useful for this purpose, and we use all of them. We can examine the results of policies that have already been tried, both in the United States and elsewhere. Where evidence about actual policies is not available, we can turn to economic theory, and even common sense.

Unfortunately, the answers provided by economic experiments are not and never will be as clear-cut as those provided by experiments in the physical sciences. Economists and policymakers can only rarely perform pure experiments because the economy is affected by many forces at the same time. Analysts try to take account of the influence of other forces when measuring the effects of specific policies, but the limitations of data and statistical science mean that they cannot guarantee total success. The measurement problem is especially acute when one attempts to determine the long-run impact of particular policies, such as increased spending on education or research and development. One reason economists so often appear to offer conflicting advice, even when they agree on basic economic theory, is that they disagree on the interpretation of evidence about past policy experiments. Another reason is that some economists require less evidence than others for boldly recommending policy changes.

We think it appropriate to acknowledge that the evidence is not equally strong for all of our recommendations. For some proposals the evidence seems solid. For others the support is reasonably strong but not absolutely conclusive. And for still others the case is admittedly speculative but plausible. We try to make clear in the discussion and the concluding chapter how strong the evidence is for specific proposals.

A medical analogy may be instructive. Physicians have been struggling for decades to determine the underlying causes of heart disease and cancer. In fact, there has been a great deal of progress toward understanding. We now have better knowledge, for example, about what foods and genetic factors are likely to increase the incidence of both diseases. This knowledge is often helpful in diagnosis and treatment. But knowing why a particular patient has heart disease or cancer may not always help cure the illness (although it may help prevent a worsening of the condition). Instead, physicians are likely to recommend various treatments—prescription drugs, chemotherapy, surgery—that bear little relationship to the underlying causes. They suggest these treatments based on how successful similar treatments have been in the past and their judgments about research evidence

on promising new therapies. Meanwhile, research scientists and physicians continue to search for new cures through experimentation,
guided by their current understanding of medical science.

Economists have a similar role in diagnosing the problems of a
faltering economy. As researchers we have developed some understanding of the functioning of the economy and the sources of its ills.
Some, but not all, of this understanding can be helpful in framing
policies that will address the problems. But when forced to prescribe
a course of treatment for a particular affliction, we cannot always rely
on the available scientific evidence to provide conclusive answers
about the exact effects of alternative treatments. This does not mean
we should abandon our research effort or refuse to suggest a direction
for policy. It does mean we should be forthright in stating the limitations of our knowledge.

Before describing the nature of our recommendations, we should
be clear in stating our policy objectives. Like most Americans we favor
faster economic growth. By faster growth we mean not only a more
rapid rate of advance in total output but also a faster rate of increase
in output, holding constant the amount of inputs used to produce that
output. Americans can always produce more by working longer hours
or placing additional people in poorly paid jobs. For many workers,
however, the added income would be worth less than the free time
they must give up to earn it. It is far preferable for the labor force to
work smarter, to produce more goods and deliver additional services
with the same level of work effort. This is achieved by raising labor
productivity, the source of economic growth we wish to emphasize.

When we speak of economic growth in this book we usually refer
to the growth of *potential* output, that is, the output that can be attained
when labor and capital are fully employed and inflation is not accelerating. In the short run, the economy frequently operates below its
potential. When this occurs, policymakers can use stimulative macroeconomic policies to make the economy grow faster than is sustainable
over a long time. In the first two years after the severe 1981–82 recession, for example, U.S. growth averaged 5.6 percent a year, a much
faster rate of advance than could be achieved if unemployment had
not been falling. In the long run the growth rate is limited by the
rates of growth of the labor force and the capital stock, and the efficiency with which both are used. One of our primary goals is to

improve the efficiency with which the nation's labor and capital stock are employed. Such improvements—producing more output with the same level of labor and capital inputs—are referred to by economists as increases in total factor productivity. They are achieved through advances in technology and improvements in worker skills and managerial practice. One of the nation's goals should be to raise the rate of annual growth in total factor productivity.

Our second goal is to reduce income inequality. We seek to reduce inequality in pretax incomes as well as aftertax incomes, that is, to reduce the disparity in market incomes, particularly wage earnings. Our proposals do not attempt to achieve more equality through reallocation of tax burdens or heavier reliance on government transfer payments such as public assistance. To reduce the deficit, tax increases and spending cuts should be concentrated on high-income Americans. We recommend this policy principally because we believe it is the fairest way to improve national saving, which is vital to improving long-run growth. However, redistributing money by means of the tax code is not the policy recommended here for improving the distribution of income. Ultimately, policies are needed to reverse the trend toward greater inequality in pretax incomes. This can be achieved, consistent with the need to encourage overall economic growth, through bettering the job skills of those now stuck at the bottom of the income distribution.

A Preview of Our Recommendations

We lay out our recommendations in chapters 4 through 7 and summarize them in chapter 8. For readers who want to know where we are going, we close this introductory chapter by highlighting several themes that run through our proposals.

First, and perhaps most important, the most reliable way to boost economic growth is to increase the share of national output devoted to investment. In broad terms, investment consists of all spending oriented toward the future rather than the present. Such spending may occur in either the private or the public sectors. It can involve the purchase of new machines, industrial buildings, roads and bridges, education and training, or the services of people working to develop new techniques and ideas. Government can profitably engage in this kind of spending itself but should do so only to fill a gap that the private sector would not fill on its own. It is often more useful for government to encourage investment by the private sector through tax incentives and reform of the legal and institutional environment than it is to undertake extra spending out of public budgets. With this in mind, in chapter 4 we present recommendations for improving the management of corporations and providing greater certainty that new products will not be subject to excessive claims for tort liability. We also offer suggestions in chapter 6 for increasing business investment in low-income urban areas where so many American social problems are concentrated.

Second, the nation will be far better off if it pays for additional investment with the saving of domestic residents. Otherwise, much of the gain from the added investment will accrue to people in other countries who supply the capital. During the past decade, net investment has fallen as a percentage of U.S. output. Net saving as a percentage of output has dropped even more. The United States has become more dependent on foreign capital than it has been in nearly a century. If this trend is to be reversed, and we believe it should be, domestic saving must rise even faster than investment.

We see little evidence, however, that the nation can rely on private individuals and corporations to raise their saving rates dramatically. It is doubtful they will increase saving on their own, and the experience of the 1980s shows it is unlikely they will do so even when encouraged by more generous tax incentives. The only certain way to increase national saving is to reduce the government budget deficit, that is, government *dis*saving. Under current policy, even when the economy achieves full employment, the deficit will absorb more than 3 percent of the nation's output—roughly half of U.S. private saving. This is the level of the so-called structural deficit in the current federal budget. Our colleague Charles Schultze has argued that the federal government should aim not just for budget balance but for a *surplus* at full employment to generate the additional saving and investment, and extra growth, that will be needed to finance the retirement of the baby boom generation early in the next century.[5]

We can suggest no novel or painless method to reduce the deficit. No such method exists. The deficit must be reduced either by raising taxes, reducing public expenditures, or some combination of the two. As a practical matter, the most politically acceptable policy will combine spending restraint with higher taxes.

But even if policymakers cannot summon the will to reduce the deficit, they can adopt a number of policies that increase growth. In chapters 4 and 6 we recommend changes in tax incentives and spending policies that would not deepen the government deficit but would expand the share of output devoted to investment. Put another way, even if the deficit is not reduced, government policy can be changed to finance increases in national investment out of domestically generated saving.

Third, it is not enough to enlarge the size of the economic pie if we do not simultaneously help less successful Americans obtain larger slices. Government policy should aim not only to boost investment in worker training but to concentrate much of the extra investment on those workers who are most deficient in labor market skills. One reason the wages of less skilled workers have stagnated or tumbled in recent years is that they find themselves in excess supply in a labor market that no longer rewards brawn without skill. The most effective way of reducing earnings inequality is to increase the relative skills of those now at the bottom of the wage and skill distribution. Many of our proposals are therefore aimed at giving special help to workers who have not gone to college.

Fourth, we strongly favor a policy of open borders for both foreign goods and foreign investment. Openness to foreign trade and investment is an essential ingredient of a strategy to promote growth. Free trade encourages U.S. producers to become more efficient and gives American consumers, including many businesses, access to the latest advances in foreign technology. Whether or not the United States "needs" foreign capital to raise its low rate of investment, additional foreign investment in businesses based in this country lowers the cost of the capital. Equally important, it accelerates the transfer of new technologies and methods of production from the best foreign producers to the United States.

The United States faces three basic choices with respect to its economic relations with the rest of the world. It can enter the twenty-first century prepared to take advantage of all the rest of the world has to offer and work cooperatively with other nations to improve the performance of the global economy. Alternatively, it can be dragged screaming into the next century, continuing to complain about other countries' trade and investment practices but doing little in its domestic policies to improve its own long-term economic performance. Or

America can attempt to turn its back on the rest of the world by withdrawing into an economic cocoon. The last course, economic isolationism, is a recipe for slow economic decline. The second strategy, economic drift, is probably a fair description of the policy America has adopted by default. It promises continued economic stagnation. Only the first course, which combines aggressive self-improvement at home with openness to foreign goods, technology, and capital, promises the kind of economic advance that Americans once took for granted.

We recognize that other countries maintain formal and informal barriers to the entry of U.S. goods and capital. Such policies provide convenient excuses for American firms and political leaders to clothe their appeals for protection in the garb of reciprocity or retaliation. In chapter 7 we discuss strategies for gaining greater access to foreign markets in ways that do not require threats of protection.

Fifth, even with a highly productive work force the American economy will continue to be buffeted by a wide variety of external shocks—in exchange rates, commodity prices, technological innovation, consumer tastes. These shocks have uneven effects: some workers and businesses gain handsomely; others lose. One certainty in a dynamic economy is that millions of workers will be forced to change jobs from one year to the next. Highly skilled and educated workers have the greatest flexibility in finding new jobs, of course. But even highly skilled workers will face problems.

Political opposition to necessary economic change can be reduced if the current safety net were both broadened and improved to assure job losers that their economic losses will be manageable. In chapter 7 we outline reforms that would speed the movement of workers from shrinking to growing industries and reduce the cost of economic dislocation.

In the end, it will take time for any progrowth, proequity policy package to achieve its desired effects. Nonetheless, a sensible combination of policies could bring at least some favorable results in short order. Despite the criticism in this book about economic policymaking in the 1980s, we recognize that the decade produced important economic achievements. Prudent, but painful, monetary policy cut double-digit inflation rates by more than half. Steady monetary growth helped sustain an economic expansion that lasted seven years and created 20 million new jobs, a record unmatched by any other industrialized country. At the same time, U.S. manufacturers discovered and implemented new methods for raising productivity. In fact, productivity growth in manufacturing grew at a nearly record pace.

The policies of the 1980s were not enough, however, to boost noticeably the pace of long-term economic growth. And whatever their other merits, they did not reverse the trend toward inequality. They probably contributed to the trend. The challenge for the 1990s is to accelerate growth while narrowing the gap that separates rich from poor Americans. In the remainder of this book, we show how this can be accomplished.

Two

Slow Growth
and Other
Economic Ills

THE UNITED STATES faces serious economic problems. The growth of productivity and income has been slow for twenty years. The federal budget is in chronic deficit. Imports have far exceeded exports for more than a decade. American competitiveness has been a source of concern for even longer. In addition, many Americans worry that foreigners are buying up U.S. companies, that the economy is losing its manufacturing base, and that the gap between rich and poor is widening. We stated in chapter 1 that slow productivity growth and widening inequality are the two most serious problems facing the economy. In this chapter we examine the problem of slow growth. We discuss why it is important to increase the rate of productivity growth. We review the main sources of growth since World War II and show why some of these sources have become weaker in the past two decades. We then point out where productivity growth might be increased. We conclude by considering the problems of declining competitiveness and continuing deindustrialization and show why they are less important than the underlying problem of slow growth.

The Slowdown of Productivity Growth

The principal reason for anemic economic growth in the United States is the sluggish pace of productivity improvement, a pace that slowed dramatically in the late 1960s and early 1970s.

Size of the Slowdown

The standard evidence showing the slowdown is displayed in figure 2-1. The left-hand bar graphs show the rate of improvement in average

FIGURE 2-1. *Measures of U.S. Productivity Growth, Selected Periods, 1948–90*

Average annual percent rates of change

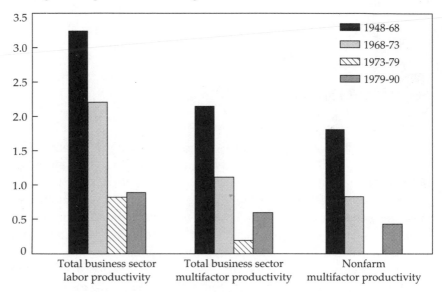

Source: Bureau of Labor Statistics, unpublished data.

labor productivity since 1948. Labor productivity is defined here as inflation-adjusted output in the business sector divided by an estimate of the hours worked in that sector. The growth rate of average labor productivity has been much slower during the past two decades than it was between 1948 and 1968.

Average labor productivity is a simple and useful measure of productivity, but most economists prefer a measure called multifactor productivity. Multifactor productivity is computed by dividing the output of U.S. businesses by an index measuring the amount of capital, land, and labor inputs used. This measure adjusts for the fact that workers, machines, and land are used in different proportions at different times in the production process. An illustration may be helpful. Consider a railroad company that hauls only grain. Suppose it doubles the number of boxcars in its stock, doubling the length of each train without adding extra trainmen. This investment might double the amount of grain hauled each year per employee, thus doubling average labor productivity. But because the increased production was achieved by adding to the railroad's capital stock, it is not clear that output rose any more than would be anticipated given the addition of extra capital inputs. Multifactor productivity measures the ratio of output to some standardized combination of all the inputs, including labor and capital, abstracting away from the growth in output that is due to the addition of capital. Changes in multifactor productivity thus provide a purer measure of efficiency improvement than changes in average labor productivity.

The middle and right-hand bar graphs in figure 2-1 show growth rates of multifactor productivity for the total business economy and the nonfarm business economy in the postwar period. How are the three indexes related to each other? The narrowest is multifactor productivity growth for the nonfarm business economy. The next narrowest is multifactor productivity in the business sector as a whole. Growth was more rapid for this broader sector than it was for the nonfarm business sector. This is true for all the periods covered in figure 2-1, but particularly for 1948–68. The difference arises because agriculture has been one of the most successful sectors in the economy in achieving sustained productivity improvement, so including it pushes up average growth.

Another reason for the difference is the movement of workers from farms to industry and commerce, which has increased overall productivity in the business economy. In 1948 agriculture had much lower productivity than the rest of the economy because many farms were small and inefficient. The sector's rapid productivity growth was achieved starting from a low base. As workers moved from farm jobs with low levels of productivity to higher-productivity jobs in the rest of the economy, average productivity in the whole economy rose. But this source of growth was nearly exhausted by the mid-1960s.

Average labor productivity, the broadest of the three measures, shows more rapid growth than multifactor productivity. This is because labor productivity grows as a result of both increases in the efficiency with which labor and capital are used (that is, advances in multifactor productivity) and new investment, which increases the amount of capital available per worker. Despite legitimate concerns about the slow pace of investment in the U.S. economy, capital per worker increased in all the periods shown.

Comparing the three measures is useful in understanding two

sources of productivity growth: capital accumulation and reallocation of resources. But with respect to whether productivity growth has slowed, all three measures tell the same story: growth fell sharply in the U.S. economy. Indeed, multifactor productivity growth vanished in the nonfarm sector from 1973 to 1979. Conventional statistics show virtually no increase in the efficiency with which capital and labor were used in the nonfarm sector in these years. All three productivity indicators show a small rebound of growth in the 1980s.

When thinking about trends in productivity growth, it is important to distinguish between the *level* of productivity and its *rate of growth*. Figure 2-1 shows that the rate fell, but productivity growth is still positive. Output per hour worked continues to rise, but not as fast as it once did. This is bad, but not as bad as it would be if the level of productivity were actually falling. Of course, aggregate productivity typically falls for a year or so when the economy goes into a recession—it fell at the end of 1990 and in early 1991, for example. But there has been no sustained decline in the level of productivity any time in the postwar period.

We have dwelled at some length on the productivity patterns shown in figure 2-1 because understanding them is essential to understanding the slowdown in U.S. economic growth. Not everyone believes the productivity statistics are as disappointing as they appear. Some economists have contended that the slow growth of the past few years should not be a matter of concern, that recent productivity performance simply represents a return to the growth pattern typical before World War II. The anomaly in the statistics, they claim, is the extraordinarily rapid climb in productivity immediately after the war.[1]

We agree that the period after World War II was one of strong productivity growth. The Great Depression and the diversion of resources during the war itself had depressed business investment and delayed the exploitation of commercial technologies. At the end of the war there were many investment and technology opportunities available, including the commercial application of military technologies that had been developed during the war. Exploiting these opportunities generated rapid productivity growth.

But the case that productivity growth is not a matter of concern is overstated. A study of the long-term data has revealed that productivity in the U.S. economy and in virtually all industrialized countries has been growing very slowly in recent years, even in comparison with growth rates that prevailed before World War II. Standard measures show that U.S. productivity growth has been especially slow since 1973.[2]

Measurement Issues and the Productivity Slowdown

The previous discussion of productivity is based on standard data. But some analysts have doubts about the validity of these data. They contend that conventional productivity measures overstate the severity of the slowdown. One source of error is the mismeasurement of output because the evaluation of improvements in quality has been poor.

Martin Baily and Robert Gordon have examined this matter with some care.[3] They concluded that standard statistics probably do understate productivity growth and have done so for many years, largely because the statistics fail to count adequately the benefits of new and better products and services. In addition, for some industries—financial services, for instance—current statistical procedures assume an absence of productivity growth. Nevertheless, Baily and Gordon show it is very hard to make the case that the *slowdown* in productivity growth is simply the result of measurement errors.

First, many measurement problems existed before 1973. To explain the slowdown in productivity growth, economists must discover measurement errors that only began to be a problem in the early 1970s or errors that became worse since then. Errors that reduced measured levels of productivity growth in the 1950s and 1960s as well in the 1970s and 1980s will not change estimates of the *decline* in productivity growth. But some errors have become more important in recent years and can help explain the slowdown in measured growth. For example, the service sector has become much more important to the economy, and the change in the quality of services has remained largely unrecorded. But many of the most serious errors (such as the assumed absence of productivity improvement in financial services) have been problems for many years. And some measurement problems tend to exaggerate recent productivity growth.[4]

A second reason it is hard to explain the slowdown as a product of measurement error is that some of the industries for which productivity is most seriously understated are those that sell much or all their output as intermediate goods. The banking industry, for instance, sells only about half its output to private consumers. Since this output raises the welfare of final consumers, any understatement of the quality improvement in banking will clearly reduce the apparent amount of productivity growth in the overall economy. However, the other half of banking services is sold to companies as inputs into their production. To the extent that the output of the banking industry is understated, the inputs of the consuming industries will be understated by an equivalent amount. This will exaggerate the productivity of these industries because their output is measured as their value added, the value of their production minus the value of purchased inputs—an amount that is clearly overstated if banking services are undervalued. In short, only half of any understatement of the output of the banking industry will show up as an understatement of aggregate output and productivity performance.

This result is surprising to many people and is a consequence of the way national income is estimated in the United States. Aggregate output is not computed by adding up the production of all of the individual industries. Instead, economists start with final sales and changes in inventories and then try to calculate the fraction of the total produced in each industry. Measurement errors often produce errors in the allocation of output to different industries but not in the calculation of total output.

On balance, standard measures of productivity understate productivity growth. They have understated growth for many years, and they have led to an overstatement of the productivity slowdown in many industries. But most of the apparent slowdown has been real. Although it may not be quite as dramatic as figure 2-1 implies, it is nonetheless large.

Why Is Productivity Growth Important?

For most people the concept of productivity may seem abstract and far removed from economic issues of immediate importance. This is a misconception. First, productivity growth is the primary source of improvement in average living standards. Second, it affects the nation's standing in the international community and helps determine American influence over international events. Third, most Americans would like to see the nation clean up its environment, improve worker safety, and better the quality of other aspects of life that are not measured in the national income statistics. Productivity growth is the only source of extra resources to pay for these improvements without reducing living standards. Finally, faster productivity growth can ease the burden of paying the huge costs that will be associated with the retirement of the baby boom generation. That generation will retire early in the next century and begin to draw social security, medicare, and other publicly supported benefits. If the benefits are to be financed without reducing the living standards of future workers, the productivity of future workers will have to increase substantially.[5]

Productivity and Living Standards

American living standards are linked in an obvious way to average labor productivity. U.S. households and government entities consume almost all that U.S. workers produce, less any saving for capital investment and future consumption.[6] If workers can produce more in an average hour of work, households can consume more, either through private purchases or additional government services.

Labor productivity and individual consumption are linked with one another through the wages workers earn in the market. Over long periods of time the compensation levels are established by the value of output workers can produce. (Labor compensation includes employer-provided health insurance, pensions, and social insurance contributions as well as money wages.) Changes in real compensation thus tend to track changes in labor productivity. The relationship is not exact in every year or even in every decade, but major improvements in the rate of productivity eventually turn up as improvements in real compensation.

This relationship is displayed in figure 2-2. Output per hour rose about 3 percent a year from 1947 through 1973. Real compensation per hour also rose 3 percent a year, more than doubling over the period. But after 1973 the growth rate of output per hour plummeted to 1 percent a year. Growth in real compensation per hour dropped even more sharply, to 0.2 percent a year.

The trend in hourly compensation is mirrored in the trend of family income because most families derive an overwhelming share of their income from wage earnings. For almost three decades after World War II, median family income grew strongly, rising nearly 2.8 percent a year.[7] But since 1973 it has grown less than 0.5 percent a year. Average family income has grown a bit faster than 0.5 percent a year

FIGURE 2-2. *Output per Hour and Real Compensation, 1947–90*[a]

Logarithmic scale (1973 = 100)

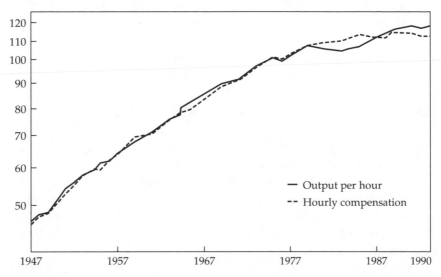

Source: *Economic Report of the President, February 1992*, table B-44. Personal consumption expenditure deflator used. Authors' calculations for 1947–58.

a. Output per hour and real hourly compensation in the U.S. business sector.

because families near the top of the income distribution have seen their incomes grow much faster than families in the middle and near the bottom, a trend we discuss in the next chapter.

Somewhat surprisingly, people's perceptions of the economy have been slow to change. Even by the end of the 1980s, most Americans remained optimistic about their income prospects. According to an August 1989 Louis Harris poll, 59 percent of adults expected their children to live a more comfortable life than they did. Less than three years later, however, just 34 percent of those interviewed held this optimistic view. Twenty-nine percent of adults believed that the living standards of their children would be *lower* than their own.[8]

The sudden turn toward pessimism is understandable given the economic downturn that began in mid-1990 and the slow recovery that has followed. Nevertheless, the American mood in the early 1990s was unusually dark, much darker than can be explained by a comparatively mild recession. Many Americans may have finally awakened to the fact that for nearly two decades average real incomes had barely risen. Young adults and poorer people probably had lower incomes, after adjusting for inflation, than people in similar circumstances received twenty years earlier.

Several factors explain why it took so long for Americans to recognize the full implications of slow growth. The long-term trend of the past two decades was obscured by strong recoveries from two deep recessions. An observer in 1978 would have been encouraged by rising trends in wages, incomes, and productivity compared to the trough of the 1973–75 recession. An observer in the middle or late 1980s would have drawn comfort from encouraging statistics about income and productivity growth after the 1981–82 recession. But both observers would have confused a cyclical upturn with a longer-term trend. Once cyclical factors are removed from trends during the years after 1973, a long-term slowdown in the growth of productivity is obvious.

The effects of these slowdowns have also been masked by two developments that made many Americans feel their living standards were continuing to grow comfortably. For most of the past two decades, the percentage of women in the labor force has risen steadily, increasing the percentage of two-earner families. Many families could thus enjoy higher consumption levels and faster rates of income growth. Yet this change has involved costs. Although many women have chosen freely to enter the labor market out of a desire to begin rewarding careers, some have been forced to work out of necessity. Many single women and dual-earner couples now struggle to meet the competing time demands of jobs and children. And women's increasing participation rates cananot continue indefinitely. In fact, the increase has already leveled off.

Average consumption has also grown at a faster rate than national income because households and the federal government have saved a dwindling share of income. Individuals and families of all ages and incomes have reduced their saving rates.[9] At the same time, the federal government has permitted its annual operating deficit to reach levels unprecedented in peacetime. Record deficits allow the nation to provide a high level of government services without paying for those services out of current private consumption. The nation's overall rate of saving fell from 8.1 percent of net national product in the 1970s (a level that by international standards was already low) to 2.3 percent in 1987, before rebounding slightly to 3.1 percent at the end of the decade.[10] The reduction in public and private saving, like the increase in labor force participation, can boost the rate of growth in consumption only temporarily. In fact, part of the increase in consumption is borrowed from future public or private consumption, since a lower rate of saving reduces the future flow of income.

For the past two decades, then, but especially during the economic expansion of the 1980s, many families have taken advantage of earnings from an extra worker and of lower saving rates to enjoy higher levels of consumption, even though individual earnings and average productivity were creeping upward slowly if at all. Future consumption gains of comparable size cannot occur unless the rate of productivity growth is increased.

If productivity growth can be increased, the simple arithmetic of compound interest ensures a powerful and fairly quick effect on future living standards. When the annual growth in output per hour is 0.5 percent a year, twenty years' productivity gains are needed to increase output per hour by 10 percent. If productivity growth rises to 1 percent a year, twenty years of productivity improvement will boost hourly output by 22 percent. With a 2 percent rate of productivity increase—a rate still lower than the one achieved in the 1950s and 1960s—the increase in hourly output is nearly 50 percent.

If these rates of productivity growth were translated into equal rates of growth in family incomes, living standards could improve dramatically. In 1990, median family income was $35,353. If incomes rose 0.5 percent a year, the median would be $39,061 by 2010. With a 2 percent growth rate, it would rise to $52,533, over one-third higher than the median income when there is slower growth.

Productivity and International Standing

In the long run, productivity can affect the nation's global influence as well as its living standard. Many policymakers and opinion leaders describe the economic challenge confronting the United States as one of "restoring competitiveness" and preventing national economic decline relative to other major powers.[11] The dissolution of the Soviet Union and the growing power of the European Community have sharpened the tone of this debate, giving it a clearly nationalistic edge. Some politicians and other observers now claim that the United States must replace its former political and military competition with the Soviet Union with a new economic competition, perhaps even an "economic war," with Europe and Japan.[12]

The United States does not appear to face imminent military peril. Its large population, advanced military technology, geographic isolation, and high average income give it decisive advantages over potential military rivals. The end of the cold war presents this and other advanced industrialized countries with a new and different kind of challenge. Our former colleague, Alice Rivlin, has argued that in this new world the United States cannot fully achieve its broad security objectives without the cooperation of other nations whose interests are also affected by events and activities that affect all.[13] If Americans want their country to have the preeminent voice in joint international efforts, to lead rather than be led by other nations, the U.S. economy must also be preeminent, or at least remain first among equals. The nation cannot count on its unquestioned military dominance to give it clout in international affairs when economic weakness makes it dependent on the wealth of other nations to achieve its foreign policy goals.

Although the military strength of the United States will probably remain unchallenged for the foreseeable future, its continued economic preeminence appears more questionable. The large advantage in worker productivity and average income levels that the United States once enjoyed is fading. Adjusted for differences in the purchasing power of different currencies, real incomes in other industrialized countries now approach U.S. levels (figure 2-3). Measured in terms of the current exchange rate values of their currencies, several countries now enjoy higher average income and output levels than the United States. More worrisome is that other major countries are outsaving and outinvesting the United States by wide margins (figure 2-4). If they continue to outpace this country in saving and investment, if they are more successful in educating and training their workers, and if they can achieve technical advances at a faster rate, U.S. economic preeminence will disappear.

Some readers may wonder whether America's loss of preeminent status would do any more than damage national pride. Would it have practical consequences for American well-being? Many economists would answer no. They would point out that what should matter to Americans is the absolute level of their own incomes and the speed of income growth, regardless of the levels or growth rates achieved elsewhere in the industrialized world. Given a choice between two outcomes—20 percent higher U.S. income together with 40 percent

FIGURE 2-3. *GDP per Capita for Canada, Germany, and Japan Relative to the United States, Purchasing-Power-Parity Exchange Rates, 1950–90*

Index (United States = 100)

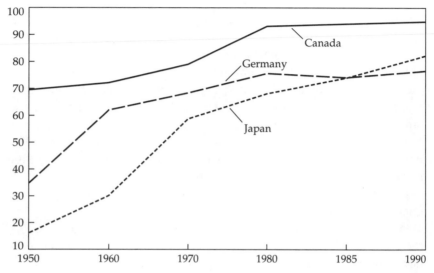

Source: Bureau of Labor Statistics, unpublished data.

higher income in Europe and Japan, or 5 percent higher incomes in all three regions—most economists would pick the first as the more desirable. Yet when former Harvard political economist and current Secretary of Labor Robert Reich posed this choice to his students several years ago, most voted for continued *relative* U.S. superiority, even at the expense of slower *absolute* growth in U.S. incomes.[14] In this respect, Reich's students may have held views close to those of other Americans.

We are not surprised that many Americans think of the economic challenge primarily in competitive terms. This attitude, however, is dangerous to the extent that it encourages the adoption of policies primarily meant to punish economic competitors rather than to help ourselves. Many such policies end up harming Americans as well as foreigners. In other respects, however, the competitive attitude could be helpful. One key to improving the nation's long-term economic prospects would be to reduce the percentage of its resources devoted to consumption so that additional resources can be freed for investment. We doubt whether the country is prepared to accept the short-

FIGURE 2-4. *National Saving and Investment Rates, by Country, 1980–90*

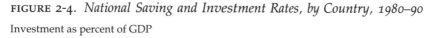

Investment as percent of GDP

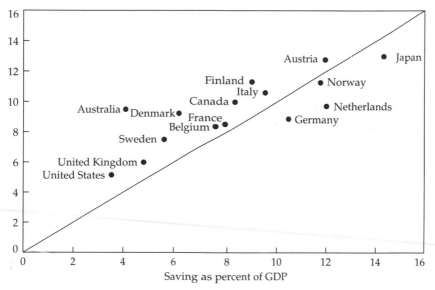

Source: Authors' calculations based on OECD data.

run sacrifices this would entail unless people are motivated by a strong competitive challenge.

Faster economic growth is in the political self-interest of the United States if it wishes to remain influential in a world where leadership requires persuasion rather than coercion. It is also in the broader self-interest of a nation whose citizens care deeply about the relative position of their country in the world economy.

Productivity and the Quality of Life

Most Americans highly value aspects of their lives and environment that do not have clear price tags attached to them—personal health and safety, environmental quality, public amenities, and so on. Although these features of personal and national life are not directly counted in standard measures of economic performance, improvements in all would be more affordable if economic growth were stronger.

Traditional economic statistics such as national output and personal income reflect only what is valued in market transactions. Activities or conditions that affect living standards but that are not traded in the market are excluded. The figures on gross domestic product, for example, do not take account of the quality of the environment or threats to personal safety or traffic congestion or increased longevity. Yet these factors significantly affect perceptions about the standard of living.[15]

One way to explain deteriorating U. S. economic performance is that standard economic statistics do not capture improvements in nonmarket aspects of life, some of which have been achieved by giving up measured economic output. Improvements in the quality of air and water are not recorded in national income statistics. These improvements, however, were only achieved by placing restrictions on production—preventing paper manufacturers from polluting streams of requiring reduced smokestack pollutants—thus reducing the apparent efficiency of American workers and capital.

Because of data limitations, it is not easy to decide whether improvements in these nonmarket aspects of American life have been very significant. Table 2-1 shows trends in a variety of nonmarket indicators of well-being. The good news is that since 1960 average life spans for both men and women have lengthened, with most of the improvement coming in the 1970s. The environment has also improved: despite a significant increase in the past thirty years in population (39 percent) and national output (149 percent), more air pollutants have decreased in volume than have increased. Some, such as particulate matter and lead, fell sharply. If market values were assigned to these environmental improvements, U.S. economic performance would almost certainly look better.[16]

But the table shows bad news as well. In the past three decades rates of violent crime have quadrupled. Traffic in major metropolitan areas has become more congested. And although the work week has shrunk, the proportion of prime-age adults at work has grown. Single parents and married-couple families with children may have less time away from their jobs than parents did a generation ago, and today's children may spend less time with their parents than did previous generations.

To the extent that society values highly certain noneconomic dimensions of life, it should also value economic growth. This comment runs counter to the conventional wisdom, which stresses the trade-offs between market and nonmarket aspects of national life. But long-

TABLE 2-1. *Indicators of Quality of Life in the United States, Selected Years, 1960–89*

Indicator	1960	1970	1980	1989
Life expectancy at birth (years)				
Men	66.6	67.1	70.0	71.8
Women	73.1	74.7	77.4	78.5
Crime rate (per 100,000)				
Violent crime	161	364	597	664
Property crime	1,726	3,621	5,353	5,078
Air pollutant emissions (millions of metric tons)				
Particulate matter	21.6	18.5	8.5	6.9[a]
Sulfur oxides	19.7	28.3	23.4	20.7[a]
Nitrogen oxides	13.0	18.5	20.9	19.8[a]
Volatile organic compounds	21.0	25.0	21.1	18.6[a]
Carbon monoxide	89.7	101.4	79.6	61.2[a]
Lead	n.a.	203.8	70.6	7.6[a]
Average weekly hours of work (nonsupervisory production workers)	38.6	37.1	35.3	34.6

Sources: *Economic Report of the President,* 1992; *Statistical Abstract of the United States* (February 1964), p. 172, and (February 1991), p. 359; U.S. Department of Justice, *Sourcebook of Criminal Justice Statistics,* 1990, p. 353.

n.a. Not available.

a. Data for 1988.

run improvements in economic well-being and many nonmarket indicators of well-being go hand-in-hand. The connection is not accidental. Richer societies have the resources to pursue environmental objectives more aggressively than poorer societies, for example. Faster growth makes it easier to devote additional resources to public health and safety, medical innovation, preservation of wilderness, and other nonmarket objectives.

To be sure, strong economic growth does not always produce improvement in noneconomic conditions, and it can cause deterioration in some areas. Crime and traffic congestion grew worse as real incomes rose, and some forms of pollution worsened as well. But strong growth at least produces the extra resources with which these problems can be addressed. If citizens and policymakers choose to devote these resources to private consumption or new public amenities, it may be that they value private consumption and new public amenities more than they do reducing crime or relieving congestion. But that does not affect the observation that the cost of crime reduction and traffic relief is more affordable out of a higher income than out of a lower one.

Productivity and an Aging Population

The aging of a population poses a special challenge when productivity and income are growing very slowly. Low birth rates and increased longevity have raised the median age of the U. S. population by four and one-half years since 1970. This aging has not proved terribly burdensome so far. The proportion of the population older than sixty-five has grown, but the growth has been modest. And the increased burden of providing for a larger number of retired elderly has been offset somewhat by the shrinking burden of providing for fewer children. But after the baby boom generation begins to retire around 2010, the ratio of retirees to workers, currently about one to three, will grow to one to two, or an even smaller ratio, as fewer new workers replace older ones.[17]

This demographic trend will make heavy demands on government budgets because a large proportion of retirees' consumption is financed through public spending. Social security benefits account for about 60 percent of the cash income received by poor families with an aged family member. They constitute more than 25 percent of the income received by nonpoor families with an aged family member and an even higher percentage of the income of older people who live alone. The cost of medicare benefits to old people is one-half the cost of social security pensions.[18] And, of course, the elderly also receive benefits under a variety of other government programs.

Even if all these benefits are not increased, which seems doubtful, the growing proportion of the population that is retired and the shrinking proportion remaining at work will raise tax burdens for active workers. Many people are alarmed by this prospect because they doubt that future workers will tolerate sharply higher taxes. The tax increases will be larger—and the intergenerational conflict more intense—if productivity and wages grow very slowly.

Because cost increases are unavoidable, one strategy to reduce their impact on future workers is to adopt policies that raise future national income. Then workers earning higher pretax wages would be left with more to consume after deductions have been made to pay for social security and medicare. If a high percentage of future earnings must ultimately be paid to finance spending on the elderly, it makes a great deal of difference to future workers whether their hourly wage is $10 or $20. A 25 percent tax is undeniably more affordable to better-paid workers. To be sure, a lower tax rate is preferable whether wages are $10 or $20 an hour, but if the higher tax is unavoidable, future workers will certainly prefer to pay it out of a higher wage.

To be fair to future generations, the nation should either increase the pace of wage and productivity growth or ask current workers to shoulder a larger part of the burden of paying for their own retirement benefits. The first strategy is not only equitable to future workers, but it can significantly improve the well-being of the current generation of workers.

Sources of Productivity Growth

Few people would quarrel with the idea that the nation's productivity performance ought to be improved. But is it reasonable to expect public policy to improve productivity growth? To help answer this question, it is useful to examine the sources of productivity growth important in the past and consider why some of them failed after the 1960s.

In 1985 Brookings economist Edward Denison tabulated the sources of productivity growth for the U.S. economy from 1929 to 1982. Table 2-2 summarizes his results. There are differences between Denison's output concept and the one that underlies the results shown in figure 2-1.[19] But these differences are not crucial for our purposes. According to Denison's calculations for the business sector, productivity growth has come mostly from improvements in worker skills and education, increases in physical capital, advances in knowledge, improved resource allocation, and growing economies of scale.

Other studies of growth have reached similar conclusions. An influential 1987 study also found that improved worker skills and education, added physical capital, better resource reallocation, and advances in knowledge were crucial to growth.[20]

We look now at these sources of growth and at the role of management in growth. Why have the sources of past growth contributed less in recent years? Could they help improve growth in the future?

TABLE 2-2. *Contributions to Average Labor Productivity Growth,*
by Type of Contribution, 1929–82

Type	Potential national income per person employed	
	Whole economy	Nonresidential business
Growth rate	1.6	1.7
Percentage of growth rate		
Labor input except education	− 13	− 23
Education per worker	26	30
Capital	15	10
Advances in knowledge	54	64
Improved resource allocation	16	19
Economics of scale	17	20
Changes in legal and human environments	− 3	− 4
Land	− 3	− 4
Irregular factors	0	0
Other determinants	− 10	− 13

Source: Edward F. Denison, *Trends in American Economic Growth, 1929–82* (Brookings, 1985), p. 30.

Resource Reallocation and the Service Sector

One important source of growth in the U.S. economy has been the movement of labor from farms to industry and commerce. Because agriculture was less efficient than the rest of the economy, the movement boosted overall productivity (a phenomenon that has been even more important as a source of growth in Japan and some European countries). The fraction of the work force in the farm sector is now very small, however, and this source of productivity growth has run its course.

But this does not mean that the impact of reallocating workers has become unimportant. Recent reallocations have, unfortunately, moved workers away from high-productivity industries toward industries with low average productivity and below average wages. In particular, the number of low-wage, low-productivity jobs in services has expanded rapidly. Employment in private-sector service companies rose from 60 percent of total private employment in 1973 to 72 percent by 1990. Average earnings of service workers are only 85

TABLE 2-3. *Average Annual Growth in GDP per Hour, by Major Economic Sector, 1948–73, 1973–89*

Sector	1948–73	1973–89	Difference, 1948–73 to 1973–89
Business	2.88	1.08	−1.80
Goods producing	3.21	1.71	−1.50
Farming	4.64	2.04	−2.60
Mining	4.02	−0.82	−4.84
Construction	0.58	−1.20	−1.78
Manufacturing	2.87	2.75	−0.12
Service producing	2.49	0.74	−1.75
Transportation	2.31	0.65	−1.66
Communication	5.22	4.63	−0.59
Utilities	5.87	2.46	−3.41
Trade	2.74	1.18	−1.56
Finance, insurance, and real estate	1.44	0.17	−1.27
Services	2.17	0.32	−1.85
Government enterprise	−0.15	0.26	0.41
General government	0.21	0.34	0.13

Sources: National Income Product Accounts data base, tables 6.2 and 6.11; *Survey of Current Business*, vol. 71 (April 1991).

percent of those in the economy as a whole and just 75 percent of those in manufacturing. And measured productivity improvement since 1973 has been much slower in services than in goods-producing industries (table 2-3).

Increasing employment in services has slowed the growth of overall productivity. But the importance of this factor should not be exaggerated. Technology improvements in service industries can lead to productivity increases just as they have in goods-producing industries. It is a common misconception that the service sector employs mainly people who work in offices or retail establishments. In fact, it includes many diverse industries. Some communications and electric utilities industries, for example, have experienced extremely high rates of productivity growth, at least over certain periods. And few people realize that annual productivity growth in services was not very different from productivity growth in the manufacturing sector before 1973 (2.5 percent in services compared with 2.9 percent in manufacturing). A big part of the slowdown since then has occurred because of the decline of productivity growth *within* individual industries, such as real estate and financial services, that make up the service-producing sector.

It would be a mistake to adopt policies that attempted to reverse the relative growth of employment in services, as we will show later. The best ways to offset the adverse effects of the growth are to increase innovation in the sector and improve the skills of its workers.

Quality of the Work Force

Investment in education has been an important source of productivity improvement (see table 2-2) and is potentially a source of further improvement. Workers now entering the labor force have more years of schooling than workers who are about to retire. This raises the average qualifications of the work force, although the rate of improvement is now slower than it was in the 1950s and 1960s. At the same time, adverse trends in skill levels have reduced productivity. These problems have come to the fore in recent years as growth has slowed down.

In the early postwar period, the U.S. work force consisted mainly of mature white males who, by the standards of their time, were well trained and generally had not been subject to forms of discrimination that would have denied them education and training opportunities. Beginning in the 1960s, however, the composition of the work force began to change; new workers were increasingly young, female, or members of minority groups, or all of these. Historically, these groups had lacked or been denied the training, educational, and work opportunities necessary to take jobs requiring high levels of skill. The growing importance of workers with less experience and training has helped reduce overall productivity growth.

The reduction created by changing demographics has been aggravated by the much-discussed problems of American education. Because the United States lacks standardized national tests of educational achievement at the high school level, the significance of these educational problems is uncertain. Policymakers concerned with education have focused on trends in the Scholastic Aptitude Test, which many high school students take to gain admission to college. The trend in average SAT scores is disquieting. After rising steadily from the end of World War II through the early 1960s, average scores went into a steep decline. The slide was briefly interrupted in the 1980s, but high school students continue to receive much lower scores on the SAT than they once did.

Part of the decline in scores is attributable to the democratization of the test-taking population as more students from disadvantaged backgrounds have sought admission to colleges. In fact, however, a more important cause is the demonstrable deterioration in the educational skills of the most talented American high school students on the academic track leading to college.[21] Independent tests of general intellectual and academic achievement corroborate these conclusions.[22]

Summarizing the findings of several studies, Martin Baily and Robert Gordon concluded that labor productivity growth after 1973 fell by 0.3 percent a year because of the combined effects of changes in the demographic composition of the labor force and the deterioration in educational skills.[23] This explains roughly a quarter of the total slowdown in productivity growth.

Policy reform can and should do little to try to change the demographic composition of the work force. In fact, future demographic changes will be more helpful for productivity as the work force becomes older and more experienced. But policy can and should sustain the high rate of investment in education and improve the quality of schooling. Policy reform can also encourage businesses to invest more in training workers, a topic to which we return in a later chapter.

Physical Capital

Economists disagree about whether depressed investment in business capital goods has been a major reason for slow productivity growth. The steep decline of multifactor productivity growth (see figure 2-1) implies that slow business investment cannot be an important contributor. Because this measure eliminates the influence of any changes in capital per worker, the sharp drop means that efficiency improvements have slowed down independently of any fluctuations in the investment rate.

The argument that inadequate capital accumulation has been important in slowing productivity growth is much more complicated. Some economists believe a high investment rate is needed to generate growth because new business investment embodies improvements in technology or causes productivity to rise in other ways. We sympathize with part of this argument, and we will return to it in chapter 6;

but the issue does not have to be resolved here. The main point is that the United States has had a low rate of saving and investment for many years; the problem has become worse in recent years; and it is likely to become still worse unless something is done about it. Economists agree that a sound strategy for improving economic growth must include a strong rate of investment. Reducing the federal budget deficit is the single most important ingredient of any strategy aimed at increasing the rate of investment.

In addition to business investment, the investment of public capital is also important for growth. Many economists acknowledge that greater business productivity depends on high-quality public infrastructure. A few have attempted to demonstrate that dwindling investment in infrastructure since the 1970s has contributed heavily to the slowdown in productivity growth.[24] We find this claim unpersuasive, but the recent interest in public capital investment is nonetheless welcome because the contribution of this investment to growth is often neglected. Weak public investment since the early 1970s has certainly abetted slow productivity growth, though the contribution is small. Boosting investment in infrastructure is a promising way to spur growth.

Advances in Knowledge

Advances in knowledge include all types of innovation, both technological and organizational. Students of economic growth generally believe that advances in knowledge represent a principal source of productivity improvement (see table 2-2). It is therefore natural to ask whether the slowdown in productivity growth since the early 1970s is partly caused by a deterioration in the rate at which new knowledge is generated and commercially applied.

We doubt that the rate of innovation has slowed. It is true, of course, that at the end of World War II many new technologies awaited development. But this does not mean that all existing technological advances have now been exploited, or even that the rate at which new ideas are developed has slowed. New ideas seem to be generated at least as rapidly today as they were several decades ago. Witness, for example, developments in the 1980s in superconductivity, genetic engineering, parallel computer processing, and optical computing. The contribution of research and development to growth has not diminished.[25]

However, productivity growth may have been slowed because

American companies have not aggressively adapted and made commercial use of advances in science. Technological opportunities can be translated into productivity gains only if some important conditions are met:

—R&D funding must be adequate or the technological opportunity will not lead to an innovation.

—A new product must be capable of being manufactured cost-efficiently; otherwise the market for the product will not develop or another company or country will take the market away.

—The users of the product must learn to employ it efficiently or potential gains to the economy will not be realized.

Some part of the slowdown in productivity may be traced to a failure of one or more of the links in the chain that connects technological opportunities to productivity gains.[26] This may apply both to manufacturing firms, which do most of the technological innovating, and to the service sector, where the new technologies are often used.

To increase productivity growth, the nation must reap more of the benefits of innovation. The pace of adding to new knowledge must be sustained or increased, and the payoff in higher productivity from new knowledge must be greater.

The Role of Management and Economic Disruptions

Management has a role in aiding productivity growth that overarches all the other factors we have discussed. Economic policy can help create an economic environment that encourages increased business investment. But it is up to managers to discover promising business opportunities, develop suitable investment plans, and shoulder the risks involved. Pure science can generate new commercial opportunities, but managers need the vision to develop them and bring the technologies to market. When workers lack the skills necessary to function in new jobs, managers must provide training and design production systems that build on workers' strengths rather than founder on their weaknesses. In view of its responsibilities, management must bear much of the blame for the disappointing productivity performance of the U.S. economy, a contention others have also voiced.[27]

One shortcoming of U.S. managers is their focus on short-term business strategies. American business management has been revolutionized during the past few decades by so-called scientific management methods that have encouraged project analysis by financial executives as the basis for investment decisions. Managers have been taught to forecast whether the discounted cash flow from a proposed project will cover the cost of funds required for the investment. If the net flow is positive, the project is to be approved; otherwise, it is to be rejected.

Financial analysis of this type is fine, but when misapplied it can lead to ineffective decisionmaking. Often it induces managers to ignore important but difficult-to-quantify aspects of a project—for instance, that developing one new product leads to ideas for additional new products. Combined with the high cost of capital during the 1980s, the misuse of financial management techniques created a bias in favor of short-run strategies. By definition, such strategies exclude investment in R&D and other projects with long-term payoffs.[28]

In 1989 the Massachusetts Institute of Technology commissioned a study of the productivity performance of U.S. manufacturing that contained a searching examination of management problems in various manufacturing industries.[29] Many U.S. companies, the study reported, suffered from outdated production strategies, short time horizons, weaknesses in development and production technology, neglect of human resources, and failures of cooperation between workers and management and between management and government. The report contended that the success of many companies during the 1950s and 1960s led to the development of rigid and overstaffed bureaucracies. Fiefdoms within companies refused to cooperate to achieve common objectives. Meanwhile, labor and management struggled over the division of profits and lost sight of the basic need to improve the efficiency of company operations.

These problems crippled productivity growth in their own right, but their effects were magnified by the economic disruptions triggered by the oil shocks of the 1970s and 1980s. Because energy is a small component of total cost in most industries, economists find it difficult to understand why energy price gyrations after 1972 could have had so great an effect on businesses. Yet the onset of a worldwide slowdown in productivity growth at the same time as the first energy crisis seems more than just a coincidence. The soaring energy prices may have been so costly to productivity growth because they diverted U.S. managers from pursuing other productivity-enhancing activities.[30]

The energy crisis was only one of several economic shocks faced by U.S. managers. Others included deregulation of the transportation and communications industries, rapid growth of regulations governing health and safety, changes in the skill and demographic composition of the work force, severe recession, soaring inflation, and major fluctuations in the cost of funds. Many American businesses tried to respond by cutting costs and adopting innovative management practices. Some companies made the innovations work. Others did not.

We agree with many of the criticisms leveled at U.S. managers, but we recognize the magnitude of the problems they faced. Rather than assign blame, we prefer to consider ways policy can help develop more effective managers. In principle, sound public policy should encourage competition and ensure that the rules of corporate governance create proper economic incentives. Policy reform can improve managerial incentives. The role of management and the improvement of rules on corporate governance will be the subject of later chapters.

Subsidiary Problems

Although slow productivity growth is the nation's foremost economic problem, it is not usually the subject of daily news bulletins. The popular media focus instead on a variety of other real and alleged economic maladies. Some are serious problems, but others are simply manifestations of the deeper difficulty of improving anemic productivity. Two of these are the supposed loss in the nation's competitiveness and the related claim that the U.S. economy is suffering from deindustrialization.

Competitiveness

Politicians, business leaders, and journalists routinely bemoan the loss of U.S. competitiveness. "Competitiveness" is often used loosely, however. Many people believe a nation's competitiveness can be directly measured by its current trade balance. But the trade balance is influenced by a lot of factors that may or may not affect the long-term competitiveness of a nation's main industries. For example, a surge in world energy prices will cause a short-term deterioration in the trade balance of a country that imports most of its oil. The imbalance does not mean that the nation's major industries have lost their competitiveness. If the industries were competitive with low energy prices, most will remain competitive when energy prices are higher. After all, overseas companies in the same international markets must pay higher energy prices too. The trade imbalance in this case simply reflects the fact that the country has experienced a loss in its terms of trade. The nation's citizens are poorer because of the energy price hike, but its industrial companies remain competitive. A nation's trade balance is also affected by currency fluctuations and sudden changes in its saving rate that are not accompanied equivalent changes in the rate of domestic investment.

What then is competitiveness? A company that is competitive in the long term is one that freely competes in world markets and can profitably maintain its market share without forcing real wage reductions on its own workers. If a firm can sell its output only by accepting subpar profits or repeatedly demanding wage concessions from employees, it is losing competitiveness. Similarly, a nation's industries can be said to be competitive if they can profitably sell their output in international markets without reducing wages (and ideally while raising wages). Viewed in this way, however, the idea of competitiveness is closely related to productivity growth because with or without international trade, the only way a nation's wages can increase over the long term is for rates of productivity to increase.

The competitiveness of U.S. industry does not look feeble when considered in terms of worker productivity. The productivity statistics most relevant to international trade are those that pertain to manufacturing, since manufactured goods account for such a large share of the nation's imports and exports. Productivity growth in U.S. manufacturing was strong during the 1980s and in fact was comparable to that in other countries. And the United States maintains very high average productivity in comparison with other advanced industrialized countries—higher, for instance, than Japan, Germany, and the United Kingdom since 1973 (figure 2-5). Even though the average productivity of Japanese workers continues to increase relative to that of American workers, there is little sign that the overall U.S. advantage will disappear any time soon.

Economists who specialize in international trade have a somewhat different concept of competitiveness than one based on average worker productivity. They emphasize long-term movements in a nation's real exchange rate.[31] When a nation's real exchange rate declines steadily, its imports (and domestically produced substitutes for im-

FIGURE 2-5. *Relative Manufacturing Productivity, Four Countries, 1973–89*

Index (United States = 100 in 1973)

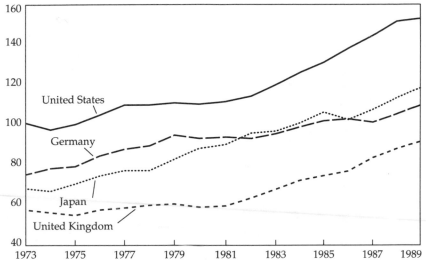

Source: Bureau of Labor Statistics, unpublished data.

ports) grow more expensive, reducing national living standards. Some trade economists consider this trend as reflecting a long-term loss in national competitiveness.

By this standard America has indeed steadily lost competitiveness. In a study completed in the late 1960s, Hendrik Houthakker and Stephen Magee found that the United States had been forced to accept a long-term decline in its real exchange rate from 1951 to 1966.[32] Robert Lawrence, who recently extended the study, found that the underlying factors forcing the decline continued through the 1980s.[33] The United States, he estimated, must accept a real depreciation in its exchange rate of 0.5 percent a year simply to maintain an unchanging trade balance. If the dollar does not depreciate this fast, the U.S. trade balance will worsen.

This view of competitiveness suggests the United States is losing ground, but fortunately the effect on living standards is slight. Imports represent only 12 percent of national income, so the 0.5 percent rate of currency depreciation implies an annual loss of purchasing power of just 0.06 percent.

FIGURE 2-6. *Share of Global High-Technology Markets, by Country, 1980, 1984, 1990*

Percent

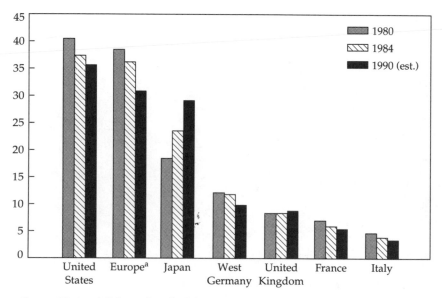

Source: National Science Board, *Science and Engineering Indicators—1991*, NSB 91-1 (1991), appendix tables 6.3 and 6.5.

a. Twelve-nation European Community.

One last way to evaluate competitiveness is to compare the rates at which nations innovate—for example, through introducing new products and production methods. Successful innovators can earn rich rewards in international trade. And such countries enjoy impressive advantages over their industrial rivals during the period before a successful new innovation has been introduced or adopted by foreign competitors. As a by-product of this market power, the exchange rates of innovating countries will appreciate, allowing their citizens to buy foreign goods at steadily cheaper prices.

Using this standard, the United State has clearly lost some of its competitive advantage, especially with respect to Japan. U.S. firms no longer enjoy a commanding lead in innovating within certain key industries, notably automobiles and electronics. The United States has lost some of its global market share in high-technology production and has endured rising import penetration in these products (figures

FIGURE 2-7. *Import Penetration of U.S. High-Technology Markets, by Type of Import, 1980, 1987, 1990*

Percent

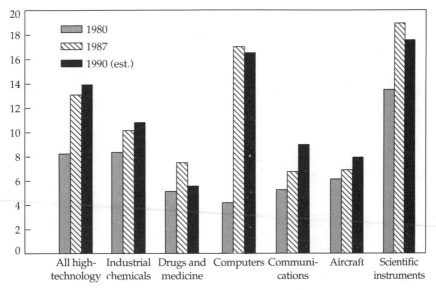

Source: National Science Board, *Science and Engineering Indicators—1991*, appendix tables 6-3 and 6-5.

2-6 and 2-7). Japan has clearly gained, while Europe has lost ground in comparison with both Japan and the United States.

The loss of U.S. competitiveness, however, is not a reason to restrict foreign competition. Japan has gained world market share by concentrating its efforts to spur innovation and productivity growth on certain key industries. But average Japanese productivity remains well behind that in the United States, partly because Japan has been unwilling to expose its less productive industries to foreign competition. Foreign competition has prodded many U.S. industries in international markets to improve their performance significantly. It is hard to imagine that the quality of American automobiles would have improved as much in the 1980s as it did if Chrysler, Ford, and General Motors had not been exposed to stiff international competition.

Deindustrialization

Headlines in the popular and business press regularly deplore America's loss of its manufacturing base. Even though millions of

FIGURE 2-8. *Share of Manufacturing in the U.S. Economy, 1929–89*

Percent

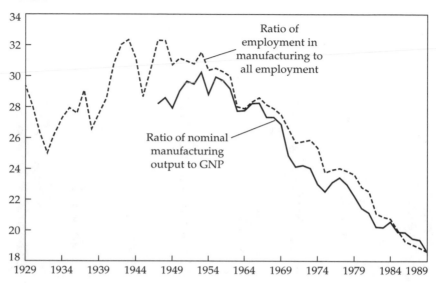

Source: Calculated from tables in the National Income Product Accounts (NIPA) data base, 1990.

jobs have been added in service industries, editorials warn that it would be folly to pin our hopes on expansion of the service sector. According to Stephen Cohen and John Zysman, the service sector can only thrive with a viable manufacturing sector, and the viability of manufacturing is threatened by the pressure of foreign competition.[34] In 1992, Democratic presidential candidate Paul Tsongas advanced similar arguments in his campaign manifesto, *A Call to Economic Arms*.[35] These arguments raise two questions: Is the United States really deindustrializing? If so, should we care?

Deindustrialization might be detected in one of two ways—as a decrease in the fraction of all national output that originates in the manufacturing industries or as a decrease in manufacturing employment, either absolute or relative. Measuring the share of all output that originates in manufacturing has been a source of some controversy.[36] On balance, the evidence suggests that the share of manufacturing has been shrinking since the early 1950s and the advent of the service revolution (figure 2-8). The percentage of employment in manufacturing has declined a bit more rapidly than the percentage of output in manufacturing in the past few years, reflecting two different productivity trends. Productivity growth in manufacturing accelerated during the 1980s, while in the service sector it slowed.

The U.S. economy has, then, indeed deindustrialized in recent years. Does this represent a serious economic problem? In one sense, deindustrialization is part of the natural evolution of the economy, and it has occurred in other advanced industrialized countries. It reflects the consequences of faster productivity improvement in manufacturing than in other sectors of the economy and changes in consumer demand for different kinds of products and services. If consumers wish to devote a larger proportion of their incomes to health services as their incomes rise, why should they be forced instead to purchase refrigerators or new automobiles to avoid the loss of manufacturing jobs? Besides, it would be very hard to do much about many of the causes of deindustrialization, whether or not it represents a problem.

Deindustrialization is linked in many people's minds with international trade. America is, they say, exporting jobs. There is a grain of truth in this argument: the rising importance of trade and foreign competition is one reason for the falling real manufacturing wages received by men with low or moderate levels of skills. The deficit in trade of manufactured goods means that manufacturing employment is lower than it would be if U.S. production and consumption of manufactured goods were equal. But the importance of foreign trade in determining manufacturing employment is easy to exaggerate. Decreases in manufacturing's share of output and employment began in the 1950s, when the United States ran a trade surplus. The shrinking relative size of the sector is caused primarily by economic forces here in the United States, not by trade.

Deindustrialization raises two legitimate concerns, however. If the manufacturing sector is shrinking because U.S. firms fail to innovate as rapidly as their foreign rivals and consequently lose ground internationally, there is a reason to be worried. U.S. citizens would be losing income-producing opportunities that would be theirs if they could innovate faster, and their real incomes may suffer. While there seems to be no slowdown in the pace of scientific discovery, the rate at which these innovations are commercially developed has fallen off. Thus the problems with the slow pace of innovations is simply a part of the larger problem of slow improvement in productivity.

Our second concern is that deindustrialization displaces people who once worked in highly paid manufacturing jobs. Many workers are forced to endure extended periods of joblessness or to accept jobs in other sectors with much lower wages and fewer fringe benefits. Displacement imposes particularly severe economic and emotional losses on senior workers with few transferrable skills. Their lack of preparation for well-paid jobs (or even for job training) can make their futures seem very bleak. A steelworker laid off from the Fairless steel plant in Pennsylvania learned that he did not qualify for retraining in either computer or appliance repair; both technical training courses required a knowledge of mathematics he did not possess. His dismal prospects are reflected in his comments to a reporter: "I was working all these years, paying the bills, paying off this house, making car payments. You don't realize time goes by and then, *bang*. It's gone. Everything is math."[37]

Reducing the economic and psychological pain caused by deindustrialization is a legitimate goal of policymaking. Many people favor adopting trade protection as a way to deal with deindustrialization. But this policy is doomed to failure because, for the most part, deindustrialization and economic displacement are not primarily caused by international trade. The only reliable prescription for improving the job prospects of unskilled displaced workers is to improve their skills and flexibility. This represents a major challenge, one that U.S. policymakers have so far failed to meet. But if the challenge can be met, the productivity of displaced workers will increase. We discuss this subject further in chapter 5.

Conclusion

We began this chapter by noting the seriousness of U.S. economic problems. The main problem is the slow growth of productivity. It underlies a number of economic maladies and makes others harder to deal with. We examined reasons for slow growth and showed why some sources for it may be amenable to change.

Several bright spots have emerged from the economic gloom. The United States continues to enjoy high average productivity in comparison with other industrialized countries. And U.S. productivity growth was faster in the 1980s than it was in the 1970s, particularly in manufacturing. Because the American work force is growing older and more experienced, there is some prospect that growth will accelerate still more in the 1990s, even if no major policy reforms are adopted.

The overall economic picture, however, is not very bright. Productivity growth remains stubbornly below its long-term level, either before or immediately after World War II. This has held the growth of wages and family incomes to depressingly low levels. One change in the economic environment that offers promise of increasing productivity growth in the intermediate run is an increase in the public and private investment rate. It is easy to identify a policy reform that could accomplish this change, at least eventually: if the federal budget were balanced, the government could raise net U.S. saving by 3 to 4 percent of national income, thus raising net domestically financed investment by more than half. Unfortunately, balancing the budget requires short-term sacrifice, since it involves increases in taxes or reductions in spending that would amount to one-fifth of current federal spending. Because the reform would be so painful, many citizens and policymakers may wonder whether it is worth adopting. We believe it is. But even if the deficit is not reduced, several other reforms that do not add to the budget deficit offer promise of improving productivity growth. These are described in later chapters.

Three

Inequality

INEQUALITY IN WAGES, in family income, and in household wealth has increased substantially in recent years. Some reasons for this have been widely reported: the weakening of labor unions, the increases in top corporate salaries, the soaring rewards to financial market speculation, and the decrease in the number of well-paid jobs in manufacturing. By themselves, however, these explanations do not account for the widening of inequality. Other sources are more important, but their exact significance has been much harder to pin down.

This chapter describes recent trends in wages and incomes to explain what is known about them. The widening of inequality began soon after the dramatic slowdown in U.S. productivity growth. The trends may be connected, but so far no one has been able to show what the connection might be. The slowdown in productivity growth began in the late 1960s and early 1970s and was at its worst between 1973 and 1979. Overall income inequality increased gradually during the 1970s and began to surge during the early 1980s, about when productivity performance began to improve, if only slightly.

The postwar trend in family income inequality is charted in figure 3-1. Inequality is represented by the Gini ratio, which economists use to measure the difference between the actual income distribution and a perfectly egalitarian income distribution. If all families received equal incomes, the Gini ratio would be zero; if all income were received by a single family, the ratio would be one. Inequality in family incomes decreased after World War II, reaching a low point in the late 1960s. Since 1969 inequality has grown almost without interruption.

The biggest jump occurred in the recession of the early 1980s, but

FIGURE 3-1. *Inequality of U.S. Family Income, 1947–91*

Gini ratio (zero is perfect equality)

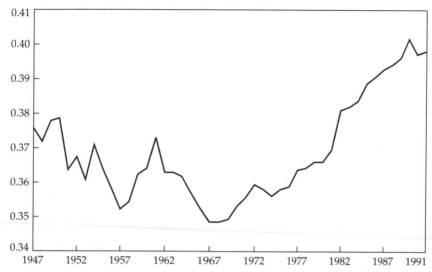

Source: Bureau of the Census, *Current Population Reports*, series P-60, no. 142 (1984), p. 47; no. 180 (1992), p. B-11.

the gap continued to widen after the economic recovery began. This pattern represented a sharp break with previous postwar experience. Until the 1980s, income and wage inequality had usually increased in recessions and shrunk or at least remained relatively constant during economic expansions. In a typical economic recovery, unemployed workers are called back to their old jobs or find new ones, boosting the wages and incomes of poor families. The incomes of more affluent families rise during expansions, too, but usually by smaller percentages. The income gap between rich and poor therefore tends to narrow whenever the economy expands. This did not occur during the 1980s. Inequality reached a high in 1989, the last year of one of the postwar period's longest economic expansions. Then strangely, inequality decreased during the 1990–91 recession, but it was still greater in 1991 than it had been in any postwar year before 1988.

Even though the economic link between the slowdown in growth and the increase in inequality is uncertain, the political connection is obvious. Middle and upper income Americans do not seem interested in expanding programs that aid people with low incomes when their own incomes are stagnant or decreasing. Poor families without bread-winners rely heavily on social security, welfare, and other public transfers. The elderly and disabled poor and many single-parent families cannot expect to see their living standards improve much unless transfer payments increase. If financially hard-pressed voters are unwilling to pay for increases when the economy expands, the income gap between working families and the nonworking poor will grow.

Earnings Inequality

One of the main reasons income inequality has increased in the United States is that wages and salaries have grown more unequal. Two-thirds of American personal income comes from labor earnings, so any increase in the inequality of earnings has a profound effect on the distribution of family income. The income distribution is also critically affected by the family living arrangements of earners. Families containing two or more potential earners enjoy a substantial income advantage over families with only a single worker. The composition of families and the distribution of earners among families has changed radically in recent decades. Later we consider the influence of these developments on income inequality. First, however, we examine what has happened to the distribution of earnings among people who work.

Inequality in wages, or in family income for that matter, occurs for a variety of reasons. Young workers typically earn lower wages than older ones. People in occupations requiring extensive training earn more than people in those requiring few credentials and little experience. Full-time workers earn more than part-time workers. Among people in the same industries and occupations, women often earn less than men, and black and Hispanic workers frequently earn less than whites. In addition, census statistics show that earnings vary greatly even among workers who share the same demographic characteristics and job qualifications and who are employed in the same industry and occupation—in fact, most of the variability of earnings in the United States arises from this last source. Even after adjusting for age, work experience, educational attainment, occupation, and other observable factors that influence earnings, a great deal of unexplained and apparently random variation remains.

When earnings inequality increases, it is natural to ask which sources can explain the increase. Some sources of extra inequality are matters

FIGURE 3-2. *Rate of Growth in Annual Earnings, Male Workers, 1967–79, 1979–89*

Percent change per year

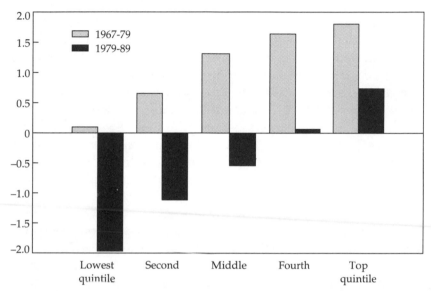

Source: Authors' tabulations from Current Population Survey data tapes.

of great social concern. If, for example, the gap between the earnings of black workers and white workers widened, most Americans would be worried that workplace discrimination was worsening. Some other sources of greater inequality should not be matters of much concern, however. Inequality might grow if the job market were suddenly flooded with new workers who had little practical work experience and who generally receive very low wages. As they obtain additional work experience, their earnings should rise and overall inequality decrease.

One way to see what has happened to the distribution of earnings is to consider the trend in earnings in different parts of the distribution. Figure 3-2 shows inflation-adjusted annual changes in earnings of male workers age 25–64 from 1967 to 1979 and 1979 to 1989. It shows these changes for five equal-sized groups ranked by annual earnings.[1] Clearly, wage inequality has increased. From 1967 to 1979, real annual earnings of men in the top quintile rose 1.8 percent a year. For workers in the bottom quintile, earnings rose just 0.1 percent a year. Earnings growth dropped sharply for workers everywhere after 1979, but while real earnings rose only 0.7 percent a year for workers in the top quintile, they actually fell 1.1 percent a year for workers in the second quintile, and 2.0 percent a year for those in the bottom quintile. Since reaching a peak in 1973, real annual earnings in the bottom quintile have fallen 24 percent, and in the second quintile 15 percent. But real earnings in the top quintile climbed 10 percent. Inequality has increased, and a smaller percentage of men earn wages that place them near the middle of the earnings distribution.

Figure 3-2 actually understates the growth in earnings inequality. Census Bureau statistics do not reflect the full extent of earnings increases among top earners because the Census survey does not record earnings higher than $100,000 a year. Data from income tax returns suggest that the earnings of workers in the top 1 or 2 percent of the wage distribution have climbed much faster than the earnings of other workers.[2]

In addition, economically disadvantaged men are worse off than implied by figure 3-2. The figure shows earnings changes among men who were successful in holding a job, at least briefly, sometime during a calendar year. Men paid low hourly wages are often without work for a year or more, find it hard to earn good wages when they hold a job, and have experienced increasing difficulty in finding a job at all. Overall unemployment rates moderated in the late 1980s, but for men who earn low hourly wages, unemployment levels remained much higher than what they experienced in earlier decades. For men in the lowest decile of the earnings distribution, the time spent in joblessness increased by 16 percentage points—about eight weeks over the course of a year—between the late 1960s and late 1980s.[3] Moreover, many poorly paid men became so discouraged that they left the labor market altogether. Labor force dropouts are not included in figure 3-2. If they were, the deterioration in the position of poorly paid workers would appear even more acute.

Employment and earnings losses were especially severe among younger workers and those with limited education (figure 3-3). For example, among men 18 to 24 years old in 1978, those with a college education earned 20 percent more than those who had just a high school education or less. By 1987 the college earnings premium had jumped to nearly 60 percent. For all men under age 44 there was a similar increase in the differential. The earnings premium for college graduates did not jump because they were receiving sharply higher

FIGURE 3-3. *Differential in Annual Income between Male High School and College Graduates, by Age, 1978, 1987*

Percent premium relative to high school graduates

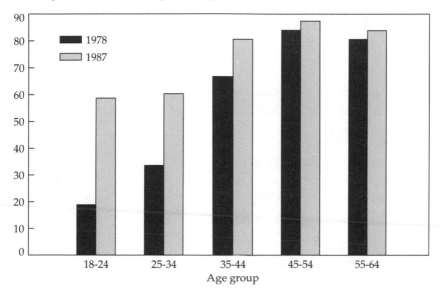

Age group

Source: Bureau of the Census, *Current Population Reports*, series P-60, no. 162 (1989), p. 145; no. 123 (1980), p. 223.

wages; their earnings rose only moderately. Instead, the premium climbed because young, less-educated men were receiving steadily *lower* real earnings. At older ages, the college premium increased too, but by a smaller amount.

Earnings trends among women have been much less discouraging. The annual earnings of adult women in most parts of the wage distribution continued to grow during the 1970s and 1980s, although much of the increase was due to longer hours of work, particularly for women from economically disadvantaged backgrounds. Longer hours or additional weeks of work a year have been needed to offset falling hourly wage rates. Women from more advantaged backgrounds have received much larger hourly wage increases. Overall, women have experienced more rapid gains in the labor market than men. Their comparative good fortune reduced economywide disparities in earnings, since women have historically received lower wages than men.

Two developments are responsible for most of the surge in earnings inequality. Real (inflation-adjusted) earnings of less skilled workers have dropped significantly. What is more, their earnings shrank relative to those received by more skilled workers, who of course earned better wages to begin with. Although this trend is apparent among many groups of American workers, younger men have lost the most ground. This is a source of serious social concern because they are responsible supporting most of the nation's children. The deteriorating economic fortunes of America's young, less skilled breadwinners has meant that the percentage of children living in poverty has shot up. The poverty rate among Americans under age eighteen reached 21.8 percent in 1991.[4]

A less well known but more important source of inequality is the steadily widening disparity over the past two decades in wages paid to workers who have nearly identical characteristics. This widening inequality has been especially pronounced among the best-compensated workers.

Hourly Wage Inequality

The growth in annual earnings inequality is primarily due to the growing inequality of hourly wage rates. Among men and women who work, there has been little detectable change in the variability of hours worked per week or weeks worked per year, but their hourly wages have become less equal.[5] This implies that the price of skill rather than the level of individual work effort is growing more unequal.[6]

The economic reasons behind the increasing disparities in wage rates and earnings are not entirely clear, but economists generally agree on a handful of important factors. These can be classified into two broad categories: the changing pattern of *demand* for workers and changes in the qualifications and *supply* of workers.

The demand for different classes of workers is affected by the overall demand for labor, the demand in different industries, and the demand for different skill categories within different industries. High overall unemployment is historically associated with reduced demand for all kinds of workers, but especially for less skilled workers. Some industries, such as manufacturing of durable goods, offer good job opportunities to less skilled workers. When these industries shrink, the demand for such labor shrinks, too. Technological change affects the demand for different classes of workers within individual industries.

The second set of explanations for recent wage developments focuses on shifts in the composition or overall level of labor supply. When young workers are in abundant supply, as they were in the 1970s and early 1980s, added competition for unskilled jobs can drive down the average wage they receive and boost their unemployment rate. When a surge of new college graduates floods the market, the wages and working conditions of all less experienced but highly qualified workers may suffer.

Demand-Side Factors

The most popular explanation for the labor market woes of unskilled workers is one that emphasizes the shifting fortunes of U.S. industries. Heavy manufacturing, which once provided millions of well-paid jobs to the less skilled, has shrunk. Its place has been taken by service industries, which are accused of offering mediocre career prospects to middle-class Americans and lousy jobs to the less skilled. The retrenchment of manufacturing, communications, and transportation is in turn linked to external economic developments. Manufacturing was hard hit by competition in international trade; communications and transportation have been profoundly affected by deregulation and freer market entry.

The loss of the comparative advantage of American industries in international trade has particularly harmed workers in autos, steel, and other industries in which U.S. advantages were once overwhelming. Wages have been restrained by international competition and, more important, hundreds of thousands of well-paying jobs have been lost as foreign producers have captured markets formerly dominated by American manufacturers.

This popular explanation for wage inequality accounts for some of the trend in wage disparities, but it falls short of accounting for most recent increases in inequality. First, the shift in the American industrial structure has been under way since the 1950s, although it certainly accelerated between 1973 and 1984. The share of American workers employed in manufacturing fell from nearly 35 percent immediately after World War II to less than 18 percent by 1989. Two-thirds of this decline occurred before the 1980s.[7] Similarly, the share of U.S. workers employed in the high-paying transportation, communications, and utility industries has been diminishing since World War II. The percentage of Americans employed in those industries actually fell faster in the twenty years before 1969 than it did in the twenty years after. The idea that recent trends in relative wages can be explained by changing patterns of industrial development is thus incomplete.

To be sure, shifts in the industrial structure partly explain long-term trends toward greater wage inequality and lower earnings for the less skilled. A detailed analysis of male wages has shown, for example, that growing industries pay average wages that are well below or well above the average for all industries, thus driving up the inequality of earnings. In addition, relative wage changes across industries have tended to drive up the average wages in some high-paying industries and drive them down in low-paying industries.[8] However, these trends came to a halt at the beginning of the 1980s, so they cannot account for any growth in earnings inequality since 1979.

Much more important than trends in the growth of high-wage and low-wage industries is wage inequality *within* industries. One notable feature of growing industries is that, whatever their average wages, the wages are highly variable. Since the inequality of wages within growing industries is greater than the inequality in shrinking industries, overall wage disparity is increasing.

Even more important, wage inequality has grown strongly within most industries, accounting for the lion's share of the growth of inequality since 1979.[9] To understand developments in earnings inequality, it is therefore important to understand why inequality is growing in so many different industries. Trade developments and industrial deregulation can explain part of the wage shift within U.S. industries. As the rest of the world adopted U.S. production methods, the terms of trade gradually turned against American producers. The worst side effects were felt by workers whose skills were similar to those of overseas workers, mainly less skilled workers. The manufacturing industries that relied on mass production methods and unskilled and semiskilled labor were particularly hard hit because their methods were easiest for foreign producers to duplicate. Even U.S. producers that have remained strongly competitive have turned to production methods emphasizing highly skilled labor, methods in which the United States continues to enjoy an advantage. International competition has thus had a disproportionate effect on unskilled and semi-skilled U.S. workers.

The effects of deregulation have in some ways mirrored those of greater international competition. Forced to compete freely with new low-cost market entrants, deregulated firms such as AT&T and Trans World Airlines have laid off less skilled workers and cut the real wages of many who remained on their payrolls. Most firms entering deregulated markets pay their workers wages only slightly above the market wage. Because these firms are not protected by regulation, they cannot afford to pay generous wage premiums to their less skilled workers. As a result, the wages of airline baggage handlers and interstate truck drivers have fallen. Wages for highly skilled workers in deregulated industries have not fallen as far because job opportunities for them have always been reasonably good outside regulated industries. The adverse effects of international trade and industrial deregulation on less skilled workers have probably had spillover effects in other industries. Unskilled workers who cannot find decent jobs in industries affected by international competition or deregulation have been forced to seek employment in other sectors. The presence of so many unskilled job seekers tends to push down the wages of the unskilled in all industries.

Aggregate demand for labor can also explain part of the trend toward more unequal wages. Slack labor markets are particularly harmful to poorly paid workers. Employees who are laid off or forced to work fewer hours always bear a disproportionate share of the burden of recessions, and many are paid low hourly wages. As a result, earnings inequality increases when unemployment climbs. The U.S. unemployment rate rose from an average of 4.6 percent in the 1950s and 1960s to 6.2 percent in the 1970s and 7.3 percent in the 1980s.[10] Gary Burtless has argued that this factor might explain one fifth of the increase in male earnings inequality between the 1960s and mid-1980s.[11] However, the gradual decline in unemployment between 1983 and 1989 did not bring any reduction in wage or earnings inequality. Lack of aggregate demand can thus explain the timing of the huge increase in inequality but cannot explain its magnitude. Nor can it explain the stubborn persistence of wage inequality during an uncommonly long economic expansion. Business cycles can account for cyclical movements in inequality but not much of the long-term trend.

Supply-Side Factors

Changes in the composition of the U.S. labor supply also contributed to increases in wage inequality over the past two decades. The most important changes in composition resulted from the entry of the huge baby boom generation into the work force between the late 1960s and the early 1980s and the unprecedented influx of women. Increases in the educational attainment of new workers, stepped-up immigration, and gradual change in the racial makeup of the working-age population have also affected the level and character of labor supply.

Changes in the supply of labor can have two kinds of effects on the wage structure. An increase in the number of less skilled workers, such as young entrants, women without recent job experience, or unskilled immigrants, will raise the proportion of all workers who receive low wages. Heightened competition for jobs requiring fewer skills will drive down the wages of the less skilled relative to the wages received by more skilled workers.

Both effects can be detected in wage trends over the past two decades. Less experienced workers entered the job market in massive numbers during the 1970s, raising the proportion of workers receiving low wages. In addition, men in this group were forced to accept lower wages because of the added job market competition from fellow entrants. The baby boomers were harmed by this development, but it was not a reason for long-term concern about the economy. On the contrary, observers were astonished that the American economy could absorb so many new workers without major disruption. But the surging supply of less skilled labor was not matched by an equivalent rise in demand. Most of the new people managed to find jobs, but their wages fell in comparison with those paid to more experienced workers.

At first, the relative wage losses were larger among college-educated young men than among the less educated. The premium received by young men for completing college fell moderately from the late 1960s until the mid-1970s, presumably as a result of the rapid rise in college completion rates. The increased supply of young college-educated men evidently outstripped demand. Starting in the late 1970s, however, the college premium began to soar (see figure 3-3).

Even though the percentage of college-educated workers continued to increase in the 1980s, the rate of increase slowed considerably, especially in the case of men.[12]

The labor force has also experienced large changes in the flow and composition of immigrant workers. The annual rate of immigration has nearly doubled in recent decades.[13] The skills and educational attainment of recent immigrants are also scantier than they once were. Immigrants to the United States were once drawn mainly from Europe or from well-educated groups in less developed countries. They are now increasingly drawn from less skilled populations in the third world. One-quarter of U.S. workers with less than a high school education are now immigrants.[14] Perhaps one-fifth of the recent deterioration in the relative wages of dropouts may be due to increased immigration of less skilled workers.[15]

Even though supply-side trends in the labor market can help explain some of the changing wage structure, they cannot account for the most important trends. Women at all educational levels have managed to reduce the gap between their wages and those of men, especially during the past decade, in spite of a continued and fairly steady increase in the proportion of women in the labor force. Moreover, wage disparities have increased within many groups in the labor force. The increases were not restricted to those age, skill, and work-experience groups that had the largest gains in relative supply. Generational crowding cannot explain all the rise in inequality among men, for example, because the trend is apparent even in the oldest age groups, where no effect would be anticipated.

Demographic shifts since 1979 should in fact have contributed to growing equalization of earnings among both men and women. Most changes in the distribution by age, education, and work experience occurring in the 1980s raised the proportion of male and female workers who would be expected to be near the middle of the earnings distribution. Workers with age, education, or experience levels that would place them near the bottom became relatively less abundant.

Technological Change

Many economists believe the most persuasive explanation for the widening wage disparities is a demand-side shift linked to the introduction of new kinds of production techniques. This technological change has occurred in service-producing as well as goods-producing industries as employers altered their production methods in ways that required a more able and skilled work force. Employers have persisted in this strategy in the face of growing wage premiums to the better skilled, a development that makes it more costly to hire a skilled work force than it was in the 1960s or 1970s.

Direct evidence about the effects of technological change on wage inequality is elusive. The Census Bureau and Department of Labor do not survey employers to determine whether and how much their skill requirements have changed. Analysts must infer shifts by looking at changes in the relative price of different kinds of labor and the relative supply of those types of labor. The shift in the industrial composition of demand can explain only a small share of the change in the structure of wages. And most economists who have carefully examined the question conclude that supply-side changes also explain only a small percentage of the growth in inequality. This leaves technological change as one possible explanation.

Some readers might assume it is inevitable that technological change will boost employers' demand for advanced skills. But even if this were true, it would not necessarily lead to wider pay differentials between skilled and unskilled workers. Relative wage changes also depend on the trends in the relative abundance of a skill. If the supply of skilled workers is keeping pace with the increased demand, pay differentials might remain unchanged, as they did during the 1960s.

More fundamentally, technological progress may not always increase the demand for advanced skills. It is widely believed, for example, that technological progress sometimes results in a "dumbed-down" production process. Many factory assembly lines require constant repetition of very simple tasks. Before the introduction of the assembly line, workers may have performed a much wider variety of tasks, which required greater effort and ability to learn. Retail clerks were once obliged to use simple arithmetic to calculate bills and make change. Many now push buttons on electronic machines that are illustrated with pictures of all items on sale. Taxes and change are computed by the cash register rather than the clerk, who may have only a hazy knowledge of arithmetic. If technological advance breeds dumbed-down jobs, it is hard to see why skill differentials would widen. They should narrow. The labor market position of unskilled labor can only improve when employers create large numbers of low-skill jobs. If skilled workers disdained employment in these jobs, the relative wages of unskilled workers would almost certainly rise.

Several pieces of evidence suggest, however, that recent technological change may have favored the more skilled over the less skilled. The pay premium offered to highly educated workers soared after 1979, particularly for men under age forty-five. In addition, pay increases have been larger in high-skill than in low-skill occupations. The fast-growing occupations within most industries are those requiring high levels of education and skill.[16] This is confirmed by projections of the Department of Labor that the most rapid employment gains have been and will continue to be in occupations requiring advanced skills.[17] Economists have also found evidence of a positive association between simple measures of technological progress and the rate of change within industries in pay premiums for advanced education. Faster technological change, as indicated for example by R&D spending, is associated with increasing pay differentials between highly educated and less educated workers.[18]

More intriguing is the discovery by Alan Krueger that workers who used computers on the job enjoyed faster wage increases in the 1980s than workers who did not use or know how to use them.[19] Although the number of computer-literate workers is comparatively small, they received a disproportionate share of all wage gains in the middle and late 1980s. Use of computers is particularly common among well-educated workers in skilled occupations; it is increasingly common among all types of workers. Krueger's research suggests that the introduction of microcomputers has conferred a significant advantage on workers who possess the skills and background necessary to learn how to use them. Unskilled workers, by definition, do not fit this description.

Although this kind of evidence indicates that technological progress has favored the more skilled, especially since 1979, it is unclear that it can account for all the wage inequality not explained by shifts in the industrial structure and the relative supply of different kinds of labor. More than half the increase in wage and earnings inequality derives from widening wage disparities among workers who have the same amount of education and previous work experience. Inequality has grown among workers within the same industry and among workers in the same occupation.

Several researchers have suggested that the sharp increase in inequality within homogenous groups defined by age, education, occupation, industry, and work experience signals larger wage premiums for unmeasured job skills.[20] Analysts who examine wage developments are constrained to study dimensions of skill that can be measured on census surveys: education, occupation, and work experience. If they could analyze other dimensions of skill or ability, such as specific job training or general aptitude, they could obtain a clearer understanding of the ultimate sources of increased wage inequality. If these dimensions could be measured, most economists believe they would find that inequality across skill categories has increased in recent years. The increases in skill premiums reflect the fact that employers' demand for highly skilled workers has outpaced the supply. To explain the surge in wage inequality that occurred in the 1980s, economists hypothesize that the trend toward increased demand for highly skilled workers that has been driven by changes in technology has accelerated. So far, however, the evidence is suggestive rather than conclusive.

Other Factors

Some labor market institutions have changed in a way that harms less skilled workers. Labor unions once were instrumental in raising the relative wages of unskilled industrial workers. This role has diminished. The decline in unions has been a particular blow to unskilled men, since many who earned middle-income wages owed their good fortune to the influence of unions. Unions have a sizable effect on wage inequality for two reasons. They tend to raise the earnings of their members in comparison with earnings received outside the unionized sector. And they strive to reduce wage disparities within the establishments they organize. The latter effect raises the wages of less skilled workers in comparison with wages they could earn in unorganized establishments. Unions appear to have very little impact on the wages of college-educated members.

Unionization rates have consistently declined since the mid-1950s, but the rate of decline accelerated in the past two decades. The rate in the private sector fell from 30 percent to 12 percent between 1970 and 1990.[21] Declining union membership might explain up to one-fifth of the rise in male wage inequality since the late 1970s.[22]

Other wage-setting institutions have also changed. Employers may be reducing their emphasis on fairness or equity when establishing a wage scale. They may focus much more on attracting or retaining workers who have particular skills that are scarce in their local labor market. To attract these workers, employers have been willing to offer larger pay differentials.

There is some evidence that workers are now willing to tolerate larger pay differentials. In the early 1980s a number of union contracts permitted employers to offer two pay scales, a high scale for those on the payroll when the agreement was signed and a lower scale for workers hired after the agreement went into effect. Before the 1980s, unions resisted this kind of wage structure because it paid unequal wages to employees with similar work experience who did the same job.

We do not argue that all increases in wage inequality can be traced to efficiency considerations or rational responses to changes in relative demand and supply. The two-tier wage structure for example, is hardly efficient. Workers on the lower wage scale undoubtedly resent the penalty they suffer because they were hired after an arbitrary date. This may reduce their productivity in comparison with what it would be under a scale in which they received the same wage paid to more senior workers. The soaring compensation given to top corporate managers is also hard to explain in terms of efficiency or supply and demand. According to a *Business Week* survey of executive pay, American chief executives earned 104 times as much as a typical production worker in 1991. In 1980 the typical CEO received 42 times as much.[23] In view of the low rates of return earned recently by large U.S. corporations, it is hard to see how the larger differential represents a rational payment for improved results. The change in corporate pay formulas probably reflects the increased power of senior corporate managers to determine their own compensation and greater tolerance of inequality on the part of shareholders and subordinate workers.

Summary

As a matter of arithmetic, increased inequality arises from two main sources: widening gaps in average pay between groups that ordinarily earn different average wages and increases in inequality within these groups. Both factors help explain recent trends. But the more important source, especially in the 1980s, was the growth in inequality within groups of workers with the same observed characteristics. Any satisfactory explanation for this increase must therefore account for the growth in wage differences among similarly qualified workers.

Among workers who differ in their qualifications the trends are reasonably clear: skilled workers are receiving higher wages, while less skilled workers, especially unskilled young men, are receiving lower wages. Two developments can account for part of this change. Industrial and occupational shifts in the demand for labor have tended to push up the demand for highly educated workers. And the relative abundance of educated labor is growing more slowly than it did in the 1960s and 1970s. Based on indirect evidence, it also appears that technological progress has pushed up employers' demand for more highly skilled workers. Demand for these workers is growing in a variety of industries. This fact, much more than deindustrialization, has hurt the job market prospects of unskilled workers.

Family Income Inequality

The earnings trends we have described have contributed to the growing gulf between rich and poor in the United States. But family income inequality has grown for other reasons as well. Inequality generally declined from 1947 to 1969, and only began to rise strongly after 1973 (see figure 3-1). It may have declined between 1947 and 1969 in part because of women's increased labor force participation. Until the 1970s, women married to poorly paid men were more likely to enter the work force than women married to well-paid men.[24] As women in poorer married-couple families entered the labor force, their earnings reduced the gap between rich and poor families. Even more important, other sources of family income became modestly more equally distributed before 1969, primarily as a result of increased public transfers to the elderly and poor.

Recent statistics on average income growth, reported in the last chapter, are discouraging, and those on income growth at the bottom of the distribution are downright depressing. Before 1973 income growth was rapid for families everywhere in the distribution, but it was strongest for families near the middle. Since 1973, growth has slumped everywhere in the distribution but has fallen fastest among families with low incomes, thus widening the gap between rich and

FIGURE 3-4. *Family Income Growth, Selected Parts of Income Distribution, 1973–91*

Index (1973 = 100)

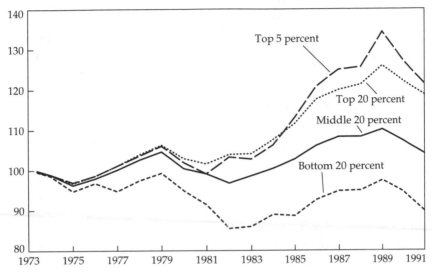

Source: Bureau of the Census, *Current Population Reports,* series P-60, no. 180 (1992), p. B-11.

poor. In fact, after adjusting for inflation, families at the twentieth income percentile received no more income in 1990 than they did in 1973. Families below the twentieth percentile received lower cash incomes in 1990 than they did in 1973. For poor families, cash income growth ended in the early 1970s (figure 3-4).[25]

In the 1970s, income growth was slow for all income groups. But at least it grew or fell only slightly, even among families near the bottom of the distribution. Since 1979, growth has partially recovered, but only among families in the top quarter of the distribution. Families near the middle continue to receive very modest income gains, but families near the bottom have never made up the sharp losses they suffered between 1979 and 1983. The severe recession and lengthy economic recovery of the 1980s obviously produced very unequal gains.

Some observers argue that family income statistics reflect too bleak a picture of recent economic progress. We agree that income growth since 1973 is understated by the Census Bureau's family income statistics, but the trend toward greater inequality is accurately reflected by those statistics. Since the late 1960s family size has declined, so the real income needed to support an average family has fallen. Between 1977 and 1989, for example, average family size declined about 10 percent.[26] Family size shrank in every income category, but shrank most among families in the middle of the income distribution and least among families at the bottom. In addition, a higher percentage of income is received by people who do not live in families, because the number of unattached individuals has increased faster than the number of families and because they have received larger income gains than families.

Another objection to the Census Bureau statistics is their exclusion of certain kinds of income thought to be especially important to families near the bottom of the distribution. Until 1979 the Census Bureau asked only about cash income sources when determining a family's income. It did not ask about in-kind income—housing assistance, imputed rent on owner-occupied homes, medical insurance, undistributed corporate profits, and food stamps. As it happens, some of these kinds of income grew rapidly in the late 1960s and 1970s and were disproportionately received by families with low or moderate cash incomes. If the new noncash sources of income had been included in the official statistics, the growth of income would be faster than shown in figure 3-4, particularly for low-income families.

It is hard to know what kind of adjustment for noncash income should be made in the Census Bureau income statistics for the 1960s and 1970s. Suitable data are simply not available. The proper adjustment for the period after 1979 is much more straightforward. Noncash benefits are now included in some census tabulations of family income. These show that, even using a comprehensive definition of income that includes noncash benefits, income inequality and poverty have increased sharply since 1979. In fact, poverty and inequality have increased by roughly equivalent amounts whether analysts use a cash definition of income or a comprehensive definition that includes in-kind benefits.

The Congressional Budget Office has adjusted Census Bureau statistics back through 1973 to reflect the shrinking size of American families and the changing circumstances of unrelated individuals. The adjusted statistics and the official census series reveal similar trends.

The adjusted real incomes of families and unrelated individuals in the poorest one-fifth of the income distribution fell 2 percent between 1979 and 1989, while the adjusted incomes of family units in the top one-fifth of the distribution rose 20 percent.[27]

Sources of income change are shown in table 3-1. The dollar figures reflect adjusted family income, that is, actual income amounts adjusted to reflect differences in the size of each family unit.[28] In calculating the figures, CBO ranked each family unit by adjusted income and then divided families into five equal groups or quintiles. The first two columns show trends in average labor earnings for male and female earners who head families. The third column shows the trend in earnings among all other members of the family unit. The other columns show changes in other components of family income and in total family income.

The first four columns illustrate the impact of growing wage and earnings inequality. Men's earnings have declined in the bottom four quintiles and risen in the top quintile. The largest declines occurred in the bottom three income quintiles, exactly as one would expect in view of the earnings losses sustained by young, less skilled men. Earnings of family members other than the male or female head rose faster in low-income families than in other families, although the differences are so small that there is little appreciable effect on the income distribution.

Changes in women's earnings have had a profound impact on family income inequality. Earnings have risen among women in all income quintiles but have risen fastest among women in the most affluent families. The percentage earnings gains of women in the richest quintile were more than three times the gains among those in the poorest quintile. In dollar terms, the gains of women in the top quintile were thirty times larger than those of women in the poorest quintile.

Earnings rose faster among women at the top of the family income distribution than among those in the middle and bottom for two main reasons. Hourly wage rates of women in affluent families climbed faster than hourly wages of poorer women, and women in the most affluent families increased their rates of employment and average hours worked faster than those in poorer households.[29] The trend in women's labor force participation is thus widening the gap between

TABLE 3-1. *Sources of Family Income Change, by Quintile, 1979, 1989*
1989 dollars unless otherwise specified

Quintile	Male earnings	Female earnings	Other earnings	Total earnings	Interest etc.	Private income	Cash transfers	Gross cash income	In-kind aid	Aftertax income
Lowest										
1979	3,005	1,512	137	4,654	559	5,213	3,106	8,319	742	8,749
1989	2,849	1,704	147	4,700	586	5,286	2,703	7,989	861	8,575
Percent change	−5	13	7	1	5	1	−13	−4	16	−2
Second										
1979	10,343	4,013	531	14,887	1,347	16,234	2,684	18,918	247	17,324
1989	9,335	4,810	531	14,677	1,585	16,261	2,895	19,156	183	17,416
Percent change	−10	20	0	−1	18	0	8	1	−26	1
Middle										
1979	16,903	5,863	1,109	23,875	2,098	25,973	2,180	28,153	101	24,488
1989	15,941	7,760	1,099	24,800	2,739	27,539	2,510	30,049	46	26,055
Percent change	−6	32	−1	4	31	6	15	7	−55	6
Fourth										
1979	24,223	8,392	1,942	34,557	3,051	37,608	1,915	39,522	55	33,210
1989	23,636	11,717	1,851	37,204	4,205	41,410	2,281	43,691	18	36,728
Percent change	−2	40	−5	8	38	10	19	11	−67	11
Highest										
1979	40,558	12,634	3,573	56,764	8,887	65,651	1,878	67,529	27	53,548
1989	44,396	18,414	3,454	66,264	12,194	78,458	2,336	80,794	9	64,496
Percent change	9	46	−3	17	37	20	24	20	−67	20
All										
1979	19,001	6,486	1,457	26,944	3,188	30,132	2,354	32,486	229	27,457
1989	19,230	8,887	1,411	29,527	4,260	33,787	2,538	36,325	220	30,645
Percent change	1	37	−3	10	34	12	8	12	−4	12

Source: 1991 Green Book, Committee Print, House Committee on Ways and Means, 102 Cong. 1 sess. (GPO, May 1991), pp. 1226–27.

rich and poor families, precisely the opposite of its effect in the 1950s and 1960s when women from less affluent families were the ones most likely to enter the work force.

One phenomenon that has contributed to the earnings patterns is the steady increase in the number of households headed by a single parent. Because one-parent families usually have only a single adult capable of earning wages, and because that adult seldom can earn as much as the primary earner in a two-parent family, single parents are handicapped in their struggle to earn good incomes. Most have incomes that place them in the bottom half of the income distribution. Indeed, the poverty rate among single-parent families has remained relatively constant (and extremely high) for the past several decades, principally because so few single parents have the capacity to earn good wages or increase their earnings if they are already at work. By contrast, married women often find it easier to increase the amount of time they work. With the help of their husbands they can often arrange to mix employment with caring for children, and higher family income makes it easier for them to arrange paid child care.

The swelling number of one-parent families is not a recent phenomenon, however. It has been part of the American demographic scene since the early 1960s, when overall income inequality was shrinking rather than growing. In fact, the trend toward single-parent families has slowed in the past decade as the divorce rate has stopped climbing.

Rebecca Blank has concluded that trends in family living arrangements are comparatively insignificant in explaining trends in low-income status during the 1980s.[30] Family composition trends were much more important in pushing people toward low-income status during the 1960s and 1970s. Nonetheless, the slow growth in the number of households containing only a single potential earner tends to boost the portion of the population at risk of becoming poor.

As a result of the trends in wage inequality, family structure, and women's labor force participation, the combined earnings of workers in the most affluent families have climbed much faster than the earnings of families in the other four quintiles (see table 3-1). Total family earnings remained virtually unchanged among families in the bottom two quintiles but rose 17 percent among families in the top quintile. Private nonwage income—interest payments, capital gains, pensions, dividends, and so forth—has climbed much faster than labor earnings.

These sources of income are more important for affluent families than for the poor, and they have increased by much larger percentages. This has further widened the gap between affluent and poor families.

Government transfer payments received by affluent families have also risen by much larger percentages than transfers received by the less well off. This is mainly because governments have cut back means-tested transfers, which are disproportionately received by the poor, whereas benefits that are not means tested, such as social security, have maintained their previous value or been increased. Government tax policy has had only a small effect on family income distribution, except at the very top of the scale. Although the federal payroll and income tax structure became somewhat less progressive between 1979 and 1989, CBO tabulations show that this had a noticeable effect on net family incomes only in the most affluent 2 or 3 percent of households.

Even if the role of government policy has been smaller than suggested by partisan commentators, it is remarkable that changes in policy had any effect at all in reducing the incomes of the less affluent. By the standards of other industrialized nations, the share of income received by poor American households was already quite small at the beginning of the 1980s.[31] Economic and demographic developments during the decade decreased this share still further. Other countries, such as Canada, that faced similar adverse trends, liberalized their income transfer systems during the 1980s to offset the effects of changes in earnings and family structure. In the United States, liberalization of the income transfer system had once played a critical role in reducing income inequality and poverty. One reason that income inequality decreased in the United States during the 1950s and 1960s is that government transfers increased. Many low-income families did not directly benefit from rising wages or falling unemployment in those decades. Families headed by retired or disabled workers or by unemployed single parents did not enjoy automatic income gains when the labor market improved. Their incomes rose principally because social security and public assistance benefits were liberalized.

Inequality of wealth also increased in the 1980s. The most reliable information about American families' wealth is based on data collected in the Federal Reserve Board's Survey of Consumer Finances conducted in 1983, 1986, and 1989. Data from the 1983 and 1989 surveys unambiguously show a sharp rise in the share of American wealth held by the nation's very richest families. The top 1 percent increased their share of total wealth from 31 percent to 37 percent.

This increase did not occur because the saving rate of the affluent climbed; in fact, it fell in comparison with saving rates in earlier decades.[32] But top wealth holders accumulated assets at a much faster pace than the remainder of the population, primarily because of rapid capital gains on stocks, bonds, and other forms of wealth disproportionately owned by the affluent. In addition, their extraordinary income gains permitted them to save greater amounts, even though the share of their income saved was declining.

Implications

Family income inequality has increased sharply over the past twenty years, especially since 1979, reaching a new postwar high at the end of the 1980s. The growing inequality of earnings, especially male earnings, explains an important part of this development. A continued increase in the proportion of households headed by single parents and steep increases in the hours and weeks worked by married women, particularly those from affluent households, further widened the disparity. Unearned incomes have also increased, conferring exceptional gains on the wealthiest families. The state and federal governments have cut back some transfers targeted at low-income people, and the federal government has made the tax system somewhat less progressive. The perception of a growing gulf between rich and poor families is amply justified. Whatever the shortcomings of any particular piece of evidence, too many pieces point in the same direction. In the past two decades low-income families have seen their incomes fall or stagnate and affluent families have seen theirs improve.

These trends would not evoke special concern if we believed the new inequality was temporary or could be sure that the trends did not imply an increase in lifetime income inequality. The inequality that resulted from the entry of the baby boom generation into the job market was probably temporary. The entry of less-skilled immigrants into the job market has also increased the proportion of workers receiving low wages. This would not be a matter of social concern unless it reduced the wages earned by workers born in the United

States. Unfortunately, economists have found some evidence that less skilled American-born workers have been hurt by the influx of less skilled immigrants. In addition, the relative decline in wages earned by the less-skilled men does not appear to be temporary. It has persisted since the late 1970s, and no reversal is yet in sight.

It is conceivable that the increase in wage and income inequality carries no implications for the distribution of well-being over Americans' lifetimes. The measures of inequality discussed in this chapter provide a snapshot of inequality at a single moment in time. Many persons and families with low incomes in a given year will receive higher incomes in the future. Young earners and families just getting established can expect their incomes to increase. Workers who are temporarily unemployed will find new jobs. Average family income measured over a period of several years shows less inequality than income measured in only a single year.[33]

Some people infer from this that growing inequality in the 1970s and 1980s does not represent a serious social problem. This would be true if the increase in inequality within a single year were matched by a similar increase in income mobility from one year to the next. It might not matter much that families in the bottom quarter of the income distribution had a low income in a given year if they also had a good chance of receiving much higher incomes in the following year.

The fact is, however, that the chance of receiving a large increase in income is not very good. More to the point, the chance of enjoying a large increase has not grown in the past few decades. Americans whose annual incomes place them in the bottom 25 percent of the income distribution have an 80 percent chance of remaining there for at least two years in succession. The probability of moving out of the poorest class from one year to the next hardly changed at all in the 1970s and 1980s.[34] This implies that the increase in income inequality within a single year is mirrored by a similar increase in inequality over Americans' lifetimes. Families at the bottom of the income distribution are not only further away from the American mainstream in a given year, they remain further away for years.

The increase in inequality represents a serious social problem as well as a major challenge to American values and institutions. Many of the worst effects of the new inequality have been felt by young breadwinners raising children. The poverty rate among American children averaged 15.7 percent during the 1970s but rose to 20.5 percent during the 1980s, an increase of nearly one-third. Child poverty rates this high are unknown in most other advanced industrialized countries.[35]

A sensible strategy to improve the U.S. income distribution must emphasize improving the job opportunities and earning capacities of comparatively unskilled workers. These workers have suffered the greatest harm from recent economic trends. Most of their income is derived from earnings. Improving their ability to earn good wages will not only raise their family incomes thus reducing inequality, it can also accelerate economic growth.

Four

Increasing the Pace
of Innovation

IN THIS and subsequent chapters we examine policies designed to increase the rate of economic growth. This chapter focuses on policies designed to increase the pace of innovation. We begin with innovation because it is the primary mechanism for achieving increased efficiency in production. Since the publication of Robert Solow's celebrated analysis of technological change, writers on economic growth have stressed the importance of improvements in technological efficiency as a source of long-term growth. The research contributions of Edward Denison and Dale Jorgenson and others confirm the significance of technological change.[1] Later chapters discuss the role of other growth-enhancing policies, including job training, which can improve labor market equity as well as average productivity.

Sustaining American Strength in Basic Research

The United States continues to enjoy world leadership in basic scientific research. The system that created this leadership is based on large-scale federal financial support, allocated by peer review of grant proposals, with most basic research carried out in universities and federal laboratories.

Academic research is the most important single element in the U.S. basic research effort. In 1989 a total of $13.9 billion was spent on academic R&D, with $9.5 billion defined as basic research and $3.5 billion as applied research (the remainder was development). Of total spending on academic R&D, $8.25 billion was funded by the federal government, with the remainder financed from state and local funds, industry, universities themselves, and foundations (figure 4-1).

The funds available for academic research are far greater in the

FIGURE 4-1. *Academic R&D Expenditures, by Type, and Funding, by Source, 1989*

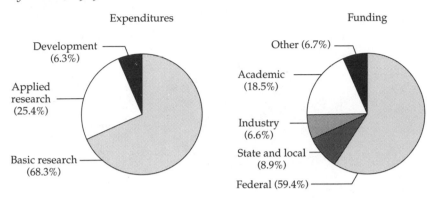

Source: National Science Board, *Science and Engineering Indicators—1989*, NSB89-1 (1989), appendix tables 5-1 and 5-2.

United States than in any of the other major industrial countries. The data in figure 4-2 are not quite comparable across the countries, but they do suggest the relative magnitudes of academic R&D and the differences in the allocation of these funds by field. The United States spends more than any other country in every academic area; in life sciences it spends half the world total.

A peer review system to allocate funds within fields works well as a method of selecting projects because scientific research in each discipline has its own logic. Basic research goes where the logic of the discipline demands, and the scientists within each discipline are usually the best judges of the most promising directions for further work.

It is hard to argue with a system that works so well and has given the nation such sustained leadership, but there are some problems with current procedures. First, scientific disciplines can become isolated and self-referencing. New studies are performed to refute someone else's study rather than because real progress is being made. Pure scientists can become scornful of applied scientists and focus on problems with the most intellectual interest rather than on ones that will lead to later advances in applied science.

The National Science Foundation should provide oversight of the peer review process to make sure that the potential for real scientific

FIGURE 4-2. *Academic R&D, United States and Selected Other Countries, by Field, 1987*

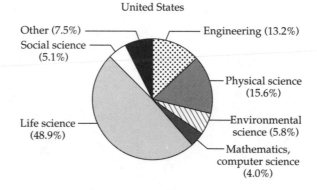

United States

Other (7.5%) — Engineering (13.2%)
Social science (5.1%)
Physical science (15.6%)
Life science (48.9%)
Environmental science (5.8%)
Mathematics, computer science (4.0%)

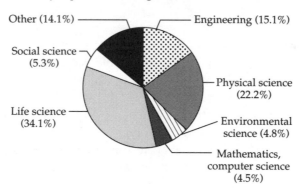

Germany, Japan, United Kingdom, France, Netherlands

Other (14.1%) — Engineering (15.1%)
Social science (5.3%)
Physical science (22.2%)
Life science (34.1%)
Environmental science (4.8%)
Mathematics, computer science (4.5%)

Source: National Science Board, *Science and Engineering Indicators—1989*, appendix table 4-23.

progress is present in each approved project. It should avoid funding projects that are motivated by a senior researcher's desire to respond to critics. The potential applied benefits of research should be given much greater weight when grant applications are reviewed.

Second, we are concerned that in comparison with the other major countries, the United States allocates such a large part of its academic R&D to life sciences. The nation is pushing out the frontiers in basic life sciences, financing advances that will benefit everyone in the world, while allocating relatively little to basic research in materials science or other areas where the spillover benefits to U.S. industry

FIGURE 4-3. *Federal R&D Funding, by Function, 1981, 1989*

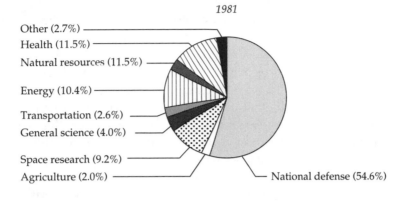

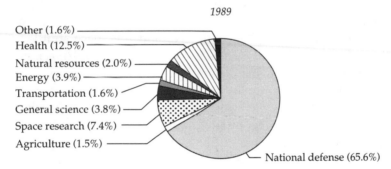

Source: National Science Board, *Science and Engineering Indicators—1989*, appendix table 4-16.

may be much higher. We do not have enough information to say whether too much or too little is allocated to life sciences, but we suggest a review of the overall federal allocation to academic R&D to determine whether the current structure has a rational basis.

Technology Development: Precommercial R&D

The federal government provides funding largely for defense-related R&D, some space and energy R&D, and not much else (figure 4-3). It provides little funding for technology development. One reason for this is a widespread and justifiable American mistrust of government policies that intervene in the market. The collapse of the centrally planned economies in Eastern Europe has provided new and compelling examples of the pitfalls of excessive government control of the marketplace. The East German economy, for instance, achieved a very high level of investment in capital goods over many years, but is now stuck with obsolete factories and equipment. The Soviet Union also had a high rate of investment and, in addition, a strong tradition of excellence in basic science. Yet Russia and the other countries of the former Soviet Union find themselves far behind the West in technology and productivity. Government intervention that supplanted market mechanisms and eliminated market incentives led to demonstrably poor allocation of investment and research effort.

Many U.S. policy initiatives have, on a smaller scale, fallen into the trap of trying to displace the market. In *The Technology Pork Barrel*, Linda Cohen and Roger Noll and their coauthors have assessed a variety of government research projects, including synthetic fuels, the supersonic transport plane, photovoltaics, the breeder reactor, the communications satellite initiative, and the space shuttle.[2] The authors' judgments of these projects are not kind. The NASA initiative on communications satellites achieved its technical objectives but was killed because the communications industry viewed the new technology as a threat to its own position and lobbied hard to eliminate government funding. The photovoltaics project also made valuable technical progress, but was cut back because political support died when energy prices declined. The supersonic transport was scrapped because of doubts about the cost and feasibility of the project and because of concerns about environmental damage. The Clinch River breeder reactor was sustained for a long time because it brought jobs to Tennessee, but it was eventually killed when the costs became too high, technical problems remained unsolved, and the price of energy fell. Little of value was learned from the project. The space shuttle survives, but its goals have been modified. The shuttle has suffered from well-known safety problems and has been subject to substantial competition from cheaper launch vehicles. The synfuels project did yield technical progress, but billions of dollars were spent on pilot and demonstration projects that failed even before the program was finally killed.

Although the authors have documented serious problems, we do not share their pessimistic conclusions. Offsetting the mixed or negative record is the widespread agreement among economists that for technology development the market does not always work well on its own. In other words, the alternative to government support of technology development—that is, no government support—may be much worse. This is the case most obviously for basic science and invention. A scientist developing new results in physics or chemistry is unlikely to make discoveries of direct economic benefit to the researcher. Research scientists publish results as quickly as possible, and developments in a field are generally the result of a worldwide effort. But even though it does not have a commercial payoff to the researcher, basic scientific research does have a payoff for the economy. Edwin Mansfield estimates that the rate of return to certain kinds of basic scientific research amounts to 30 percent.[3]

One consequence of American reluctance to provide government support to technology development is that the United States now ranks low among industrial countries in nondefense R&D as a percent of GNP (figure 4-4). Total R&D in the United States in the 1980s was 2.6 percent of GNP, a little less than the comparable figure for the 1960s and also a bit less than the figures for West Germany and Japan. Spending on R&D for other than defense has been only 1.8 percent of American GNP compared with 2.6 percent in West Germany and 2.8 percent in Japan, countries that invest very little in defense R&D.

Since the late 1960s, it has been said that the United States does not invest enough in what has variously been called precommercial, precompetitive, middleground, or generic research.[4] The social rate of return to precommercial research is much higher than the private return. New ideas and new ways of approaching technological problems are very hard to keep secret. For precommercial projects in particular, the risk of failure is very high. Even if a project is successful, its applicability may be too wide for one company to make full use of the innovation. We see a strong economic case for government support of precommercial technology development if this can be accomplished in a way that is not excessively wasteful. In fact, the government has successfully supported precommercial R&D projects in the past, especially in computers, telecommunications, and aerospace engineering.

Many of the most successful projects were funded by the Department of Defense. In *Creating the Computer*, Kenneth Flamm found that DOD, and the Defense Advanced Research Projects Agency (DARPA) in particular, provided crucial support for many of the main developments in semiconductors and computers.[5] Federal government sup-

FIGURE 4.4 *Total and Nondefense R&D Expenditures as Percent of GNP, by Country, 1971–87*

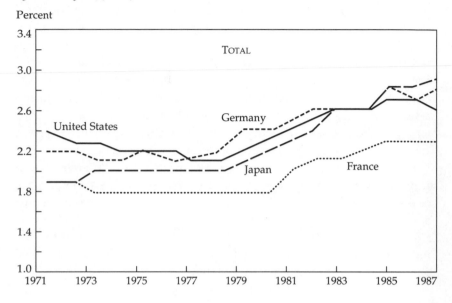

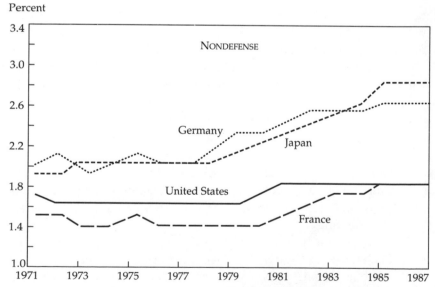

Source: National Science Board, *Science and Engineering Indicators—1989*, appendix table 4-20.

port also played a key role in the development of commercial jet aircraft and telecommunications.[6] The evolution of some of the nation's leading high-technology industries was driven by government support of technology. Federal funds can play a vital role in building U.S. industries that later enjoy global competitive advantage. Overall U.S. competitiveness is stronger today because of the strong position of the computer, telecommunications, and aerospace industries.

But the nation's industries can no longer count on federal agencies to provide support for developing technology that has important civilian applications. Defense technology has moved away from civilian technology in many areas. Civilian firms do not need stealth technology, for example. In other cases civilian technology is being transferred to the military rather than vice versa.[7] America cannot rely on DOD to generate new high-technology industries. The weakness of the government's civilian R&D effort is likely to be a handicap for industrial competitiveness.

Many policymakers share our concern about government technology policy. Some agree that federal funds once needed for defense should now be used to support precommercial technology development. We agree with this plan. But it is a plan with potential pitfalls.

Cohen and Noll found a pattern in the difficulties faced by federally sponsored technology development projects. The projects began during crises and were given large initial budget allocations. Results were expected quickly, and the focus of the early research was narrow. Even though this research revealed serious technological problems to be overcome, and even though changing economic circumstances often showed the initial focus to be incorrect, substantial federal funds were committed to pilot demonstration projects. As inevitable problems surfaced in these projects, political support waned and program budgets were cut. Yet the only hope of eventual success in the projects lay in increased funding, since the development stage of R&D is always vastly more expensive than the research stage. Pilot projects were often killed before any benefit had been obtained. Alternatively, the projects dragged on for a while, largely because of the employment created in particular congressional districts.

If federal support of technology development is to bear fruit, policy reforms are needed. First, project ideas should come from the private sector, mainly corporations and small businesses but also universities and other nonprofit institutions with strong technological capabilities.

This would ensure that the projects are not dreamed up by federal agencies or politicians with no clear sense of their ultimate commercial usefulness. Participating private companies should be required to provide part of a project's funding. This is particularly important if projects go beyond early technology exploration and include funding for pilot plants. Second, the basic support strategy should include a wide variety of projects directed toward the same general goal, each one of which receives modest funding. This strategy serves a dual purpose. It allows the exploration of many options, rather than encouraging early commitment to a particular technology strategy.[8] And it reduces the dangers of pork barrel funding because no single project generates enough jobs to be a focus of massive local lobbying efforts. Third, congressional oversight should not lead to congressional meddling into exactly which projects are funded and how the research ought to proceed. Congress should determine the rules of the game; it should not call the plays. Finally, it is vital that Congress extend its time horizon. The time horizons of U.S. corporate managers may be too short, but those of members of Congress are often even shorter.

It is not easy to decide what kind of institutional structure would be best suited to achieve these objectives. A panel chaired by Harold Brown from the Committee on Science Engineering and Public Policy of the National Academy of Sciences–National Academy of Engineering endorsed the concept of increased support of precommercial technology development, and suggested establishing a Civilian Technology Corporation to administer the program.[9] The corporation would be a quasi-governmental institution with an independent board of governors that would have strong links to the private sector. Brown's panel argued that this arrangement would encourage greater independence from political interference.

The Carnegie Commission on Science Technology and Government has also made suggestions for improving support for precommercial technology.[10] The National Institute of Standards and Technology (NIST) within the Department of Commerce should have responsibility for supporting precommercial research. And it should also help diffuse new technology. Second, DARPA should be transformed into a National Advanced Research Projects Agency (NARPA). The Defense Department should be instructed to use NARPA to promote dual-use technologies, those developed for military use that can also have civilian applications. The Defense Department, through NARPA, should encourage developments that serve both commercial and military users. And other departments and agencies, such as NASA, the National Science Foundation, and the National Institutes of Health, should be instructed to support and diffuse precommercial technology when it comes under their purview.

The Carnegie Commission also suggested a new structure to coordinate initiatives for advancing and diffusing technology. It recommended that the Office of Science and Technology Policy exercise responsibility in the Executive Office of the President for identifying and evaluating policy issues related to the national technology base. And the commission also asked that the National Security Council consider broad issues of science and technology policy as part of their decisionmaking process.

Of these alternative institutional arrangements, the idea of a Civilian Technology Board looks most attractive. If the increased effort in technology development is to be successful, there must be independent review panels free of congressional and White House interference to allocate funds. A Civilian Technology Board that operates like a kind of National Science Board for precommercial technology would have the best chance of avoiding political interference. We have no objection to the suggestion that other federal agencies consider how their research efforts could foster commercial applications of technology developed for government use, but this strategy is unlikely to have much effect. Most current federal research is geared to specific goals. Trying to introduce commercial considerations into the grant-approval process may simply confuse the funding agencies and the grant recipients.

One concern with a Civilian Technology Board is that it may avoid political influence but fall prey to anticompetitive influence from the private sector. The board must avoid becoming a supporter only of existing technologies and companies, and it should not provide a forum for oligopolistic industries to collude. NASA's satellite program was killed by political opposition from entrenched communications companies that did not want additional competition.[11] And the development of high-definition television has been slowed and transformed as a result of the lobbying efforts of the broadcast industry.[12]

The best way to avoid political interference and anticompetitive influence is to foster diversity and to use peer review of project proposals. Within any technology board there should be independent panels of technology experts, each of which solicits peer review of proposals before deciding on funding. These panels must stress support of many diverse, small, lean, and potentially competitive projects.

Technology Development: Critical Technologies

Three groups, the National Critical Technologies Panel, the Department of Commerce, and the Department of Defense, have now attempted to identify technologies that are critical for the United States (table 4-1). One idea behind these competing lists is to provide an organizing framework for federal funding of technology development. Another is to help mobilize political support for that funding. Designating certain technologies as critical may loosen congressional purse strings in a time when budgets are tight.

One problem is that the lists may not convey much new information. Several of the technologies are clearly critical, but almost everyone already knew that. There is little value in telling the public that software or biotechnology are vital technologies. Informed observers may question whether the other technologies designated really are the most important ones or ones from which the United States can obtain the highest payoff.[13] In compiling such lists, panels tend to search for technologies in which Japan or some other nation is ahead, and then claim it is vital to catch up. This happened in the recent past when the Japanese began an ambitious government-sponsored effort to develop the fifth generation of computers to overtake a wide U.S. lead in computation. The project was launched with great fanfare in the early 1980s, yet in 1992 Japan's Ministry of International Trade and Industry effectively canceled it, replacing it with a new Real-World Computing project.

Another danger with designating critical technologies for development is that doing so may lead to the problems described by Cohen and Noll. To gain funding, proponents of a particular technology sound the alarm about its importance, are given large budgets, and are then forced to come up with immediate results to justify public support.

We are therefore skeptical about the critical technologies approach, although we do not want to dismiss it out of hand. The Department of Defense has a successful record in identifying areas where important technological breakthroughs can occur. We have already argued in favor of an overall framework for funneling R&D funds into technologies of importance to the economy. Identifying critical technologies can be useful as a broad guide to the allocation of funds. But this approach should not be used in isolation to justify large projects or ones that have failed the test of scientific peer review.

Technology Development: Service Sector

Specialists have engaged in a vigorous but largely fruitless debate about whether the manufacturing sector is particularly important to the economy. Without manufacturing, some argue, good jobs in the service sector will disappear. We mentioned this debate in our earlier discussion of deindustrialization. We agree wholeheartedly that manufacturing is a vital sector of the economy. Most commercial R&D in the United States is carried out in manufacturing. New technology developed in manufacturing is then diffused to the rest of the economy through equipment and materials.

We are nonetheless skeptical of some of the extreme claims made about the paramount importance of manufacturing. It seems self-evident that the overall productivity of the economy depends heavily on the performance of the service sector. More output originates in services than in manufacturing, and services account for a much greater percentage of employment. If productivity growth in the economy as a whole is to be revived, then productivity growth in services must grow. There is scope for technology development in the service sector that can help achieve this goal.

One puzzle about slow productivity growth over the past twenty years is that this has been a period of rapid technological change in computers and electronics. The puzzle is even more complex than it might first appear, for the slow pace of productivity growth is most notable in service industries, yet they have invested heavily in the new technology.[14] The investment should by itself have boosted productivity as the ratio of capital to labor increased. Much more important, the new capital goods embodied a massive improvement in technology. The revolution in information technology caused or facilitated tremendous change and innovation in the service sector.

But the information revolution has not brought much recorded productivity growth in the service sector. Part of the growth is not captured by current statistics or is being misallocated to other industries because of the inadequacies of the system of measurement. In some cases, too, problems in particular service industries have offset

TABLE 4-1. *Government Lists of Important Technologies*[a]

National critical technologies	Commerce emerging technologies	Defense critical technologies
Materials		
Materials synthesis and processing	Advanced materials	Composite materials
Electronic and photonic materials	Advanced semiconductor devices	Semiconductor materials and microelectronic circuits
	Superconductors	Superconductors
Ceramics	} Advanced materials	} Composite materials
Composites		
High-performance metals and alloys		
Manufacturing		
Flexible computer-integrated manufacturing	Flexible computer-integrated manufacturing	
Intelligent processing equipment	Artificial intelligence	Machine intelligence and robotics
Micro- and nanofabrication		
Systems management technologies		
Information and communications		
Software	High-performance computing	Software producibility
Microelectronics and optoelectronics	Advanced semiconductor devices	Semiconductor materials and microelectronic circuits
High-performance computing and networking	Optoelectronics	Parallel computer architectures
High-definition imaging and displays	High-performance computing	Data fusion
Sensors and signal processing	Digital imaging	Signal processing
Data storage and peripherals	Sensor technology	Passive sensors
Computer simulation and modeling	High-density data storage	Sensitive radars
	High-performance computing	

Biotechnology and life sciences		Machine intelligence and robotics
Applied molecular biology	Biotechnology	Photonics
Medical technology	Medical devices and diagnostics	Simulation and modeling
		Computational fluid dynamics
Aeronautics and surface transportation		
Aeronautics		Biotechnology materials and processes
Surface transportation technologies		
Energy and environment		Air-breathing propulsion
Energy technologies		
Pollution minimization, remediation, and waste management		
		No national critical technologies counterpart: high energy density materials, hypervelocity projectiles, pulsed power, signature control, weapon system environment

Source: National Critical Technologies Panel, *Report of the National Critical Technologies Panel* (Washington, 1991).

a. National critical technologies were designated by the National Critical Technologies Panel; emerging technologies were designated by the Department of Commerce; defense critical technologies were designated by the Department of Defense.

the benefits of the new computer technology. For example, computers helped banks greatly improve productivity in check clearing, loan processing, and other services, but at the same time the industry lost a fortune through bad loans. In some ways the new information technology actually promotes waste. Computerization's main task is to process and analyze information, and information is a commodity that is very hard to value. A company report can go through thirty drafts rather than five because revising is so much easier. Are managerial decisions any better as a result of this extra effort? Based on first-hand experience with our own manuscripts, we are at least skeptical.

Another explanation for computers' apparent lack of impact on productivity is that information technology is often used as a marketing device rather than as a method of improving efficiency. For example, maintaining frequent flyer programs requires that airlines make a substantial investment in information processing equipment. These programs were initiated as a marketing strategy and as a method of increasing brand loyalty. They are one reason that the large airlines have been able to withstand the onslaught of small, low-cost airlines since deregulation. They have not added to airline productivity once all the major airlines adopted such programs, however.

Finally, and perhaps most important, information technology's impact on productivity may simply be slow in coming. Whenever a new technology is introduced, it takes years before it is assimilated. Electric motors were introduced at the turn of the twentieth century and rapidly became popular. But their immediate effect on productivity was not dramatic. It took many years before they were fully integrated into production processes. One reason it may take a long time for information technology to pay off is that developing software, re-engineering work processes, and training personnel are all time consuming. In addition, the systems keep changing, requiring constant retraining.

At this point it is not clear which explanation for weak productivity growth in services is the most important, but the slow learning process, with the concomitant waste of resources in the short run, is almost certainly a significant part of the explanation. This means that there is a role for systems research—precompetitive or middle-ground research—that could speed the transition to a more productive service sector. In a way this is an ideal area for government or cooperative sponsorship of generic precompetitive R&D. Almost every private company and every public agency or nonprofit organization has an office bureaucracy to administer operations. An analysis of methods of office automation could contribute to across-the-board efficiency improvements, not just to improvements in the service sector.

Technology Development: Commercial R&D

In several studies Martin Neil Baily and Robert Z. Lawrence have argued for favorable tax treatment of commercial R&D.[15] From empirical work by Edwin Mansfield and others, they find compelling evidence that commercial R&D has a rate of return to society of 50 percent or more, much higher than the private rate of return.[16] The market does provide some incentives for companies to perform commercial R&D. Firms can earn profits from the new products and processes that they develop. But the new products and processes also confer benefits on companies that copy, borrow, or purchase them. Ultimately consumers also benefit from the competition that then develops. The result is that the incentive provided by the market is inadequate. As a practical matter, the company that sponsors the original R&D does not collect market rewards from its investment that are commensurate with the return society receives from the investment.

The federal government provides a tax credit to encourage private firms to invest in R&D, but it has serious imperfections. Although the credit was supposed to offer an incentive of 25 percent when it first went into effect in 1981, the true incentive was smaller.[17] Various policy changes since then have further weakened the incentive. Despite these problems, however, Baily and Lawrence found that the credit did boost R&D spending in the early and mid-1980s. The provisions of the tax code affected spending with an elasticity of between 0.8 and 1.0, which implies that a tax incentive that reduces the cost of R&D by 10 percent raises R&D spending by 8 to 10 percent.[18]

This research is not the only reason for believing that tax incentives have an impact on R&D. Since 1987 multinational companies have been required to allocate some of their R&D spending to their foreign operations. In 1987, regulation 861-8 of the tax code required 50 percent of R&D to be allocated. This figure was reduced to 36 percent for 1988 and later. Shares of foreign sales or foreign income were used as the basis for the allocation. For companies with a deficit of foreign tax credits, this regulation has no impact on total tax burden. But for companies with excess foreign tax credits, the regulation effectively

FIGURE 4-5. *Ratio of R&D Spending to Industrial Production, 1960–89*

Ratio (1980 = 100)

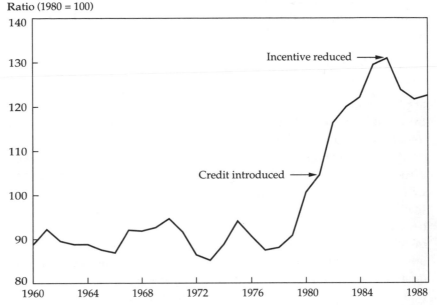

Source: Martin Neil Baily and Robert Z. Lawrence, "Tax Incentives for R&D: What Do the Data Tell Us?" Study prepared for CORETECH, Washington, D.C., January 28, 1992, figure 1.

eliminates the deductibility of part of their U.S. R&D expenses. In effect, it raises the cost of performing R&D for many U.S. companies with substantial foreign operations.

The 861-8 allocation rules have caused U.S. multinational companies to reduce domestic R&D spending substantially, according to James Hines, even though the regulation has been only partially implemented.[19] By comparing companies with excess foreign tax credit and those with deficit foreign tax credit, he found that the companies facing the 861-8 disincentive have performed significantly less R&D than those that did not. He concluded that the 861-8 provision has reduced U.S. R&D by $1.4 billion to $2.2 billion a year, for an estimated gain in tax revenue of $1.2 billion a year.[20] The *combination* of the evidence from the two kinds of studies is compelling: tax incentives do influence the amount of private R&D spending.

The conclusions drawn in the statistical analyses are confirmed in figure 4-5, which shows that the ratio of R&D to industrial output rose dramatically in the 1980s. The tax credit was not the only reason for this increase, since spending had started to rise before the credit came into force. But the credit was almost certainly one reason for higher R&D spending. The weakening of the tax incentives for R&D in the late 1980s probably had a negative effect on spending.

There is no guarantee, of course, that generous tax incentives for R&D will dramatically boost spending. The credit that has been in effect for the past few years has a modified structure that provides a greater incentive per dollar of tax revenue lost than was the case with the earlier version. Under current laws, a company that decides to increase R&D spending does not raise its R&D spending base and does not reduce the credit it can expect in the future. But even if current proposals are adopted, the credit will provide only $1 billion a year in support for company R&D, which will have at most a modest effect on total R&D spending. This is, however, better than nothing at all, and it does provide a policy signal. It is one of the few policies favoring growth that have remained in effect in a period of tight budgets. The credit should be doubled.

Direct government support for technology development is no substitute for a high level of company-funded R&D. The MIT Commission has pointed out that the United States was once the main innovator in a number of technologies but lost its competitive position in the world market by failing to make improvements in technology.[21] Continuing incremental innovation is important to improving productivity and national competitiveness, more important perhaps than basic innovation. A high level of corporate R&D is a key to achieving incremental innovation.

Lengthening Time Horizons

Innovation requires patience as well as the willingness to take risks. Corporate America has been criticized in recent years for its unwillingness to take the time necessary to develop new technologies. We do not agree that this criticism applies to all U.S. companies. U.S. chemical companies, for instance, have been willing to take fifteen years or more to go from initial R&D to final production.[22] But chemical companies may be unusual. A recent study that compares the United States with other countries concludes that time horizons are indeed shorter among managers in U.S. companies.[23]

American companies are not entirely at fault for focusing on the near term and avoiding large investments in projects with long-run payoffs. The current interest rate reflects the rate at which society is willing to trade extra income in the future for income in the present. When interest rates rise, rational investors will be less willing to invest in the future. As we discuss in greater detail in chapter 6, real interest rates on long-term debt soared in the 1980s, largely as a consequence of record federal budget deficits. Corporate managers would have been irrational if they had done anything other than shorten their time horizons or, in the words of the former director of the Office of Management and Budget, Richard Darman, become practitioners of "now-nowism."

Critique of American Corporate Governance

Critics of American business argue that managers and investors have become even more short-sighted than would be expected from the increase in interest rates, primarily because of the way U.S. companies are owned and managed.[24] The outlines of the American system are familiar. Corporations are owned by shareholders who elect boards of directors to represent them in determining basic business strategy. The directors in turn appoint managers who should be provided incentives to maximize the long-run value of their companies. In this simple framework, corporations and their managers are induced to engage in long-term planning, investment, and innovative activity to the extent that can be justified by the prevailing cost of capital.

As early as the 1930s, however, Adolph Berle and Gardiner Means argued that managers of major American corporations might well stray from the theoretical pursuit of profit maximization, both in the short and long runs.[25] Because corporate shareholders are widely dispersed, they lack the ability and incentive to carefully monitor the companies they own. In practice, directors are often chosen by the managers rather than by the shareholders and thus may not safeguard shareholders' interests. By implication, managers and directors will receive excessive salaries and corporate perquisites. This theory appears much more persuasive today than it did when first advanced.[26]

In one important respect, today's corporate world is very different from the one envisaged by Berle and Means. Corporate shareholding now is much more concentrated in the hands of pension funds, insurance companies, mutual funds, and other institutional investors that have large stakes in individual companies. In principle, these large stakeholders have strong incentives to monitor managers and to ensure that managerial decisions are consistent with the long-term interests of the stockholders.[27] In practice, however, these stakeholders have not actively monitored managers' performance; they have remained on the sidelines as passive investors. To a significant degree, their passivity has been the product of tradition and lack of expertise. Institutional investors have tended to live by the "Wall Street rule": when dissatisfied with the performance of a company, sell its stock rather than complain.

During the 1980s, many institutional investors found excellent reasons to sell the stock they owned. They were induced to do so by a wave of corporate buyout proposals, which often turned into bidding wars between raiders, who wanted to displace existing managers, and white knights, who were recruited to save the managers. In principle, corporate buyouts appeared to resolve the dilemma of corporate management by concentrating control in the hands of a small number of opportunistic investors. Even when takeover proposals failed, the attempt could produce a similar effect by causing the target companies to buy out shareholders and narrowly concentrate control among a small number of remaining owners. In short, the market for corporate control made it possible for shareholders themselves, or potential future shareholders, to ensure that corporate managers took actions that were consistent with maximizing the value of their companies.

Critics of the takeover movement have argued that, in fact, buyouts and the defensive restructurings of corporate balance sheets they provoked did little to improve, and have actually harmed, the long-term performance of the target companies. The reason is that, unlike the wave of corporate mergers of the 1960s, which were financed by exchanges of equity, the takeovers of the 1980s were financed by corporate debt: target companies borrowed heavily from banks and issued low-grade corporate bonds (junk bonds). As a result, these companies had to make large annual interest payments, which forced cutbacks in investment and R&D. Even if the takeovers concentrated ownership and succeeded in aligning the interests of managers and shareholders, they injured the national economy because they discouraged target companies from investing in projects with long-term payoffs.

The Brookings Center for Economic Progress and Employment sponsored a number of studies to investigate competing claims about the effects of the wave of corporate takeovers. At least initially, take-overs did have a beneficial effect. One study found that, on average, corporate buyouts completed before 1984 led to some improvement in the performance of target companies.[28] Another analysis of more than 4,000 plants whose ownership changed hands between 1972 and 1981 found statistically significant improvements in productivity after the acquisitions.[29]

Unlike the conglomerate merger wave of the 1960s, many mergers of the 1980s were between firms in similar lines of business. Indeed, many hostile takeovers in the 1980s that initially may have looked like conglomerate transactions were followed by later sell-offs of plants and divisions to firms in similar lines of business, thus effectively serving as vehicles for completing horizontal combination.[30] More lax enforcement of antitrust policy during the 1980s no doubt played a major role in allowing these transactions. And they do seem to have improved productivity. For example, factories owned by less diversi-fied firms had higher productivity than factories owned by conglom-erates.[31]

Recent studies nonetheless provide ample ammunition in support of the critics of takeovers. Investment and R&D activity appears to have slowed in target companies.[32] This does not necessarily mean that the takeovers were undesirable. In fact, according to apologists for the takeovers, investment and R&D *should* fall in companies with poor investment prospects. If it takes an increase in debt to force the managers of companies to operate cost effectively and thus to con-strain their investment and R&D spending, the outcome is beneficial.

This hypothesis may be true, but there is also mounting evidence that as the corporate takeovers continued through the 1980s, the bene-fits gradually fell short of the undeniable costs. One study, for exam-ple, found that the postacquisition performance of firms bought out after 1984 was generally poor. Another found that after 1986 takeovers and other restructuring activity no longer were principally concen-trated in industries with subpar returns, as theory would predict.[33] Numerous companies that increased debt in the 1980s, either on their own or as a result of acquisition, have since run into financial trouble, especially those financed with junk bonds issued in the latter half of the decade. The financial woes of these corporations have caused many workers to lose their jobs and many communities to suffer needless disruption.[34]

The challenge now is to find new mechanisms to ensure that managers behave in the interests of shareholders and that shareholders pay heed to the long-term welfare of the companies they own. Three kinds of proposals have been advanced to do this. One is to enable and encourage shareholders and directors to become more active in corporate decisionmaking. A second is to relax legal restrictions that limit or prohibit institutional investors from exercising influence over the companies they own. In theory, after all, these large stakeholders are primarily interested in long-run corporate performance. A third proposal would provide incentives for managers and directors to pay greater attention to long-run considerations in decisionmaking.

The following sections review each of these suggestions. We caution, however, that the evidence is far from clear that the proposals would promote socially worthwhile long-term investment and innovation without creating potentially costly difficulties. We favor the third approach—providing stronger incentives for managers and directors to assign greater weight to long-term projects. In light of the uncertainties, the potential gain from this strategy seems far greater than its possible cost.

Encouraging Greater Shareholder and Director Involvement

Given the costly side-effects of debt-financed corporate takeovers, one logical set of reforms would encourage shareholders and directors to become more active monitors of corporate managers, thus reducing the need for takeovers as a method of disciplining wayward managers. Or, as John Pound has said, let the "marketplace of ideas" and "political markets" replace the financial marketplace as the principal means for disciplining corporate managers.[35]

There is already some evidence of greater shareholder activism. After a shareholder-mounted challenge, USX decentralized its operations and split up ownership of its steel, energy, and other divisions. Similarly, a dissident shareholder helped push Sears to cut costs, add three new outside directors, expand the size of the board's nominating committee, and explore various restructuring options. Other corporations, including Georgia Pacific, ITT, Pfizer, Textron, Time Warner, and United Airlines, adopted changes in bylaws and executive compensation packages in 1991 and 1992 in response to shareholder initiatives. The most significant development occurred at General Motors. GM's outside directors forced a major change in management, in large part to accelerate the restructuring and streamlining of the company. In addition, several of the nation's largest shareholders, notably the California Public Employee Retirement System (Calpers) and the New York State Pension System, have become more aggressive in pushing underperforming companies to make changes in their governance structures and operations.[36]

Some reforms could encourage these developments. One would make it easier for shareholders to communicate with one another and thus to become more effective in mounting challenges to corporate managers. The Securities and Exchange Commission has adopted rules that would allow groups of shareholders collectively owning 5 percent or less of the total stock outstanding to discuss how they plan to vote on certain corporate issues without filing material to that effect with the commission. In addition, the commission has eliminated advance SEC review of proxy materials, allowing shareholders to place advertisements, send letters, or write newspaper articles on corporate matters without clearing the contents first with the agency.[37] The SEC has also made it easier for shareholders holding some minimum portion of stock to propose alternative slates of directors to run against management's slate.[38]

The problem with this approach is that it does not guarantee that corporations will be encouraged to undertake investment and R&D projects with long-term payoffs. On the contrary, if shareholders are myopic, giving them greater influence over corporate decisionmaking could actually discourage innovation. The shareholder activism movement is still young, so there is essentially no evidence on these concerns. Although we are sympathetic with reforms that improve shareholder and director control as a method for aligning shareholder and managerial interests, we do not consider them a panacea for eliminating corporate myopia.

Creation of Long-Term Owners

Because greater shareholder democracy has uncertain effects, some reformers suggest that corporate ownership should be further concentrated in the hands of institutional investors, who are likely to have a special interest in long-term corporate performance. Special attention has been focused on bank ownership of corporate equities, which is currently prohibited in the United States. In contrast, Japanese banks may own up to 5 percent of the equity of any corporation. Japanese bank participation in *keiretsu*, tight alliances among different corporations cemented by cross-shareholdings, is in fact common. Bank involvement in corporate life is even more entrenched in Germany, where the large banks control directly or by proxy more than half of all equity in German corporations.[39]

Those who argue that the United States should adopt such a policy rest their case on the claim that bank ownership of corporate equities in Japan and Germany has permitted their companies to take a longer-term view than is true in U.S. companies. If banks both own shares in and lend to the same companies, they are likely to be interested not only in seeing their loans repaid but in ensuring that their borrowers profit handsomely from their long-term investment projects. As proof, supporters of such ownership arrangements note that German and Japanese financial institutions are more likely to extend credit to the companies whose shares they own when the firms encounter financial trouble. This helps lower the cost of capital to firms facing short-term financial pressure and gives them the freedom to take a long-term view.[40]

Significant changes in U.S. bank ownership laws may be necessary, but permitting direct bank ownership of corporate equities has dangers. It ties banks' capital positions and thus lending ability directly to the fortunes of the stock market. In 1991 and 1992 Japanese banks, which invest heavily in the shares of nonbanking companies, saw their capital-to-asset ratios plummet when Japanese stock market prices plunged by more than 50 percent. The loss of bank capital constrained lending both at home and abroad by Japanese banks and thus helped deepen a mild downturn in overall Japanese economic activity.

This vicious cycle might have been avoided if Japanese bank accounting rules had not counted a portion of the unrecognized appreciation in stock values as part of bank capital; or, in other words, if the stock investments had been valued at the "lower of cost or market." Alternatively, banks that make equity investments could be required to meet stricter capital requirements than other banks. In fact, however, neither of these technical fixes removes the procyclical effect of equity investments by banks. Regardless of the accounting rules or minimum capital-to-asset ratios, any substantial decline in the market values of stocks held in bank portfolios will affect the economic values of banks, which in turn is likely to make their lending behavior cautious until the stock market recovers. Bankers' caution can deepen any initial decline in economic activity, which in turn causes stock market values to fall.[41]

For these reasons, if bank investment in corporate equities is to be permitted at all, it should only be allowed through bank holding companies, which are not funded by insured deposits, rather than through the banks themselves. In fact, current law permits bank holding companies to make equity investments, provided the equity stake in any single company does not exceed 5 percent of the outstanding stock of that firm. A similar 5 percent limit applies to direct shareholding by Japanese banks. Nevertheless, despite their ability to do so, few U.S. bank holding companies have made major equity investments in other companies. One reason is that holding companies are discouraged from investing in equity by the bankruptcy doctrine of equitable subordination. Under this doctrine, any shareholder who has extended credit to a company in bankruptcy will find its claims subordinated to the claims of other creditors who do not own stock. If banks or their holding companies are to be encouraged to make more extensive investments in corporate equities, the doctrine of equitable subordination must either be revised or eliminated. Even if this reform were made, it still is not clear that banking organizations would be willing to make equity investments.

Michael Porter and others have suggested additional legal changes that would permit other major institutional shareholders, such as insurance companies, employee pension funds, and mutual funds, to own larger stakes in corporations and to place their representatives on corporate boards.[42] In effect, these shareholders would be allowed to move away from passive investing in a highly diverse group of companies and toward an active managerial role in a smaller number of firms.

We see dangers in this kind of reform. Concentration of investments in a smaller number of companies increases the riskiness of a portfolio and reduces the liquidity of the individual holdings. Institutional shareholders may also suffer from short-termism if their managers are compensated or judged primarily on the basis of their short-term investment performance.[43]

Nor is it clear how many institutions would take advantage of expanded opportunities to become active on boards of directors. Our suspicion is that mutual funds and insurance companies would be reluctant to become actively involved in corporate management, at least for the foreseeable future, largely because both have developed a money management mentality based on the previously noted Wall Street rule. Corporate pension funds, which are usually controlled by corporate managers, will probably be unwilling to become actively involved in the management of other corporations.[44] The reluctance of these institutions helps explain why some public employee pension funds have thus far been the most active shareholders, together with maverick individuals. Neither group of investors is bound by the conventions of the corporate culture.

In sum, there is a modest case for encouraging greater equity ownership by bank holding companies, but not banks themselves, through modification of the doctrine of equitable subordination. However, in view of the uncertainties and potential risks of relaxing current diversification restrictions on institutional shareholders, we are much less confident that a move in this direction would produce major benefits in promoting long-term planning.

One proposal has recently been advanced to encourage pension funds in particular to lengthen their investment horizons. To discourage high turnover in pension portfolios, some analysts have argued for a tax on short-term profits earned by these funds and possibly by other tax-exempt investment vehicles (such as mutual funds). Penalizing short-term investment behavior is appealing on the surface. Indeed, in a widely noted study, Josef Lakonishok, Andrei Shleifer, and Robert Vishny found that pension fund managers using active investment strategies achieved lower returns than were available simply by investing in the Standard & Poor's 500 index, suggesting that short-term trading did not generate additional shareholder returns.[45]

By discouraging trading, however, a tax on short-term profits probably would encourage pension funds to adopt strategies for indexing investments, a trend that Lakonishok and his colleagues predict will occur in any event. Additional index investing will not necessarily induce corporate managers to lengthen their time horizons. For one thing, pension funds that are invested in an index such as the S&P 500 have little incentive to become active shareholders because by investing in the index they are already assured of doing as well as the market average. In addition, index investing would give the companies whose stocks belong to the major indexes, such as the S&P

500, an advantage in raising capital in comparison with the thousands of unlisted companies whose stocks are actively traded. It is far from clear that it is a good idea for the government to confer additional advantages on the nation's largest companies. Finally, taxing trading by pension funds and other tax-exempt institutions could reduce liquidity in the market, which could raise the cost of equity capital for firms wishing to issue stock. This concern is not a trivial one, since most trading, by volume, on the major exchanges is conducted by institutional investors. In sum, given all the reservations as well as the absence of hard evidence of the relative costs and benefits of any proposal to tax short-term profit taking by otherwise tax-exempt institutional shareholders, we would recommend against its adoption.

Manager and Director Compensation

Ideally, compensation for executives and directors should be structured to encourage them to perform in the long-term interests of the shareholders of their companies. In fact, however, current compensation practices have attracted strong criticism from two directions.

One reason for complaint is the loose connection between executive pay and corporate performance. Analysts have found little correlation between executive compensation, including base salary, performance bonuses, stock options, and other types of compensation, and company performance. A widely publicized study of the 1,000 largest U.S. companies found that just 4 percent of the variation in executive compensation across companies in 1990 was traceable to differences in shareholder returns.[46] These results are especially surprising since much of the compensation of many corporate executives consists of stock options, which in principle should be highly correlated with corporate performance. Indeed, for many companies, the value of these stock options has been extraordinary, reaching many millions of dollars. The absence of a correlation between executive pay and company performance strongly suggests that many executives are overpaid.

Second, high executive pay—which in many cases comes to more than one hundred times the earnings of average company employees—has been criticized not only for draining corporate resources but for harming employee morale, especially in companies that have had to shrink to survive. Japanese compensation disparities are not nearly as large as those in the United States, and Japanese employees appear much more loyal to their employers than are their American counterparts.[47] Anecdotal evidence supports this view. Two of the more successful American companies, Nucor (the leading steel minimill) and Walmart (the nation's largest retailer), are well known for their relatively low levels of executive compensation (but substantial stock options).

In light of the publicity surrounding them, it is not surprising that high executive salaries have attracted political attention. In 1992 Congress considered a proposal by Senator Carl Levin to prohibit corporations from deducting the costs of executive compensation packages of more than $1 million a year. President Clinton endorsed this idea during his campaign.

In our view, this response would be far too broad and is potentially harmful. Assuming that such a ceiling actually worked as intended and were not evaded through use of hidden corporate perquisites, it could severely discourage successful companies from properly motivating their executives. This is especially the case with stock options, which in principle represent a highly desirable form of compensation because they give managers a direct stake in the health of their companies. Under current tax law, stock options become an expense to a company only when they are exercised by their holders and their values become fixed. But since the decision to exercise an option is made by the holder, companies would face great uncertainty as to when the value of stock options granted would push the total compensation of any employee and option holder beyond the limit. If this occurred, the company would lose the right to deduct some portion of that employee's compensation package. As a result, any cap that took stock options into account probably would induce companies to stop using them, reducing the kind of compensation that is most likely to align the interests of managers with those of shareholders.

From the shareholders' perspective, there should be limits even on compensating executives with stock options, which after all dilute the value of existing shares. Stock options are not in shareholders' interest unless they cause executives to improve the performance of their companies. In 1992 the Securities and Exchange Commission took a number of steps to improve shareholder discipline in this regard. Specifically, it abandoned the longstanding principle that executive compensation was part of the ordinary business of a company and therefore off limits to shareholder votes. The SEC also adopted a comprehensive proposal to require public companies to disclose in a standardized fashion the elements of compensation paid to their five highest-paid executives and to explain how the board of directors' compensation committee determined executives' pay. Some critics have attacked these initiatives on the ground that shareholders might oppose giving talented executives appropriately generous compensation. Even if this were true, which appears doubtful, the criticism is fundamentally misplaced. Shareholders, after all, own the company, and it is their right to have it managed as they see fit.

Companies should be provided stronger incentives to pay their executives and directors in a way that encourages them to plan for the long run. To achieve this goal, we favor incentives that discourage companies from offering their executives stock options that can be exercised within a relatively short period. Typical stock options can now be exercised in three years or less. This period is too short to create appropriate incentives.[48] Michael Porter has argued for prohibiting executive stock options that can be exercised within five years. He would also limit the portion of the total option that could be exercised at the close of the five-year holding period.[49]

We favor less draconian measures that would nonetheless create better managerial incentives. The Internal Revenue Service should impose a tax penalty on capital gains income realized from the exercise of any stock option granted to an employee or director of a corporation when the exercise date is less than a designated period after the date on which the option was awarded. The penalty could be gradually reduced the longer the option is held before it is exercised. For example, income realized from exercise of a stock option might be subject to a 20 percent penalty tax if the option were exercised within the first three years of award. The penalty could fall to 15 percent if the option were exercised in the fourth year, to 10 percent in the fifth year, and so on until the penalty is phased out entirely after the seventh year. Since the tax penalty is imposed on corporate employees who hold stock options, the system would discourage executives and directors from cashing out their stock options early, and thus it would give them a grater stake in the long-term performance of their companies.[50]

Along the same lines, the tax laws could also be changed to encourage companies to shift executive compensation from cash payments, which offer no strong incentives to monitor corporate behavior, toward stocks or stock options, which do offer such incentives. One possibility would be to limit or reduce the deductibility for corporate income tax purposes of cash payments made to directors but to continue full deductibility for director compensation paid in stock or stock options. If this reform were combined with our proposal to penalize the early exercise of stock options, directors as well as executives would be offered strong incentives to see that actions taken by their corporations are consistent with maximizing the value of corporations over the long run.

Liability Reform

Companies planning to develop new products or processes sometimes fear that the new technology may expose them to costly liability suits. Their fear may deter them from investing in innovation. In response to this potential problem, the Reagan and Bush administrations, businesses, and the property-casualty insurance industry have sought to reform the nation's tort or liability laws. These are the laws that oblige firms and individuals found to be responsible for accidents to compensate the victims for their injuries.

In principle, tort rules will efficiently deter accident-causing behavior if they assign the costs of injuries to those who can avoid or prevent them at least cost. Supporters of the current tort system argue that an expensive liability system will do just that. Critics of the tort system respond that liberalization of tort doctrines in the past three decades has unleashed a rising volume of costly suits. In addition, juries have become more liberal in their damage awards. Together the trends have increased tort costs. And the variation in awards has created growing uncertainty among firms about the nature and extent of their liability exposure. This uncertainty directly affects innovation by deterring risk-averse firms from introducing new products and services, because it raises the risk premium that investors require to compensate them for accepting possibly devastating liability risks.

The Center for Economic Progress and Employment at Brookings has sponsored research to help sort out these conflicting claims. Researchers have tried to determine whether existing tort laws are efficient, whether they discourage innovations in a way that is not justified by the threat to safety actually posed by the innovations. The research challenge is daunting. Economists and statisticians do not have good data on the liability costs faced by different industries over a sufficiently long period to estimate reliably the effects of tort costs on innovation. But researchers have drawn two conclusions from the limited evidence that is available.

The first finding should hardly come as a surprise. American firms face higher liability costs than those faced by companies headquartered in Europe and Japan. And the gap is growing. In 1980, tort costs, including the costs of workers' compensation and auto insurance, amounted to 1.5 percent of GNP in the United States. By 1987, costs had risen to 2.6 percent. Meanwhile, tort costs range between 0.5 and 0.7 percent of GNP in Japan and major Western European countries.[51]

These ratios measure the gross cost of the tort system, much of which in the United States is paid to attorneys rather than to victims. The costs exclude the benefits of added safety that the tort rules may produce. In fact, U.S. tort law does appear to have produced safety benefits in certain industries, especially automobiles and general aviation, principally because the negative publicity generated by adverse tort rulings deters firms from exposing consumers to excessive dangers. In addition, tort cases occasionally push regulators to crack down earlier than they otherwise might on dangerous products or practices.[52] We unfortunately lack comprehensive estimates of the safety effects generated by tort rules. It is thus impossible to know whether the gross expenditures on the tort system produce commensurate improvements in safety.

Even if the costs of the U.S. tort system outweighed its benefits, it would not follow that the system discourages innovation. Liability costs are relatively modest, less than 3 percent of GDP. As long as these costs are predictable, companies should have little trouble passing them on to consumers in the form of higher prices. Higher liability costs thus need not have a detrimental effect on the willingness of investors to support innovation.

In some industries, however, liability costs are not easily predictable. For this reason, the tort system may inhibit innovation in some sectors of the economy. Industries with only modest liability costs in 1980–84 increased their investment in innovation. Where liability costs jumped sharply, innovative activity, and indeed output generally, fell off substantially.[53] This suggests that a large change in liability costs, and the associated increased uncertainty about future levels of liability costs, dampens innovation.[54]

We see modest empirical support for reforms in the laws that would make tort costs for U.S. firms more predictable. Many proposals have been advanced to accomplish this. Some have been adopted by a handful of states.[55] We favor several of the reforms. Companies should be allowed to defend their products using a broader "regulatory defense" that would shield manufacturers who are in compliance with relevant state and federal regulations from liability for defective product design. Damage awards for pain and suffering should be determined by fixed schedules based on the age of the victim and the severity of the injury, with the damage ranges adjusted upward over time in proportion to the growth in nominal incomes. States should consider eliminating "joint and several" liability for pain and suffering awards (but not for economic loss). This liability doctrine exposes defendants to responsibility for paying all the losses in a case when other responsible defendants are unable to pay. These proposals would continue to allow injured parties the right to collect compensation for their losses, but the availability and amount of compensation would be more predictable.

Each of these proposals is controversial. Only the first has been included in the modest product liability reform bill that Congress has considered in various forms for the past several years. No federal reform package has yet passed. One reason that liability reform has not gained congressional support, despite Bush administration backing, is the argument of consumer groups and plaintiffs' attorneys that any weakening of liability law would significantly reduce incentives for firms to produce safe products.

This argument will continue to be successful so long as the insurance and business interests seeking tort law reform do not at the same time seek an improvement in federal safety regulation. Safety regulation and enforcement could be strengthened in a variety of ways. Congress could provide larger budgets for research and development by the federal regulatory agencies charged with worker and product safety and environmental protection. If necessary, regulated firms could be taxed to support the cost of better regulation. While our suggestion is likely to be controversial, it is one that attempts to address the political reality that has stymied reform up to now.[56] The hard fact is that businesses are unlikely to gain significantly greater predictability in liability costs, and thus a significant reduction in the risk premium that some industries must pay for capital, unless those industries can assure the public and Congress that legitimate safety objectives will not be compromised. There is of course no guarantee that opponents of liability reform will accept a compromise along the lines we have proposed. But we see no harm in trying to achieve reasonable compromise, since the prospects for liability reform in the near future are otherwise virtually nil.

Encouraging Joint Ventures

Another way to reduce the riskiness of innovation is to encourage joint activities among firms, not only in research and development, but also in production. The U.S. government has encouraged joint research in two policy initiatives taken in the past decade. In 1984 a legal change gave partial insulation from the antitrust laws to cooperative research efforts. The government actually provided funding to Sematech, a consortium formed by fourteen of the nation's leading electronics and computer firms to promote research in the production of semiconductors and the specialized equipment needed to manufacture them.[57]

Joint research ventures can be justified on a variety of grounds. They can, for instance, enable firms in the same industry to avoid unnecessary duplication of effort while reducing the risks of failure that each faces. But several counterarguments have been raised against permitting companies to pursue joint research projects. Such arrangements permit firms to collude in the development of new technology and thus to produce less of the technology for the market (just as price collusion reduces the amount of output available to final consumers). Companies may also lend only second-rate researchers to the joint projects, viewing the projects as long shots for success. Top-level researchers and valuable proprietary information will be kept in-house for each firm's own use. In principle, government subsidies, such as those provided for Sematech, can overcome both problems. In addition, direct subsidies can be defended on the traditional ground that R&D produces spillover benefits to the economy as a whole that cannot be captured solely by the firms engaging in it.

It is unknown whether joint R&D activities, funded by the government or not, are worth the potential antitrust risks. It is a question that is very hard to answer, since no one can know what innovations would occur in the absence of cooperative arrangements. Nevertheless, between 1985 and 1989, nearly 170 joint R&D consortiums were formed pursuant to the 1984 National Cooperative Research Act, principally in the telecommunications, computer and semiconductor, and automobile industries.[58] The success of these consortiums is unknown, but the fact that many continue to be supported by their participants suggests that the participating firms believe the efforts are worthwhile. The best-publicized joint R&D consortium is Sematech, which apparently has developed one important advance, a device that can print millions of circuits on a microchip and thus help make possible the development of the 256 megabit chip.[59]

One issue debated by Congress in recent years is whether to extend the relaxation of current antitrust rules to joint production arrangements as well. Many, if not most, economists specializing in industrial organization are opposed to such an extension, fearing that it could represent a dangerous step toward the cartelization of industries.[60] We are inclined to agree.

Joint production arrangements should not necessarily be outlawed, however. Many have already been established, not only among companies within the United States, but increasingly among companies in different countries. These arrangements do not pose an antitrust concern if they do not lead to excessive concentration of market control. The critical question for antitrust purposes, therefore, is the scope of the relevant market. Other things being equal, the broader the geographic market, the less likely it is that any particular joint production arrangement will lead to excessive market concentration. For this reason, antitrust law should leave ample room for production joint ventures to form where the markets in which they compete are truly global, where there are no trade restrictions, and where the global market will not be excessively concentrated after the joint venture has been established.

Should America Adopt an Industrial Policy?

Many readers of this chapter may feel that we are advocating industrial policy. We disagree. Industrial policy involves the government in making decisions about the potential profitability of *specific* companies or industries. A government pursuing an activist industrial policy might provide direct financial support to a company that would otherwise go bankrupt. Or it might decide to support a particular industry because of the industry's alleged growth prospects. We do not advocate such policies. The policies we propose are far less intrusive. An R&D tax credit, for example, is available to any company that performs R&D, without reference to whether the government believes a specific project will be profitable.

This distinction is important because government decisionmakers lack the information necessary to make market-oriented decisions and because they do not bear the financial risks involved in the outcome. We agree with critics of industrial policy who point out that political rather than market criteria would be used to pick the winners if an industrial policy were adopted.[61] Resources poured into an industrial policy would be allocated no better than resources devoted to past government large-scale efforts, including agricultural subsidies, the breeder reactor, and the supersonic transport.[62]

We see an important difference between targeted assistance for certain generic technologies that are chosen on the basis of scientific peer review and assistance to specific companies or industries that are deemed necessary for the economy. While it may be tempting to label government support of generic technologies as a form of industrial policy, the label would be misleading.

Given current budgetary limitations, it is unlikely that the federal government will be prepared to pour massive subsidies into a general industrial policy any time soon. We see a distinct danger, however, that a far-reaching industrial policy could be implemented through more aggressive trade protection, which does not have a direct budgetary cost attached to it. Indeed, trade protection raises revenues if it is provided through tariffs. The problem is that protection is more likely to inhibit innovation than to advance it because protection weakens the discipline of market competition and raises the costs of inputs for some of our most progressive industries. We oppose both protection and other forms of industrial policy.

Conclusion

We have argued for specific steps that can strengthen America's position in advanced technologies and raise the rate of innovation and productivity growth. These policies include sustained support for basic research, increased support for precompetitive or generic technology development using R&D funds now used for defense

R&D, more generous tax credits for commercial R&D, reform of the institutions of corporate control to encourage longer time horizons, reform of liability laws, and steps to encourage joint ventures in R&D.

The policies we advocate are promarket and progrowth. Where market incentives are weak, we attempt to supplement them without usurping the market's strengths in promoting efficiency. The proposed technology development policies need not be terribly expensive. In commercial R&D we should double spending on the R&D tax credit to $2 billion a year. Direct funding of precommercial technology development has been most successful when the budgets have been lean.

One essential element in raising productivity and in facilitating the diffusion of new technologies is job skills. We next consider the training of workers to ensure that jobs created by technological advances are filled by Americans.

Five

Improving the Labor Market

BOOSTING AMERICAN PRODUCTIVITY will require more than added investment in machines, buildings, and research and development. It will also require more and better organized investment in human beings.

American workers continue to enjoy substantial strengths in comparison with workers elsewhere. Their average productivity remains extremely high. They are hard working. Unlike workers in most other advanced industrialized countries, Americans continue to put in long hours, are rarely absent from their jobs, and take relatively few holidays or paid vacation days. Among major industrialized countries, only Japan has a labor force that works as many hours a year (see table 5-1).

But productivity in other countries is increasing faster than it is in the United States, and in some industries the productivity of foreign workers now exceeds that of U.S. workers. The long hours of American workers are partly explained by the trend in real wages. As those at the bottom and in the middle of the earnings distribution have seen their wages fall, they have increased their hours on the job to maintain their standard of living. This strategy has not been successful for all workers. Those with the fewest skills have seen their incomes fall in spite of their longer hours.

Formal schooling and workplace training decisively affect productivity and earnings. To improve the flagging performance of U.S. workers, it is necessary to improve their formal schooling and increase the workplace training that employers offer. This chapter diagnoses the educational and labor market problems faced by U.S. workers in general and less skilled workers in particular. The educational preparation of non-college-bound Americans is inadequate to the de-

TABLE 5-1. *Average Annual Hours Worked in Manufacturing,*
Seven OECD Countries, 1989

Country	Hours per year	Rank
Canada	1,850	4
France	1,611	5
West Germany	1,602	6
Japan	2,155	1
Sweden	1,540	7
United Kingdom	1,861	3
United States	1,940	2

Source: Bureau of Labor Statistics, "Underlying Data for Indexes of Output Per Hour," unpublished data (December 1991).

mands of the modern workplace. And training in the workplace does not offset their educational disadvantages. The difficulties faced by these workers have contributed to the economic problems addressed by this book: slow productivity growth and greater earnings inequality.

A good diagnosis of labor market problems would be of only academic interest if it did not also suggest remedies. The remedies we recommend will be controversial and politically difficult to achieve. Because they represent major departures from current practices, we cannot be certain what their exact effects will be, although we believe the effects will include a more equal distribution of education and training opportunities and faster overall wage growth, especially for low-wage adult workers. Most of our suggestions are aimed at improving workers' general skills and job-specific skills. We have fashioned the proposals to upgrade the skills of the least skilled Americans, thus addressing the issue of equity. But we have also tried to ensure that extra training will take place where it can be provided most efficiently. Our proposals thus emphasize improvements of training in the workplace rather than sharply increased spending on formal education in public or private schools, colleges, or proprietary training institutions.

Even if readers reject our specific proposals, they should consider carefully whether the nation can afford to do nothing about the problems we describe. For the least skilled workers, weak productivity growth has not simply meant slow growth or stagnation in wages. Their wages have actually decreased. For some, especially young men, the losses have been large. Benign neglect would be a callous response to this reality.

Work Force Preparation

American high school graduates bring comparatively few skills to the workplace. In spite of some recent improvement, they continue to rank low in international comparisons of student knowledge and ability. A small gap in achievement is noticeable in primary grades, and the gap widens as students get older. In science, for example, junior and senior high school students fare dismally on international tests of achievement (figure 5-1). American seventeen-year-olds also score lower than students in almost all other countries in tests of mathematics competence.[1] Nearly half cannot convert nine parts out of one hundred to a percentage.[2] Shortcomings in educational achievement are reflected in high rates of functional illiteracy among seventeen-year-olds who are still in school.[3] Yet many if not most of these illiterates will receive high school diplomas in spite of their inability to read and write at a primary school level.

The effects of poor high school education are offset for many students by enrollment in postsecondary schools. Approximately 57 percent of high school graduates go on to college or other postsecondary programs, a much higher percentage than in other advanced industrialized countries (figure 5-2). But many Americans must learn in college what their Japanese and European counterparts are taught in high school.

Graduates of the finest U.S. colleges and graduate institutions undoubtedly receive a superb education. Their formal preparation for work is equal or superior to that received by the best college graduates of other advanced industrialized countries. Unfortunately, fewer than one in five twenty-five-year-olds has graduated from a four-year college. Students whose postsecondary education ends after one or two years at a community college have probably received a less demanding education than that received by many high school graduates in northern Europe or Japan. Americans who get no schooling after high school are far less educated than high school graduates from other industrialized countries. Taxpayers also spend much less on educating and training workers who do not pursue postsecondary education (figure 5-3). The poor preparation of high school graduates combined with the superb education received by graduates of the nation's best colleges is one factor that tends to widen earnings disparities.

If American schools do not prepare their graduates adequately for

FIGURE 5-1. *International Performance on Tests in Science and Mathematics, 1980s*

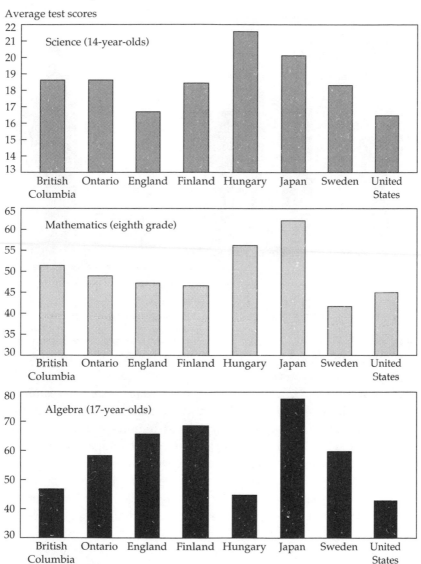

Average test scores

Sources: Lawrence R. Mishel and Jeffrey A. Frankel, *The State of Working America, 1990–91* (Armonk, N.Y.: M.E. Sharpe, 1991), p. 244; and John Bishop, "Incentives for Learning: Why American High School Students Compare So Poorly to Their Counterparts Overseas," in Commission on Workforce Quality and Labor Market Efficiency, *Investing in People: A Strategy to Address America's Workforce Crisis* (Department of Labor, 1989), p. 64.

FIGURE 5-2. *Enrollment Rates in Postsecondary Education, Selected Industrialized Countries, Late 1980s*

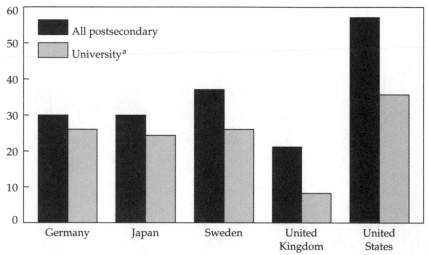

Percent of cohort that enrolls

Legend: All postsecondary / University[a]

X-axis: Germany, Japan, Sweden, United Kingdom, United States

Source: General Accounting Office, *Training Strategies: Preparing Noncollege Youth for Employment in the U.S. and Foreign Countries* (May 1990), p. 12.

a. Enrollment in an institution that confers baccalaureate degree or higher.

work, employers rarely remedy the deficiency. Few companies invest very much to improve the work skills of their young employees, perhaps in part because of employers' traditional reliance on public schools and on workers themselves to make necessary investments in general skills. In the past this strategy made sense. The United States was one of the first industrialized nations to offer free and compulsory schooling to all children younger than age fifteen. Compared with their counterparts in other industrialized nations, young American workers joined the labor force with a great deal of formal schooling. This advantage has largely disappeared, at least for the three-quarters of Americans who will never graduate from a four-year college.

The reluctance of employers to invest in their young workers is based on hard-headed economic calculation. Few young workers remain on the payroll long enough for an investment in training to pay off. High turnover rates among teenage workers and workers in their early twenties may not be surprising; many of them are trying to combine work with schooling. But high turnover persists even when

FIGURE 5-3. *Average Public Spending per Person Age 16–24 for Education and Training*

Thousands of dollars

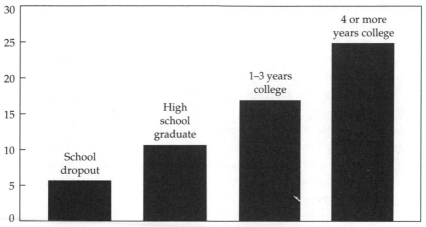

Source: General Accounting Office, *Training Strategies*, p. 24.

they reach their late twenties. In 1988 one in three male high school graduates between the ages of twenty-nine and thirty-one had held his job for less than a year. Among male dropouts of the same age, one in two has held his current job for less than a year.[4] When job tenures are this short, employers will logically assume that training is a high-risk investment.

Unlike American employers, companies in Germany and Japan invest heavily in training young employees. Workplace training in Germany occurs in the context of an extensive and long-established apprenticeship system. After completing compulsory full-time schooling at age sixteen, most German youth enter apprenticeships that typically last two or three years. For each occupation in which apprenticeships are offered, the training curriculum is developed through negotiations between representatives of the government, unions, and employers' associations. Training is constantly modified and kept up to date to reflect technological progress and recent developments in industrial practice. Apprentices spend one or two days each week in school studying vocational and academic subjects and the remainder of the week receiving on-the-job training from their employers. They are expected to learn more than they will actually use on a specific job: sales clerks may be taught about the manufacturing process for shoes or clothing, for example. This extensive training not only gives them a deeper understanding of their chosen occupation, but it also provides a basis for later promotion to more demanding jobs within the occupation. Upon completing their apprenticeships, trainees take comprehensive examinations to certify their mastery of occupational skills.[5]

The Japanese system of postsecondary training entails less government involvement but is equally extensive. Japanese employers assume most of the responsibility for developing the occupational skills of their employees. They use a variety of methods for company-based training, but the most important is the routine reassignment of workers from one job to another within an establishment and between establishments. On-the-job training teaches workers a new set of skills for each new assignment. This kind of training might seem terribly wasteful: many workers trained in a specific task will not perform it very long, and a high proportion performing a task may be recent trainees. Nonetheless, Japanese companies evidently feel the heavy investment is worthwhile. And the MIT Commission on Industrial Productivity has contended that frequent job rotation yields a work force with broad experience and the capacity to deal with a wide variety of production tasks, problems, and new technologies.[6]

A second aspect of Japanese company-based occupational development consists of training at specialized centers. Attendance in programs at these training centers is routine. Each year, for example, the Sanyo Corporation provides at least three days of training at its corporate educational center to one-third of its work force. Workers are also encouraged to seek occupational training through correspondence courses, with employers picking up the tab for those that are successfully completed. Many employers require their workers to participate in quality circles or other organized groups dedicated to improving the company's performance. Three-quarters of Japanese companies use one or more of these methods to provide training for their workers.[7] Of course, large Japanese companies take it for granted that nearly all young male workers will remain with the same firm for most of their careers.

Young Americans get little formal training in their first jobs. Only 12 percent report receiving any at all in the first year, and only one-sixth of this training occurs in a formal company training program.[8] (In West Germany 70 percent of young people age sixteen to eighteen enter paid employment through the apprenticeship system.)[9] The

FIGURE 5-4. *Probability of Receiving Training after Completion of Formal Schooling and Entry into Employment, Young American Men*

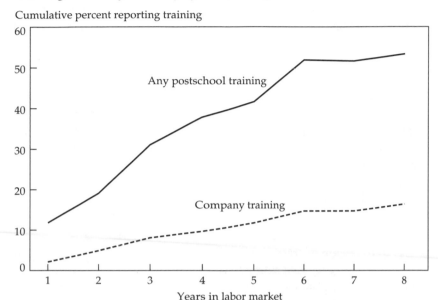

Cumulative percent reporting training

Any postschool training

Company training

Years in labor market

Source: Hong Tan and others, "Youth Training in the United States, Britain, and Australia" (Santa Monica, Calif.: Rand, 1991), p. 8, based on the National Longitudinal Survey.

situation improves as Americans grow older. By the sixth year after completing full-time schooling and entering the job market, more than half report receiving some postschool training, but only 15 percent report that the training was obtained under a formal company training program (figure 5-4). The amount of company-financed training is modest in comparison with training in either Germany or Japan.

The deficiencies of the education system for Americans who do not attend postsecondary schools are not corrected by company training programs. Only 40 percent of U.S. workers say they have taken company training to improve their skills in their current job.[10] Moreover, the probability that a worker will receive company training is strongly related to the worker's educational attainment. Highly educated workers are much more likely than less educated workers to receive company training. Many of the benefits of company training are concentrated on workers who have already received extensive schooling. The distribution of companies' investment in training reinforces the inequality that arises from unequal investment in public education. This situation contrasts sharply with the one in Germany, where company investments in apprenticeship training are heavily concentrated on the majority of German workers who do not go on to college.

Why do U.S. employers invest so little in training young workers? Certainly not out of complacency about the quality of young job applicants. Two-thirds of employers believe that applicants for entry-level jobs are inadequately prepared in basic academic skills.[11] Many employers, especially small ones, do not invest much in training because high turnover, particularly among the young, prevents them from capturing enough of the benefits of training to make the investment worthwhile. Bureau of Labor Statistics surveys suggest that the average American worker will hold eleven jobs during his or her work career, most before the age of thirty. Even after age thirty, a typical worker will change jobs four or five times.[12]

Many economists, including those who study the matter closely, deny that turnover represents a major barrier to investment in postschool training. According to one popular theory, workers themselves will pay to obtain training in general skills, that is, skills transferable from employer to employer. General skills include the ability to read, write, type, add, subtract, and solve challenging mathematical problems. Employers, on the other hand, will invest in developing workers' firm-specific skills. The company that invests in these skills can recoup its investment only if its workers remain on the job long enough for the training to pay off. But employers should not find it difficult to retain workers who have been taught firm-specific skills. Because the skill is only useable in one firm, acquiring it has not raised the worker's potential wage at other firms. If the company that provides training offers its workers slightly higher wages than they can obtain elsewhere, they will not be tempted to quit. Thus by paying a small wage premium the company can recoup its investment.

In theory, workers will invest in improving their general skills up to the point at which the cost of an extra course in school or college is no higher than the financial benefits they expect to receive from the schooling. Companies will invest in job-specific training up to the point at which the cost of the extra training is equal to the increase in productivity and profits they can expect to derive from it. This explains why workers should invest in formal schooling and employers should invest in firm-specific training. It does not really explain why American firms in fact invest so much less in training than do companies in Germany and Japan.

Although American employers face higher turnover among their young workers than employers in Germany and Japan, the turnover rates are at least partly a result of American employers' own personnel practices. Companies in Germany and Japan try to retain and retrain their career employees during business downturns; many American companies resort to layoffs.[13] If workers believe their employers will routinely lay them off during recessions, they have less reason to accept temporary wage sacrifices to partially finance their own training at a company. Reasoning that a layoff is likely anyway, many U.S. workers may demand jobs with comparatively high initial wages rather than jobs that offer extensive training, promotions, and wage increases but low initial wages. The lack of job security therefore discourages workers from making the commitment to their employers that would justify large investments in training.

Some American companies do not face this kind of problem, of course, at least until recently. IBM rarely laid off its workers and thus easily persuaded them to participate in company training programs. On any given day, the company trains 22,000 employees somewhere in the world, at a total annual cost of $1.5 billion, exclusive of the cost of the participants' time.[14] Larger American companies generally invest much more in training their workers than do mid-sized and smaller ones. Many large companies have developed good reputations for loyalty to their employees during good times and bad. Most offer better wages and job opportunities than do smaller companies that compete in the same industries. Large firms can credibly promise to pay rising wages over time if workers participate in training programs financed partly out of company resources and partly out of short-term wage sacrifices on the part of the workers themselves. Low employee turnover ensures that both the company and the trainee share in the benefits of training. As a result, larger employers help provide both general and specific training to their employees. These firms account for a dwindling share of U.S. employment, however. Since 1980, *Fortune* 500 companies have shed 4.4 million workers while civilian employment as whole has grown by 17.4 million. Employment in smaller companies mushroomed during these years.[15]

Smaller companies typically cannot afford to offer programs that combine general with firm-specific training. Most pay wages just high enough to attract and maintain a minimum work force. Many do not explicitly or implicitly promise to pay their employees higher wages at some future date. Even if they offered such a promise, it is doubtful whether it would be credible. Workers might be skeptical about the firm's existence in five or ten years when the higher wages would be expected. They will be unwilling to participate in a training program that is costly to them if the payoff is uncertain. Companies will be unwilling to commit funds to general training when high turnover means that much of their investment will walk out the door. High employee turnover thus leads to an undesirable outcome: small and medium-sized firms do not invest very much in their workers.

The economic model of training implies that employee turnover will prevent small employers from participating in the general but not the firm-specific training of their work force. As a practical matter, however, it is not easy to distinguish between the two. When a company helps a worker upgrade occupational skills, the training usually helps the worker increase productivity on jobs both inside and outside the company. To improve a worker's job-specific skills it is often necessary to improve his or her general skills at the same time.

Firms attempting to reform their production methods often find it essential to upgrade both the general and the specific skills of their workers. When the Phoenix Specialty Manufacturing Company in Bamberg, South Carolina, changed its production methods in the early 1990s, it discovered that the basic reading, writing, and mathematics skills of its work force were inadequate for the new methods. Its workers could not be relied on to implement a production system in which initiative and resourcefulness were paramount. As a result, the company had to upgrade both the job-specific and the general skills of its work force.[16]

The problem of inadequate general skills would not be serious if workers invested more in their own general training. Many, of course, do go to the effort and expense of enrolling in proprietary vocational schools, community colleges, or formal apprenticeship programs. But most make no investment, relying instead on the training they will receive from employers. The result is that they obtain only informal, on-the-job training that provides few skills that other employers value.[17] This arrangement might be appropriate for workers who will spend their entire careers working for a single firm, as is the case in Japan, but such careers are rare in the United States.

A crucial shortcoming in the American system of postschool training is thus apparent. Because of high employee turnover, many employers, especially small businesses, fail to invest in developing the general occupational skills of their workers. Of course, high turnover offers some compensating advantages. The U.S. labor market is renowned for its responsiveness to large economic shocks. Part of this flexibility comes from American workers' willingness to quit unsatisfying jobs and employers' willingness to discharge redundant workers. Labor markets in many Western European countries are much more rigid. But the high U.S. turnover rates can lead to low rates of employer investment in general occupational skills. For reasons of their own, including shortsightedness, poor information, or inadequate access to credit, many workers do not invest enough in improving their own general skills, either. They are thus left stranded in low-productivity jobs with little prospect of promotion within the company or upward mobility outside it. Their inadequate general skills contribute to America's two primary economic problems: slow growth and increasing economic inequality.

Remedies

We have highlighted two shortcomings in the job preparation of American workers. Young people who are not bound for college receive substandard formal schooling before entering the job market. Many then receive very poor and spotty training in general skills after they become employed. These two problems require distinct solutions, one focusing on the nation's secondary school system and the other on the labor market institutions providing postschool training.

Secondary Schools

The growing recognition that American schools are deficient and the suspicion that their slipping performance may help explain slow productivity growth has forced voters and policymakers to consider thoroughgoing reforms. Although the topic of education reform is important, our focus is on a narrower set of reforms aimed at improving the job market preparation of youth who are not college bound and strengthening the links between secondary schools and the world of work.[18]

It is widely acknowledged that American schools are unsuccessful in motivating pupils to work hard at learning academic subjects. This problem is particularly acute for students who do not expect to go to selective four-year colleges. One reason for poor motivation is that hard work in school has no immediate or obvious payoff after students leave school, except for those who go on to selective colleges.

Employers do not go out of their way to hire new high school graduates who have performed well in school, nor do they reward their more able young workers by paying them higher wages than they pay to new workers who performed poorly in school.[19] Few employers even bother to ask for the high school transcripts of their job applicants. They may feel that the information would not be helpful or that young workers will not remain on the payroll long enough for the information to be worth the effort of collecting it. This attitude contrasts sharply with that of many employers in Japan. Good Japanese employers hire young workers on the basis of nominations from local high schools, which prepare lists of recommended new graduates based on their grades and school performance. If Japanese students work harder in school than their American counterparts, one reason might be that the benefits of hard work and good grades are so immediately tangible after graduation: better students get better jobs.

Although the United States cannot completely adopt either the Japanese or German systems of linking school performance to good job and apprenticeship opportunities, it can strengthen the connection between learning basic skills in high school and receiving good job opportunities later. This will require three kinds of reforms, all of which must be widely advertised to students, parents, and employers. First, the high school curriculum for young people not bound for college must contain certain common elements in schools throughout the country. These subjects should be closely tied to later productivity on the job—reading, writing, mathematical reasoning, basic science, and so on. Although much of the school curriculum would remain under local control, the nation ought to specify core elements that must be included in all secondary curriculums, and it must develop specific standards identified with "sufficient," "good," and "superior" knowledge of each subject.

Second, students should be required to demonstrate mastery of the core subjects on nationally recognized tests. Their scores would clearly signal to employers their level of knowledge. The assessments should not be tests of aptitude and should be very different from the norm-referenced multiple choice exams that currently dominate standardized testing. Test results along with simple school transcripts should be routinely provided to employers who request them when school graduates apply for jobs.

The Bush administration proposed that high school seniors take American Achievement Tests currently being developed in five core subjects. However, the administration also proposed that taking the tests (or, for schools, offering them) be voluntary. Although this is in keeping with the strong American tradition of local control over public education, it robs the tests of much of their meaning. If employers can request information about basic skills for only a few of their young job applicants, it is not clear why they should request the information for any of them.

The United States currently offers only one widely recognized credential indicating mastery of the skills taught in schools, the high school diploma. This credential is generally required by employers, but it is a very crude indicator of the specific skills students have mastered. Two goals of nationally recognized scholastic tests should be to increase employers' knowledge of young job applicants and to boost the incentives for high school students to work hard to acquire useful skills. Unless the scores are commonly available for recent high school graduates, it is hard to see how the tests can achieve either goal.

Some readers may question whether greater emphasis on standardized achievement tests, both in the schools and on the part of employers, can lead to improvements in labor market equality. Such tests are frequently criticized because they create distinctions between otherwise similar people that may not be justified by actual differences in their productivity. Appropriate tests of general and specific skills can, however, improve labor market efficiency by showing students something about their own comparative advantages in the job market and indicating to employers which applicants have the general skills needed for specific jobs. If employers actually use this information in hiring, students who hope to obtain good jobs will be offered powerful incentives to improve their achievement in school so that they can score well on the tests. This incentive should increase the average effort (and raise achievement levels) of high school students who do not intend to go to college. The present system already provides strong incentives for students who hope to attend selective colleges. If equivalent incentives were provided to those who do not go on to college, the amount they learn in the classroom might increase and their earnings capacity improve once they leave school. This should improve their labor market performance in comparison with that of well-paid college graduates.

Our last recommendation may be the most challenging. School officials and teachers must be held accountable for the academic and job market success of their students who are not college bound. At first, of course, it would be unrealistic to do this. Few schools now seem interested in what happens to their graduates after they leave school. Most do not even know whether they find jobs. But schools do know about the academic accomplishments of their students. Nationally recognized tests of student performance could provide still more information. Even more important, the test scores would provide parents, employers, and interested public officials with reliable information about the success of individual schools in improving the job-related skills of their students. But it is not enough that this information become widely available. It must also be used to retain, promote, and reward successful teachers and school administrators. Whether this is accomplished through a system in which parents and students choose their schools, as advocated by our former colleague John Chubb, or through drastic reform of the current system of hiring public school principals and teachers, the effect should be the same. Schools that succeed in improving the basic skills and knowledge of their students should be rewarded, and schools that fail should be reformed or closed.

Postschool Training

Although school reform can ultimately improve the job market performance of workers who receive no schooling beyond high school, it can do nothing to remedy the problems of today's working-age population. To increase the productivity of current workers, the nation must increase their investment in their own skills or their employers' investment in their general skills. Alternatively, the government can raise the amount it invests directly in the skills of the country's most disadvantaged workers—for example, by increasing outlays on the Job Corps program or the Job Training Partnership Act (JTPA).

We favor a policy that stresses increasing employer investments in training. The government already offers a variety of inducements to workers to invest in themselves. By providing generous subsidies to community colleges, state and local governments make many low-cost training opportunities available. Heavily subsidized student loans and outright educational grants to the economically disadvantaged help unskilled workers pay for schooling in community or four-year colleges or in proprietary vocational schools. But many workers never take advantage of these opportunities. One-fifth of high school students do not even take full advantage of free public schooling. In spite of the large and growing economic advantage of holding a high school diploma, they drop out before graduating. It is questionable whether boosting public subsidies for general training would change the behavior of people who now refrain from investing in themselves.

More fundamentally, we question whether the investments that less skilled workers would make in themselves offer the same high payoff as the self-directed investments of more highly skilled workers. If a worker lacks the good sense to remain in a free public school long enough to earn a high school diploma, it is not obvious he or she would make a prudent choice when offered more generous subsidies to attend any training institution he chooses. In the 1992 presidential campaign George Bush and Bill Clinton both proposed schemes in which workers could draw on public funds to pay for self-improvement through education or training. In some cases the loans could be repaid by taxing a percentage of the worker's earnings over the remainder of his or her career. Although this kind of scheme can help bridge a critical gap for some hard-pressed students and workers, it will not do much to improve the productivity of the large majority of active workers who have little inclination to return to school.

It would be valuable to enlarge and strengthen government programs such as the Job Corps that offer training directly to the disadvantaged. (We offer some suggestions for reform later in this chapter.) But government programs suffer from serious problems. Public training programs are ordinarily focused on the economically disadvantaged and the unskilled. They do not enjoy a good reputation among less skilled workers, many of whom also need added training. Moreover, government officials seldom have a clear idea about the most appropriate training to provide workers who ask for help. Although public administrators seem to do no worse than workers—and may actually do better—in selecting specific courses of training, public trainees often end up with skills they do not use on their next jobs.[20] Private employers, who at least understand their own training needs, enjoy significant advantages in assigning workers to courses of instruction. Chances are good that if an employer is paying for part of the training investment, the training will be used in the worker's next job.

To promote new investments in training by employers, the nation needs to do more than simply exhort companies to invest more. Exhortations have been made for more than a decade by public officials and business-sponsored organizations, with little apparent effect on typical employers. Small and medium-sized businesses ignore these pleas for the most natural of reasons. Few of them can improve their bottom-line results through a unilateral policy of added investment in the basic skills and occupational training of their workers.

Many employers would benefit if the American work force possessed better basic skills. Jobs could be made more challenging, work could be organized in a more demanding way, and greater responsibility could be transferred from line managers to workers themselves. But employers cannot expect to capture the benefits of extra investment in general skills unless they pay high enough wages to retain the workers they have trained. Some companies can afford to pay such wages after they have paid for training. Those who cannot will be better off hiring, at the going market wage, workers who already possess necessary skills.

To raise the level and quality of workplace training, we propose a public-private venture with three main components: establishing nationally recognized credentials to certify occupational skills; imposing a required employer contribution toward the workplace training of non-college-educated workers; and creating a national apprenticeship system to help youth who are not bound for college move from school to work through a carefully designed program of firm-based occupational training.

NATIONALLY RECOGNIZED CREDENTIALS. The U.S. labor market is extremely decentralized. Occupational training is provided by thousands of public schools, community colleges, and proprietary institutions and hundreds of thousands of employers. There is little coordination among them in defining the training necessary to acquire particular occupational skills. Except for the professions and a handful of industrial and construction trades, few occupations described in the Department of Labor's *Dictionary of Occupational Titles* offer broadly recognized credentials proving a worker's mastery of the occupation. This reduces the information available to employers when they are considering the qualifications of individual job applicants, and it greatly diminishes the transferability and hence the value of occupational skills learned on a particular job.

The value of training would be enhanced if mastery of occupational skills picked up on a job were certified with a nationally recognized credential. The credential would have to be developed by a public institution that includes employers, worker organizations, federal and state departments of labor, and, where appropriate, educational institutions. The public authority would define an occupation, specify the minimum competencies needed to practice it, describe a training plan that guides employers or training institutions in developing the timing, sequencing, and organization of appropriate training for it, and develop tests that would prove a worker's mastery of the occupation.

Some observers believe that such standards can be developed through purely voluntary organizations, possibly with limited assistance from the federal government. This seems doubtful. In the German system, apprenticeships are available in nearly 400 occupational categories, representing more than 20,000 blue-collar and white-collar occupations. Standards and tests of competency are needed in all these occupations. A public authority, the Bundesinstitüt für Berufsbildung, coordinates the system. It is difficult to see how voluntary private organizations in the United States could develop authoritative occupational definitions, standards, and competency tests on the required scale without substantial public funding. As a practical matter, public expenditure would bring public participation in the creation and implementation of the standards. The system will require active government participation, but not government domination, if it is to work.

The development of recognized occupational standards and competency tests offers important advantages. Public loans and grants to students in community colleges and proprietary training institutions could be tied to progress in attaining skills in a recognized occupation. This could reduce the fraud and wasteful training that now takes place in postsecondary vocational institutions. Proprietary institutions frequently persuade disadvantaged students to enroll in poorly designed programs and help them finance their training through guaranteed student loans. When the training turns out to be worthless, the students default on their loans. In 1986 the default rate on loans to students at these institutions was 40 percent.[21]

In addition to paying for Pell grants and student loans, the federal government also finances private sector on-the-job training through subsidies under the Job Training Partnership Act. Participating employers promise to hire and train disadvantaged workers for a limited period—typically, two to five months—in exchange for a direct government subsidy covering part of the wage and training costs. Although the Department of Labor has published rules describing the kinds of jobs and training appropriate for these subsidies, meaningful standards are difficult to enforce when there are no broadly recognized standards of occupational qualification or mastery. Once these standards have been developed, the Department of Labor could simply insist that employers certify their subsidized trainees in recognized occupations before the subsidy could be paid. Although this burden might seem onerous to employers, it is reasonable to impose it when the public is paying for some or all of the firm's on-the-job training expenses. To persuade more employers to participate in the program in spite of the added burden, the subsidy rate could be raised.

MANDATORY CONTRIBUTION TO TRAINING. To pay for the development of occupational credentials, company-based training programs, and a nationwide apprenticeship system, it will be necessary to generate funds. We believe that a straightforward assessment on company payrolls is the most defensible and appropriate source of financing. To create an incentive to provide general training for non-college-educated workers, the government could excuse employers from paying some or all of this tax if they invest certain amounts in their own internal training programs, including certified apprenticeship plans.

The French government imposed a similar training mandate in 1971. French employers must invest 1.1 percent of their annual money wages in worker training and an additional 0.5 percent in approved apprenticeship programs. If they fail to invest this much, the difference between their actual investment and the mandatory minimum must be forfeited to the state, which in theory uses the money to finance public training programs. The policy has had little effect on large French employers, which, like big American firms, typically invest more than the required amount anyway. It has had a significant effect on smaller companies, however. In the first eight years after introduction of the tax, the share of workers in small firms who received training increased from less than 2 percent to 4 percent a year. Small firms doubled their spending on worker training.[22]

The French system needs major modification if it is to work in the United States. Many U.S. companies pour funds into an activity that they call training or employee development, but little of this spending contributes to improving the general skills of less skilled workers. It is focused instead on developing management proficiency or rewarding senior white-collar personnel. Sometimes "employee development" occurs in comfortable surroundings in the Caribbean or Hawaii. Much of this spending should properly be classified as part of employee compensation rather than worker training. Companies do not need added incentives to provide these kinds of emoluments. Nor do they need special encouragement to upgrade the skills of senior managers and white-collar professionals, most of whom have already received extensive formal schooling, much of it at public expense.

If government intervention is needed, it must be aimed at expanding company-sponsored training provided to less skilled workers, the ones whose slumping wages have contributed to recent increases in economic inequality. Their deficiency of basic skills limits the demands that employers can place on them when defining the content of jobs. If jobs cannot become more challenging, many workers cannot be made more productive either. Thus employers should be required to devote a specified percentage of their payroll to training workers whose formal education ended with high school or with no more than a year of college. If less skilled workers are considered those with one or fewer years of college education, 55 to 60 percent of all workers would qualify and would be eligible for publicly promoted training investments.

For the immediate future, employers' obligation to train the less skilled could be met if they could demonstrate that they are devoting, say, 2 percent of their payroll to expenses directly related to training or to the wages of workers who are being withheld from current production so that they can be trained. If the nation develops a credentialing system, a company could be required to show that its training investment actually yields mastery of skills in publicly recognized occupations. This obligation could be met, of course, if the employer offered apprenticeships in approved programs to a sufficient number of new employees. It is, however, pointless to impose a detailed obligation of this kind before occupational standards have been defined and a national apprenticeship system has been established.

Within the first several years after a training obligation is imposed, approved training expenses should be defined rather loosely. Looser rules would reduce the shock of the new mandate and minimize the potential adverse effect on unemployment, but would still signal to employers the social significance attached to worker training. Gradually the definition of approved training should become more strict and follow the recommendations of the joint public-private certification authority described earlier. Politicians will be tempted to exempt small employers from the obligation, but this would be a mistake. The shortfall in workplace training is greater in small firms than in larger ones. Imposing a common obligation on all private employers to invest in worker skills would require small firms to bear a proportional share of the costs of improving the work force. Besides, the ultimate cost would not be entirely borne by businesses. Part would be passed on to consumers in the form of higher prices and to workers in the form of slower immediate wage growth. In the intermediate and long runs, wages would grow faster as a result of improvements in the skills and productivity of average workers.

Employers will naturally object to a government training mandate that requires them to invest in less educated workers. Some companies have very few unskilled workers. Others prefer to invest only in highly compensated employees, since poorly paid workers do not remain on their payrolls long. Of course, this unwillingness makes government intervention desirable. Nonetheless, employers should be offered a less expensive alternative if they do not believe they can usefully invest in training less skilled workers. If the specified minimum percentage is 2 percent, employers that devote less than 2 percent of their wages to approved training should be obligated to contribute one-half the difference between 2 percent of wages and their actual training expenses to a public fund. Thus a company that spent no money on approved training would be required to contribute 1 percent of wages; one that devoted 1.5 percent of wages to training would contribute 0.25 percent to the fund.

This proposal reduces by 50 percent the cost to employers of investing in their less skilled workers, at least for investments that total less than 2 percent of employers' payrolls. For each $1.00 a firm spends on approved training, it avoids paying $0.50 to the public training fund. If it can find no useful way to spend $1.00 on training, however, it would be better off contributing $0.50 to the fund. This provision reduces the temptation for companies to waste money on unnecessary training, an unfortunate feature of the current French system. It also provides a source of public funds for developing occupational standards and establishing a national apprenticeship system.

A training contribution of 2 percent of payrolls would generate $46 billion a year.[23] In comparison, public spending on education now amounts to $360 billion a year. The training obligation would increase private companies' training investment by less than $46 billion, of course, because most employers spend at least modest amounts on certified training already. In the long run, the impact of a training mandate on companies' behavior would increase. They should eventually be obliged to spend part of their training funds on publicly sanctioned apprenticeship programs for young workers, or, for more senior workers, on training programs that lead to certification in publicly recognized occupational skills.

NATIONAL APPRENTICESHIP PROGRAM. The most effective training program for non-college-bound young people would be one that dramatically expands the formal occupational training they receive in their first full-time job. In America this training is typically slight, and young workers who do not go to college often flounder for years before beginning a career that involves much chance of training or advancement. A national apprenticeship system modeled on the one in Germany offers promise of correcting this problem.

The advantages of an effective apprenticeship program have been described elsewhere.[24] A primary feature is the signed agreement between a young worker and an employer. The agreement clearly specifies the wage as well as the obligations of the two parties. The employer agrees to provide occupational training meeting the minimum standards established by the national authority for occupational certification. The young worker agrees to remain employed for a specified minimum period, typically two to four years, and to achieve certification.

Employers would provide on-the-job training in retail stores, banks, industrial plants, offices, and other business locations. Formal classroom training, provided either by the employer or by a local training institution, would usually supplement on-the-job training. Companies would not be obliged to offer a permanent job at the end of an apprenticeship, but most would probably offer jobs to their successful trainees—apprenticeship programs give employers a good opportunity to try out prospective workers before placing them on their permanent payrolls. Even apprentices who are not offered a permanent job by their apprenticeship employer will obtain something that few existing jobs offer, general training and a certificate proving mastery of a recognized occupation.

Apprenticeships now train less than 2 percent of U.S. high school graduates. In comparison to the 13.5 million students enrolled in two- and four-year colleges in 1990, a little over 280,000 workers were registered in 43,000 apprenticeship programs, mainly in the construction trades. Few apprentices are recent high school graduates. In 1990, more than 80 percent were age twenty-three or older.[25] By contrast, most German teenagers enter full-time paid employment through apprenticeships. One result is that youth unemployment rates are far lower in Germany than they are in the United States or in other industrialized countries that lack an apprenticeship system. The youth unemployment rate even remained below the rate in the United States during the middle and late 1980s when overall German unemployment exceeded the U.S. rate. Young German workers also spend less time in idleness or moving between jobs than their U.S. counterparts. Moreover, seven of ten graduating German apprentices end up working in occupations for which their training has equipped them.[26]

An apprenticeship system would also provide the opportunity to teach young people general skills in the context of practical assignments. Reading, writing, public speaking, and mathematics can seem more interesting if they can be put to daily practical use. For many American youngsters, apprenticeships might increase the amount of useful knowledge that is absorbed and retained. Because some young people do not flourish in a classroom setting, particularly if the material is divorced from day-to-day experience, a carefully structured apprenticeship program that combined classroom with on-the-job training might represent a better learning environment than a traditional secondary school.

To realize an apprenticeship system, standards must be established for training and occupational certification in a wide variety of white-collar and blue-collar occupations. We have already suggested a cooperative public-private mechanism for accomplishing this. In addition, the job expectations of high school students and the training practices of many private employers must be changed. High school sophomores and juniors who are not thinking of going to college should be encouraged to consider enrolling in an apprenticeship or preapprenticeship program. This may not be difficult. The number of people who currently apply for apprenticeships often exceeds the number of available positions. Many more young workers would become apprentices if more employers could be persuaded to establish programs.[27]

Not all employers need offer apprenticeships. Only one-quarter of West German companies, some 400,000, actively participate in the apprenticeship system.[28] However, the participating companies offer enough positions so that nearly all Germans who want to become apprentices can find an opening. Some firms find apprenticeships attractive because they provide low-cost labor. Others welcome the opportunity to train and observe young workers who have the potential to become good employees. The United States will not be able to achieve a high rate of company participation in apprenticeship training overnight: Germany's system has been in place for decades, and many firms depend on the system to provide most of their new workers. To encourage American firms to move toward an apprenticeship system, we suggest that they eventually be obligated to devote a minimum percentage of their wage bill, perhaps 0.5 percent, to occupational training in certified apprenticeship programs. (This obligation should be part of the 2 percent training contribution rather than in addition to it.) Firms that spend less than the specified amount should contribute one-half the difference to a public apprenticeship fund. Money in the fund can be used to maintain and update apprenticeship training standards and certification exams as well as to subsidize apprenticeships for economically disadvantaged workers who are eligible for help under the Job Training Partnership Act. It might also be necessary, at least initially, to provide public subsidies to exemplary apprenticeship programs.

Improvements in Labor Market Institutions

Although the best prospect for improving the work preparation of Americans will come from reforms in secondary schooling and workplace training, other measures can also boost productivity or improve the allocation of labor. We suggest measures that will require reforms in existing federal programs and in the compensation and management systems of private employers.

Research and Development in Federal Training Programs

The federal government spends $4 billion a year on training programs aimed at improving the skills and employability of displaced and disadvantaged workers. Most of this money is funneled to state and local government agencies and to nonprofit training agencies that actually run the local programs. The federally sponsored training programs also provide employment services to a wide range of program applicants, including welfare recipients, teenagers and adults in poor and near-poor families, and workers who have recently lost their jobs as a result of economic displacement. State and local governments are given some flexibility in the types of services they can offer, but most services fall within a fairly predictable range. One-third of adult trainees receive classroom instruction, either in specific occupational trades or in remedial skills such as reading and arithmetic. Smaller numbers receive subsidized on-the-job training provided by private firms or unpaid work training within nonprofit organizations and government departments. A large percentage of people who enroll receive assistance in finding jobs and preparing for job interviews. The training and other services rarely last longer than six months; two or three months is more typical.

Federal training programs enjoy a mixed reputation, both among the target population and the general public. Voters and policymakers may applaud the idea of job training in principle, but many believe government programs have proven ineffective. This reputation, while not entirely undeserved, is a bit unfair. Federal training programs have been the subject of many evaluations, and contrary to popular belief, the evaluations indicate they are moderately effective. Most studies suggest that the main programs have helped increase participants' average earnings, at least in the short run.[29] A recent evaluation of the main federal training programs, for example, found that adults enrolled in JTPA-funded programs enjoyed earnings gains of $500 a year during the first eighteen months after they signed up for the programs.[30]

The perception that the programs have failed is thus not based on evidence but on the popular impression that thirty years' spending on training programs has failed to yield a noticeable reduction in poverty. Although the impression is almost certainly accurate, it has little to do with the programs' effectiveness. The nation annually spends comparatively little on training—about 0.1 percent of GNP. Even a favorable return on the investment, one as high as 10 percent a year, would have only a very small impact on poverty. If voters and policymakers really want the programs to improve the position of less skilled workers, it is hard to avoid the conclusion that they will have to spend more money. In the previous section we suggested a source of funds and a practical way to use them.

We also believe, however, that existing funds can and should be spent more effectively. The federal government should undertake a systematic program of research and development to improve publicly funded training. For example, a recent evaluation showing that JTPA programs for adults are modestly effective also showed that similar programs for disadvantaged sixteen- to twenty-one-year-olds are ineffective and possibly harmful.[31] Although these results are comparatively new, they were foreshadowed by previous evaluations. Congress and the Department of Labor have been slow to use the results in program administration, and local training operators virtually ignore them when designing programs for economically disadvantaged young people.

While the Labor Department imposes detailed performance standards on program operators, it has yet to devise a systematic program of research and development that would generate new information about the programs that are most helpful in raising the employability and earnings of less skilled workers. The nation spends $700 million a year on JTPA programs aimed at disadvantaged out-of-school youth, for example. These programs are doing no good, and they may actually be harming the employment prospects of participants. Young people and taxpayers would be better off if the nation used the $700 million systematically appraising some alternatives. If members of Congress and Labor Department officials lack good ideas about how to improve the programs, they should solicit proposals from other government agencies and the private sector. For example, the Labor Department could offer five-year grants to state and local governments or to private organizations to design and implement plausible alternative training programs in a handful of local areas. Winning proposals could be selected in a fair competition. Resulting programs should be subjected to careful outside evaluation. States and local governments already have some flexibility in designing their training programs, but few try innovative alternatives to standard practice. Even when they do, national administrators and officials in other localities have little idea whether the innovations have worked.

We should scrutinize, assess, and improve public training programs just as private firms evaluate their own business activities. If a program is unsuccessful in improving the employability and earnings of participants, it should be scrapped and a better one found. This will not occur as a matter of routine unless the government implements a rigorous research and development plan for its training programs.

Improvements in the Employment Service

In a dynamic economy, millions of jobs are lost each year and millions more are created. To speed up the movement of workers from shrinking to growing industries and to minimize earnings losses, the government offers job search help to the unemployed through state employment services. The Employment Service, called the Job Service in some states, was established by the Wagner-Peyser Act of 1933. The act established a nationwide network of state-operated, federally financed Employment Service offices to serve as a labor exchange, matching job seekers with available jobs. Each local Employment Service office takes job orders from local employers and matches them with job applications. In addition, it offers employment counseling to job seekers and standardized tests to assess their qualifications.

Although efficient Employment Services should reduce the hardship and uncertainty that workers face as a result of economic change, it is doubtful whether the existing state services provide this function. Employment Services do perform a crucial role in enforcing the work test so that unemployed workers can qualify for unemployment insurance, but they are mostly ineffective as a labor market exchange. Few people find jobs through an Employment Service referral: most are found through informal referrals from friends, direct applications to company personnel offices, or responses to want ads. Businesses typically rely on their own recruitment efforts rather than the state Employment Service, possibly because they doubt the quality of people who would be referred. The main labor exchange function provided by Employment Service offices is referral of less skilled workers to low-paying and often temporary jobs listed by local employers.

The main problems with the Employment Service derive from two sources. The service has been weighed down over the years with the obligation to help the most disadvantaged class of job seekers—unemployment insurance recipients, people collecting food stamps and public assistance, residents of public housing, and poor teenagers seeking access to targeted employment and tax subsidy programs. This obligation gives rise to a problem of adverse selection. When the clientele of the Employment Service became younger, poorer, and less skilled as a result of new government regulations, employers searching for good workers began to look elsewhere. As more good employers stayed away from Employment Service offices, average workers had less reason to file job applications there, further reducing the average quality of the clientele.

As a practical matter, the Employment Service office does not know where the job vacancies are. It therefore also lacks detailed knowledge of the training that would be most helpful for job applicants who might enroll in college or vocational training programs. To enforce the work test for jobless benefits or public assistance, it requires that applicants fill out endless forms, attend fruitless interviews, and wait in lengthy queues. None of these measures helps many people find jobs. But the burden on benefit applicants probably reduces fraud and abuse in the programs.

Adverse selection would not arise if employers were obliged to list their job openings with the local Employment Service. Sweden and some other European countries insist that employers advertise their job openings at the public employment agency. As a result, the public job service has extensive knowledge about local employment opportunities and the qualifications needed to fill them. Swedish workers trying to find new jobs will naturally visit the public employment service to get good leads, and Swedish employers can be confident that the public agency will send them workers who have decent employment credentials. But the United States has chosen instead to allow employers wide scope in their hiring strategies.

The state employment agencies can become substantially more effective as a labor exchange if they provide services to a broader cross-section of workers and offer listings for more of the good job openings. This can be accomplished in one of two ways. The United States could, like Sweden, require businesses to list job openings with the service. Employers would not be required to hire from among the applicants referred by the Employment Service, nor would they be required to list openings that are supposed to be filled through internal promotions and job reassignments. But they could be required to notify the service of vacancies available to outside applicants and to describe realistically the skill requirements that the applicants will need.

Since the United States is unlikely to force employers to cooperate with the public labor exchange, an alternative strategy would be to improve the quality of service that workers and employers can expect. More workers and businesses might use the Employment Service, reducing the problem of adverse selection. We believe that existing services can be improved using recent innovations in computers and telecommunications. Some of these innovations have been adopted by state Employment Services, but budget pressure has forced the federal government to shy away from investing in many others.

The U.S. Employment Service has been slow, for example, to exploit computers to refer workers to distant job openings. According to official statistics, fewer than 10,000 job openings a year are filled as a result of interstate job referrals. This is a tiny proportion of the workers who find jobs through interstate moves and an even smaller proportion of the job seekers who might find work if job availability in other areas were advertised in local Employment Service offices. Although developing software for interstate job referrals is a formidable problem, it is solvable given the dramatic reductions in the cost of computation over the past two decades. Moreover, the burdens of writing job referral software are hardly unique. Missile defense, the space program, and air traffic control all required enormous investments in software development. We wonder whether the problems of the U.S. Employment Service have received less attention because policymakers erroneously believe that labor market exchange is a straightforward and relatively unimportant public function.

Investments in new software should be supplemented with investments in more sophisticated telecommunications equipment. For example, technical developments now permit people in widely scattered sites to participate in face-to-face communications through teleconferencing. This innovation should be exploited in selected employment service offices to allow company personnel officers to interview job applicants at distant sites. Jobless workers in areas with high unemployment often find that the best route to a good job is the road leading out of town. But long-distance job seekers are forced to invest in costly and often fruitless in-person searches. Their costs could be substantially reduced if their local Employment Service offices provided good job leads from labor markets around the country as well as a low-cost method of conducting interviews with prospective employers in those markets. The U.S. Employment Service does not offer this opportunity because its primary mission has involved local job referral and enforcement of the work test. Its mission should not be viewed so narrowly.

Relating Pay to Performance

Mounting evidence suggests that lagging U.S. productivity results not only from slow domestic investment and inadequate worker training but also from the country's system of industrial management and labor relations. Many American firms continue to make rigid distinctions between the prerogatives of managers and those of line workers. Managers design jobs and organize work; line employees carry out assigned tasks that are often defined in astonishing detail. This managerial system, known as the Taylor system, was a marvel of efficiency in the past, when most large enterprises were involved in high-volume production of autos, ironing boards, and other goods or services. It appears less successful today, at least in the United States. American firms now must compete with foreign firms, which can adopt the same or similar methods but do not need to pay high U.S. wages.

Then, too, the Taylor system was adopted in an age when the qualifications of U.S. line workers were suspect. Many were immigrants who could speak, read, and write English only with great difficulty, if at all. Native-born American workers frequently came from depressed rural areas where many had received poor schooling. The challenge was to devise a way to use these unskilled people efficiently without overburdening the managers who supervised them. The characteristic American solution was to divide production into small steps, each of which could be easily learned, and to assign each worker a task involving only a very limited number. Since each job was so narrow, the performance of each worker could be monitored with comparative ease.

Workers were typically paid a straight hourly wage, regardless of their productivity. Indeed, any other method of payment might have seemed nonsensical. Most workers had little scope for increasing their productivity because output resulted from a team effort in which the role of each worker was narrowly circumscribed. To be sure, some were paid piece-rate wages or compensated on a commission basis, and their output determined their income. But most were and continue to be paid straight hourly, weekly, or monthly wages, and many establishments are still run under the Taylor system.

Although these management and compensation systems were amazingly successful in their heyday, they have proven less effective in recent years. The Taylor system fails to exploit fully the knowledge that workers develop on their jobs. If workers know more than managers about personnel needs or the efficiency of particular production methods, it can be profitable for owners to pay attention to them. Many companies have suggestion boxes, of course, but the rigid division between the responsibilities assigned to managers and line workers may discourage workers from making suggestions. In addition, the system offers no powerful incentives for workers to cooperate with business owners: they receive the same wages whether they do or do not supply helpful information.

A decade ago American economists became interested in alternative compensation schemes, particularly the Japanese pay system, under which workers receive large annual bonuses in addition to straight hourly wages. Because the bonuses are ultimately linked to a company's profitability, some economists felt that the system gave workers a vital stake in the profitability and ultimate success of their employers.[32] Although scholars were initially interested in the effect of the system on inflation, aggregate unemployment, and other macroeconomic outcomes, they have also investigated the influence on employee productivity.[33]

Several kinds of evidence suggest that tying pay to output or company profitability increases productivity. First, in contrast with workers paid under the standard straight-wage contract, similar workers paid on a piece-rate basis typically receive a wage premium.[34] If employers pay piece-rate workers higher wages, we presume it is because those workers are more productive. Second, case studies of individual firms suggest that profit-sharing schemes generally also increase productivity.[35] Finally, an amazingly large body of statistical evidence shows that employers who link workers' pay to output or profitability enjoy an edge in productivity.[36]

An unexpected finding has been that the impact of pay-for-performance on productivity is further increased when the pay is linked to more flexible worker-manager relationships. Profit sharing, gain sharing, and production bonuses have proven effective in increasing worker productivity. Other schemes, such as employee stock ownership plans, appear to be less consistently successful. But each of the alternative pay systems is more successful when it is combined with basic reform in the employee-employer relationship.

A logical inference is that many businesses should reform both their compensation system and their style of management. Part of each worker's compensation, perhaps as little as 5 or 10 percent, should be tied to worker output, company profitability, or company performance. This gives every employee a stake in improving productivity. It helps reduce the separation of interest that divides workers from business owners: both have a tangible and immediate stake in the productiveness or profitability of the enterprise. Conceivably, the reform might reduce the feeling of "us versus them," an attitude that often colors relations between line workers and managers.

In addition to the change in the compensation system, managerial systems should allow workers to use their knowledge to help improve the firm's performance. This requires that managers share some traditional prerogatives, permitting line workers to exercise some direct control over the design, organization, and assignment of work. Ways for accomplishing this might include quality-assessment circles or direct worker representation on corporate boards. However, neither innovation, by itself, may produce much change on factory assembly lines or the shop floor. For real change, workers or teams of workers must be permitted real decisionmaking authority in the workplace.[37]

A change in law or government regulation cannot reform management systems or the pay policies of private companies. These changes occur mainly as a result of economic pressure on individual companies and better information about the effects of alternative pay policies and management systems. If the nation's industrial relations system is to move toward greater worker-manager cooperation and greater worker participation in shop floor management, the change will have to occur one company at a time.

Six

Promoting Investment

ECONOMIC GROWTH requires investment—in plant and equipment, in people, and in the development of new ideas. Other things being equal, the more resources a society devotes to investment, the faster its economy can grow.

In this chapter we concentrate on methods for increasing investment in plant and equipment. As discussed in chapter 4, a strong relation may exist between such investment and success in innovation, which is also essential for promoting growth. In addition, we examine the claim that specific kinds of investment and investment in particular locations promise especially large gains to society as a whole. Because these returns are claimed to be much higher than the returns earned by private investors, investment in these areas may warrant special government incentives.

Encouraging Investment

Individuals must finance their investments either with their own savings or with money borrowed from others. So, too, nations must finance their capital investments either by using the savings of domestic residents or by borrowing from residents of foreign countries.

From just after World War II until 1980 the United States financed almost all its investment with its own savings. Net national investment and net saving ranged between 7 and 8 percent of annual U.S. output. Net investment is the nation's total or gross investment in a given year minus the depreciation on its capital stock that occurs during the year; net saving is similarly calculated by subtracting annual capital depreciation from the gross saving of individuals, companies, and

FIGURE 6-1. *Net Private Investment and Private and Public Saving as Percent of GDP, 1970–91*

Percent

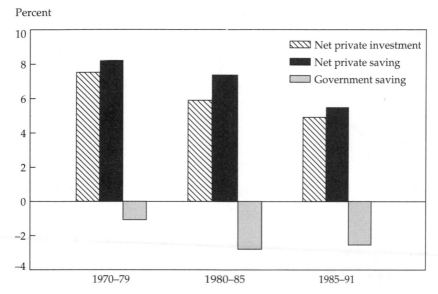

Source: Authors' calculations using data from *Economic Report of the President, February 1992.*

governments. As noted in chapter 2, the share of U.S. income devoted to investment was low compared with levels in other industrialized countries, but the United States consistently maintained the highest living standards because it was the world's technological leader. Though foreign residents and foreign firms invested their funds in the United States throughout the postwar period, their investments in this country were a little less each year than the investments made abroad by U.S. residents.

All this changed in the 1980s. Net national saving plummeted to about 2½ percent of GDP during the second half of the decade. Half the decline in the saving rate came from a drop in private saving, the other half from an increase in the total (federal, state, and local) government deficit (figure 6-1). With less money available to finance domestic investment, real interest rates rose sharply during the early part of the decade. Though falling somewhat by the end of the decade, they remained much higher than the levels of the 1970s (figure 6-2). Not surprisingly, the rise in interest rates discouraged net private

FIGURE 6-2. *Nominal and Real Interest Rates for Moody's AAA Corporate Bonds, 1971–91*

Percent

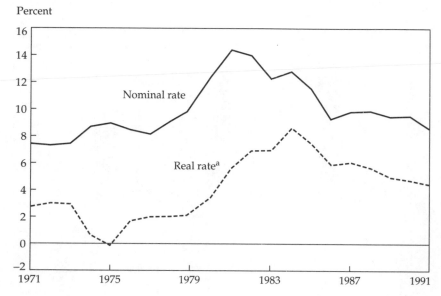

Source: Authors' calculations using data from *Economic Report of the President, February 1992,* pp. 378–79.

a. Real long-term rate calculated by subtracting from the nominal rate the two-year moving average GDP deflator for personal consumption expenditure.

investment, which fell as a share of national output to 4½ percent by the end of the 1980s.

The fall in investment could have been even worse; the investment share of output might have fallen as steeply as the saving share. That did not occur because of the willingness of foreigners to lend the United States funds to bridge the large gap between its saving and investment. Without those funds, U.S. interest rates would have risen even more sharply, and the investment share of output would have fallen even further.

A key economic challenge for the United States in the 1990s is to reverse the investment and saving patterns of the past decade and dramatically increase the share of output it devotes to investment. At a minimum, the nation should aim gradually to expand the investment share to its pre-1980 level—that is, to at least 7 to 8 percent of GDP. Ideally the share should be increased even further, perhaps to 10 percent of GDP, an investment share much closer to that of other industrialized nations. The United States is now so far from reaching even our minimum objective—in 1992 the net investment share was less than 3 percent—that to return to the investment rates attained in the 1960s and 1970s would be a considerable achievement.

Borrowing Our Way to Higher Investment?

Given the willingness of foreigners to finance so much of U.S. investment in the past decade, why not rely on foreign residents and companies to finance an increase in that investment? For example, the federal government might boost tax incentives for private investment or increase spending on infrastructure projects without paying for these policies with higher taxes. Following this strategy, the government could shift more national resources into investment, although it would do so by enlarging the federal deficit. It would not match the increase in domestic investment with a larger pool of national saving, leaving it to foreigners to finance the extra investment. So long as the return from the added investment exceeds the cost of the funds borrowed to finance it, expanded borrowing from foreigners seems to make sense.

The main flaw in this argument is that the nation can do better by financing added investment with its own added saving. Creditors get first call on the returns from any investment. If the creditors are domestic residents, the interest paid to them remains in the United States. If the creditors are foreign investors, the interest income flows abroad. A concrete example illustrates the difference. Suppose the extra investment the government might stimulate with tax incentives or with direct expenditures earns annual returns of 15 percent. If the investment is financed with foreign credit, foreign residents may receive annual interest or dividend payments amounting to perhaps 10 percent, leaving 5 percent annual returns for U.S. residents. If, however, the investment is entirely financed by U.S. residents, all 15 percent remains here.

The globalization of financial markets has increasingly divorced national saving levels from investment decisions. In the old world order, where capital was segmented by national boundaries, nations could invest only what they saved. When capital began to flow more freely between countries, countries could invest more than they saved, and vice versa. In an extreme case, moving capital across national boundaries would carry no more risk than moving capital within the same country. Real interest rates, adjusted for expected changes in exchange rates, would be the same in all countries; saving and investment levels within any country would be completely independent of each other.

International capital markets do not currently approach this extreme. Economists at the Organization for Economic Cooperation and Development have examined the relation between domestic saving and investment rates (as shares of national income) for the OECD countries since 1963.[1] These economists found almost a perfect one-to-one relationship between national saving and investment in the early and middle 1960s, which implies that capital markets were effectively segmented at that time. But the correlation between investment and saving has declined steadily since the late 1960s. By the mid-1980s only 58 percent of any increase (or reduction) in the saving rate within a country was associated with an equivalent increase (or reduction) in the investment rate. Extrapolating these estimates suggests that in the early 1990s only about half of any change in the saving rate will be translated into a change in the investment rate.

If the United States wishes to reverse the pattern of the 1980s—when the saving share of output fell by twice the amount of the decline in the investment share—the nation may have to increase the saving share of output by roughly twice any targeted increase in the investment share. Only about half of any added U.S. domestic savings may remain in this country; the rest may flow abroad. In 1991 net investment represented less than 2 percent of output, a share that was temporarily depressed by the very weak economy. Without any major changes in fiscal policy, this share will probably eventually increase to about 5 percent, where it was before the 1990–91 recession. Even at that level, the private investment share will remain 3 percentage points below its average between 1950 and 1980. To increase the investment share by 3 percentage points of output, the United States may have to increase its anemic national saving rate by a full 6 percentage points. And doing so would return the investment rate only to its level before 1980.[2]

Private Saving

The nation cannot count on a large and sustained increase in private saving to boost overall national saving. During the 1990s, aging baby boomers will reach a stage of their careers when they might be expected to save more in order to pay for the college educations of their children and to accumulate wealth for retirement. But it would be a mistake to rely too heavily on this trend to increase national saving. The large decrease in U.S. personal saving in the 1980s did not occur because of the change in the demographic composition of the population. Demographic changes in the 1980s should have increased private saving, since a shrinking proportion of the adult population was under age thirty, an age when Americans typically consume more than they earn. The private saving rate fell because saving rates of Americans in all age categories declined. The decline was particularly large among Americans older than forty-five, who would ordinarily be expected to have the highest saving rates.[3] We see little reason why demographic changes in the 1990s and afterward should significantly increase the overall saving rate.[4]

An important part of U.S. private saving consists of corporate contributions to pension funds. The private saving rate might increase somewhat in the 1990s if corporations increased their contributions to defined-benefit pension plans. During the 1980s corporations were able to greatly reduce their contributions to pension plans as prices of bonds and stocks in pension portfolios increased. The sharply increased valuation of pension portfolios meant that corporations did not have to contribute as much money to their funds to cover the cost of future pension liabilities. But because capital gains in the stock and bond markets may be much lower in the 1990s than they were in the 1980s, corporations may have to boost their annual contributions. Again, however, such an outcome cannot be counted on. Even if it materialized, it would be unlikely to increase the private saving rate by any more than a percentage point of GDP.

Many policymakers believe the private saving rate could be raised by restoring or improving several saving incentives in the tax code. Between 1981 and 1986, for example, the tax code permitted income deductions of up to $2,000 per wage earner for contributions to individual retirement accounts (IRAs). The tax code currently allows self-employed taxpayers to contribute before-tax income to Keogh plans. Other provisions permit some employed taxpayers to make tax-deductible contributions to 401(k) retirement plans. The effects of these saving incentives have been exhaustively studied.[5] On balance, the evidence is not encouraging. Several studies have shown that these incentives have no perceptible effect on increasing private saving.

Others have yielded more optimistic results. A few have shown that private saving is significantly increased by the tax incentives. But whether the incentives raise overall national saving is still not clear. Even if they did increase some people's saving, the effect would have to be large enough to offset the loss of government revenue before any increase in total saving would be achieved. The tax incentives undeniably reduce tax revenues, because they permit some earned income to escape taxation. And by reducing tax collections, they increase the federal deficit and reduce government saving. If the tax incentives are to raise national saving (that is, the sum of private and public saving), they must increase personal saving by more than the amount they add to the federal deficit. Even using optimistic estimates of their effects on private saving, one cannot be sure if the saving incentives produce a large enough effect to raise overall saving.

The Federal Budget Deficit

Because private saving is unlikely to increase much even with new tax incentives, it is natural to consider whether national saving can be raised through an increase in government saving. Saving by state and local governments is already positive. It is unrealistic to expect state and local authorities to run larger surpluses for the benefit of the nation as a whole. The only other way to boost government saving is to eliminate the federal budget deficit, which in the 1980s drained almost half of annual private saving. The federal deficit reached 6 percent of GDP in 1992, almost exactly the amount needed to expand the investment share of output by 3 percent.

Part of the 1992 federal deficit, however, reflects one-time expenditures on savings and loan deposit insurance. The need for this spending should disappear within the next few years. Another part of the deficit, equal to 2.5 percent of GDP, reflects the poor state of the economy. The rest of the deficit, equal to 3 percent of GDP, is the full-employment budget deficit, the portion of the deficit that will remain even after the effects of the recession and the savings and loan bailout are eliminated. In early 1992 the full-employment deficit was projected to remain at 3 percent of GDP through 1997 (figure 6-3).

There are no mysteries about how the federal deficit can be reduced. Expenditures must be cut, or taxes raised. Almost certainly both steps will be needed. As this book went to press, the nation had been offered several far-reaching plans for deficit reduction. The one proposed by

FIGURE 6-3. *Government and Full-Employment Deficits, Actual and Projected, as Percent of GDP, 1970–97*

Percent

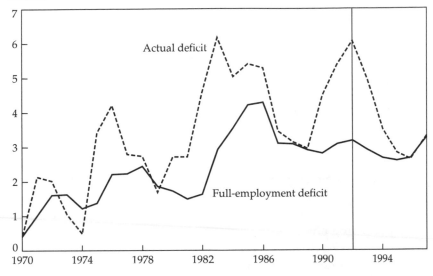

Source: Authors' calculations using data from Congressional Budget Office, *The Economic and Budget Outlook, Fiscal Years 1993–1997* (January 1992), p. 29.

independent presidential candidate H. Ross Perot is perhaps the best known. On the expenditure side his plan would cut agricultural price supports, medicare, and medicaid. To raise revenues, he proposed a 50-cents-a-gallon increase in the gasoline tax and additional taxes on social security recipients with annual incomes higher than $32,000.[6] A similar plan was advanced by a commission headed by Senators Sam Nunn (Democrat of Georgia) and Pete Domenici (Republican of New Mexico), which relied on a new value-added tax for additional revenues.[7] Our colleague Charles Schultze has also proposed a VAT to finance a national health insurance program that, combined with other tax increases and expenditure cuts, would eventually produce a balanced budget.[8] The "Concord Coalition," a bipartisan effort headed by former Senators Paul Tsongas and Warren Rudman, has urged adoption of a far-reaching deficit reduction plan.

We do not consider the details of these proposals here, largely because the details of any successful plan will be determined more by political than economic criteria. But we do believe that equity considerations should be important in determining the final plan. Most of the burden of deficit reduction should fall on those Americans who can bear it most easily; namely, those with higher incomes (including the authors and many of the readers of this book). In the final analysis, however, the economic effects of any of the deficit reduction plans would be roughly the same. Each would raise national saving and investment in the long run.

Admittedly, there are crucial issues of timing in implementing any deficit reduction plan. Because the recovery from the 1990–91 recession has been unusually slow, there may be a case for providing some temporary fiscal stimulus, which would enlarge the deficit in the short run. However, any short-term stimulus should be combined with long-term deficit reduction measures, scheduled by law to become effective eighteen months to two years after the adoption of the stimulus package. If the deficit elimination steps are phased in, perhaps over five to seven years, the Federal Reserve should try to offset their output-reducing effects with easier monetary policy.

What could the nation expect to gain in the long run from an aggressive program to eliminate the deficit? Using standard economic theory, Schultze has suggested that each additional percentage point share of national output devoted to domestic investment would increase output growth by 0.1 percent a year by the end of a decade. Put another way, the higher investment rate would raise the level of national output after ten years by about 1 full percentage point.[9] A deficit reduction plan that would increase the national saving rate by 3 full percentage points, combined with a modest increase in private saving equivalent to another 1 percentage point of output, could produce a total increase in the saving rate of 4 percentage points. Given the estimated relation between domestic investment and domestic saving, such a plan should allow an increase in the investment share of output of 2 percent. Schultze's estimates suggest that added investment of this amount could by the end of a decade increase the growth rate of potential output by 0.2 percentage points a year and the level of total output by 2 percent.[10]

Because of the intense political pain that would accompany any deficit elimination program, such a gain, at first glance, seems slight. But when accumulated over a generation (thirty years), this increase in the growth rate would yield a 7 percent increase in average incomes, not just in a single year but for every year thereafter. Indeed, the output gain could be even larger if some of the additional investment is channeled toward activities and regions where it could provide spillover benefits to other firms, as we discuss later.

Moreover, U.S. residents benefit from additions to national saving that are not invested in the United States. Recall that if national saving is increased by 4 percent of GDP in every year, domestic investment is likely to rise by only 2 percent of GDP. The remaining 2 percent of GDP will be invested abroad, where it will earn the rate of return available from foreign investment. Or it will replace capital imports into the United States equal to 2 percent of U.S. GDP, so that the nation will pay less interest and dividend income to foreign investors. In either case, U.S. residents will be left with more future income.

The political problem, of course, is that presidents and most members of Congress do not hold office for a full generation. They are not in a position to reap the full political rewards for the benefits their programs may provide in the future. Also, as bad the deficit problem is, it does not pose the kind of immediate risks to the United States—a flight from the dollar, a sudden jump in interest rates, or a severe recession—that might force political leaders to take immediate corrective action. Instead, the real danger of continued large deficits is long term. In the words of Charles Schultze, the danger is akin to termites in the woodwork. Because the nation faces no imminent crisis, the president and congress would have to exert extraordinary political leadership to implement an orderly deficit-elimination program.

Advocates of deficit elimination have so far rested their case primarily on how it will help future generations. The effort might enlist broader support if political leaders pointed out that, despite the sacrifice deficit elimination obviously entails, many businesses and workers can benefit immediately.

One immediate effect of reducing the deficit would be to lower real interest rates. According to estimates made by Data Resources Incorporated, the implementation of a five-year deficit-elimination program, if coupled with offsetting monetary stimulus, would decrease the ten-year government bond rate by almost 2 full percentage points in four years and by almost 3 points in ten years. Lower interest rates, in turn, would help stimulate purchases of such consumer durables as cars and houses. Lower rates would also lead to a decline in the exchange value of the dollar and thereby stimulate exports. By encouraging private investment, a deficit-elimination plan would be good for manufacturers of producers' equipment. In sum, though deficit elimination entails immediate pain, it also promises immediate gain for many sectors of the economy. In the intermediate and long run, it is probably the most certain way to increase the growth rate of the economy.

Critics of Deficit Reduction

We have offered a conventional account of the benefits of reducing the federal budget deficit. Critics of deficit reduction question the dangers posed by the deficit and, by implication, the merits of doing something to eliminate it. Robert Eisner, among others, believes the harmful consequences of recent deficits have been overstated, because the deficits themselves are exaggerated as a result of measurement error.[11] That is, official budget figures fail to adjust for inflation, which, Eisner argues, steadily erodes the real value of the national debt. Once this effect of inflation is taken into account, the deficit is smaller than it appears in official figures. The deficit is thus a much smaller drag on economic growth than conventional analysis suggests.

Though technically correct, Eisner's critique is irrelevant to the implications of deficit financing for long-run growth. While government dissaving is indeed lower when the market value of federal debt is eroded by inflation, the saving of the private sector, which owns the federal debt, is also decreased by inflation. Eisner is correct that government dissaving is overstated, but because private saving is overstated too, the effects of inflation on overall saving—private saving plus public saving—are nil. The relative size of the two components of overall saving matters little. Eisner's analysis does not undermine the clear message of figure 6-1: total saving in the United States, as a share of total output, fell sharply after 1980.

Another critic, Allan Meltzer, has suggested that the effects of deficits are more benign than popularly supposed.[12] He observes that virtually all the deficit consists of interest paid on the federal debt (figure 6-4).[13] Interest payments merely represent a transfer payment from taxpayers to purchasers of government bonds and, according to Meltzer, have no significant economic effects. This argument, too, seems incomplete. Because aside from interest, the rest of the government's budget is essentially balanced, annual payments of interest must be financed by additional yearly borrowing. When the government issues bonds to finance interest payments, it must borrow do-

FIGURE 6-4. *Federal Interest Payments and Budget Deficits as Percent of GDP, 1962–91*

Percent

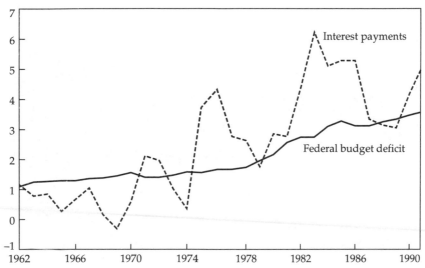

Source: Congressional Budget Office, *Economic and Budget Outlook, Fiscal Years 1993–1997*, pp. 29, 48.

mestic saving that would otherwise be available to finance domestic investment. Government interest payments support the current consumption of bondholders to the extent bondholders consume their interest proceeds rather than save them. National saving is thus decreased because of the government's deficit. Like Eisner's argument, Meltzer's criticism ignores the decrease in national saving caused by federal deficits.

The rising share of interest payments, both in total output and total federal expenditures (figure 6-5), not only helps crowd out private investment but may also crowd out desirable *public* investment. Some conservatives who are hostile to public spending view the persistent federal deficits with equanimity. The deficits serve as a useful deterrent to additional, potentially wasteful government spending. We hold a different view. Given the public's strong aversion to tax increases, the large deficits inhibit the federal government from increasing support for research and development, education, training, and public investments that would expand long-term economic growth.

FIGURE 6-5. *Main Components of Federal Expenditures as Percent of GDP, 1962–91*

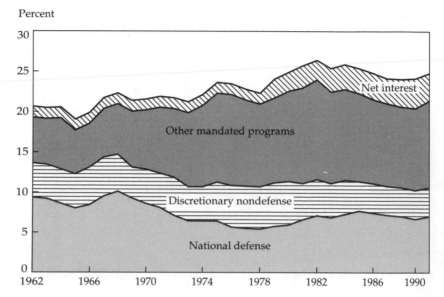

Percent

Source: Congressional Budget Office, *Economic and Budget Outlook, Fiscal Years 1993–1997,* p. 48.

The rising interest payments on the federal debt absorb government resources that could be used more constructively, and they act as a powerful deterrent to growth.

In thinking about the large federal deficits, some economists draw comfort from the view that the deficits, because they are offset by additional saving in the private sector, do not affect total national saving. This argument has its origins in the nineteenth century writings of David Ricardo, but it has been resurrected and popularized by Harvard economist Robert Barro.[14] Barro's reasoning is straightforward. He believes citizens take a very far-sighted view of government borrowing. When the government increases its deficit, it must ultimately pay interest on the added borrowing. This must eventually either increase future tax burdens or reduce future government services. Current citizens or their heirs will have to pay for the additional current spending one way or the other. Recognizing this fact, citizens will reduce their current consumption (that is, increase their current saving) so as to make the resources available to pay for the inevitable tax increase or future reduction in public services.

Like many other economists, we find this reasoning implausible. Few people are likely to be as rational, well-informed, and far-sighted as Barro's theory assumes. In fact, even well-informed citizens might disagree with Barro's prognosis. Older people might reasonably believe that the "inevitable" tax increase will not occur in their lifetimes. Why should they set aside additional saving today for a tax increase that will occur after they have died? Perhaps more important, trends in public and private saving during the 1980s flatly contradict Barro's hypothesis. After government deficits mushroomed in the 1980s, the private saving rate fell rather than rose—the first significant and sustained decline in saving in the postwar era.

Like some conservatives, some liberals believe the popular concern about federal deficits is overblown. They reason that a high proportion of federal spending consists of investment rather than consumption and thus adds to the nation's stock of physical, human, and intellectual capital. Just as private corporations finance much of their investment by borrowing, so too should the government. By this reasoning, the nation can afford to live with the current deficit. Of the roughly $200 billion in the 1993 full-employment deficit, approximately $130 billion represents borrowing for federal spending on physical capital. If spending on worker training and R&D were added, the "investment" total might well exceed the structural deficit.

Advocates of this "capital budgeting" approach to the deficit overlook one critical fact, however. The *depreciation* of the existing stock of federally financed infrastructure is a *current* expense and should not be financed by additional borrowing. This depreciation averages more than $100 billion a year. Whereas gross federal spending on nondefense capital equipment and structures totals roughly $130 billion, federal investment net of depreciation amounts to only $10 billion.[15] If the financial behavior of private companies is the proper benchmark for the federal government, as advocates of capital budgeting claim, the government, like the private sector, would need to finance depreciation out of current revenues. And because very little of the current budget deficit finances a net addition to the public capital stock, very little of it can be excused.

Occasionally economists argue that, contrary to popular belief, the national saving rate did not decrease during the 1980s if saving is defined to include realized capital gains and the equity buildup in owner-occupied homes.[16] The supposed implication is that policymakers need not concern themselves with reducing the government deficit.

The premise of this argument is true. The saving rate did not decline as much in the 1980s as generally assumed so long as one defines national saving to include increases in the market values of real assets. But the supposed implication is incorrect. Higher market values of existing assets do not create resources for additional investment in new physical plant and equipment. Investment occurs only when part of the flow of current real output is set aside from current consumption and used to purchase new machines, buildings, and other capital goods. These investment goods, in turn, can be used to raise the future productive capacity of the economy.[17]

In sum, there is compelling evidence that large structural government deficits reduce growth over the long run by raising real interest rates and discouraging investment. A program to eliminate the federal budget deficit, combined with measures to modestly raise private saving, can reduce long-term interest rates and boost economic growth over the next few decades.

Encouraging Investment with High Social Returns

Investment projects are not all of equal value. Some promise especially large gains for the wider economy. Several types yield social returns that are much higher than the returns earned by the private firms that make the investments. It makes sense to subsidize such activities. If there are positive spillovers from investment, so that investment in one company or industry yields benefits for others, the growth benefits may be greater than those estimated by Schultze and others who have used conventional techniques to measure the long-run effects of additional investment. In chapter 4 we discussed how the social returns on research and development are likely to exceed the private returns; here we consider four other types of investment for which similar claims have been made.

Investment in Equipment

A new theory of economic growth has recently become popular among some economists. In the old growth theory, capital combined with labor and technology to produce output. The contribution of capital to growth was assumed to be independent of the separate contributions of labor and the production technology. The new growth theory rests on a different assumption—that capital and technology closely interact, so that the gain to society from new investment exceeds the private benefits precisely because investment activities themselves stimulate the development of new technology.

Recent empirical work by Bradford DeLong and Lawrence Summers suggests that investment in producer equipment yields especially large spillover benefits that can lead to substantial increases in productivity, much larger gains than those previously estimated.[18] The gains in growth from investment in equipment far exceed the gains from other kinds of investment, including investment in housing or business structures. DeLong and Summers base this conclusion on a large multicountry analysis that attempted to determine what factors accounted for differences in growth among the countries between 1960 and 1985. They found that countries investing more heavily in equipment were able to achieve more rapid growth. The analysis has been criticized, principally on the ground that high overall growth rates may have caused the high rates of investment in equipment rather than the other way around. But the authors provide reasonably convincing evidence that the causation runs from equipment investment to growth. Their results are plausible, since it is well known that new equipment usually embodies the latest technology and thus serves as a vehicle for the introduction of new technology. When new equipment is introduced, firms must often retrain their workers, so that human capital accumulation accompanies the physical investment.

We see a reasonably compelling case for government provision of special incentives for investment in equipment. Conversely, we see no special merit in providing additional incentives for investment in commercial structures.[19] The most effective way to encourage equipment investment is to allow firms to deduct a part of such investment directly from their federal income tax liability. In fact, this type of investment tax credit was available over much of the period from 1962 through 1986. The tax subsidy rate gradually rose from 7 to 10 percent during these years.

Economic research provides clear evidence that the investment tax credit was successful in stimulating equipment investment. The authors of the classic studies of the subject, Robert E. Hall and Dale Jorgenson, concluded that "the investment tax credit, essentially a subsidy to the purchase of equipment, has had a greater impact than any of the other changes in tax policy during the postwar period."[20] Joseph Pechman, a well-known opponent to most tax preferences, argued that the credit provided a "sizable incentive for investment" by reducing the cost of a capital investment and hence increasing its rate of return.[21]

The investment tax credit was criticized not because it was ineffective but because it allegedly distorted investment decisions by favoring equipment over other forms of investment. If indeed equipment investment has larger social payoffs than, say, investment in structures, this objection actually represents an argument in favor of the credit.

With this evidence in mind, we recommend the implementation of a permanent 5 percent credit for new equipment investment. At recent levels of investment in producer equipment, the annual cost would be approximately $15 billion. We propose to pay for the credit by raising corporate income tax rates by approximately 5 percentage points (from the current 34 percent to 39 percent).[22] Given the need to raise overall national saving by reducing the federal budget deficit, it would be a mistake to introduce a credit without finding a way to pay for it. To keep personal income tax rates approximately equal to the corporate rate, we would also favor an increase in the top marginal rate from its current 31 percent. Additional revenues from the personal income tax should be devoted to overall deficit reduction.

Some have suggested that if an investment tax credit is introduced, it should be applicable only to *incremental* investment, that is, investment above a certain base amount, such as a company's investment in the previous year. This provision would significantly reduce the revenue loss and thus the need to have an offsetting increase in the corporate income tax rate. But an incremental tax credit would provide far less incentive for businesses to invest in equipment, especially in recession years when investment can fall well below the threshold amount that determines eligibility for the credit. It is precisely when economic conditions are weak that the government should offer clear incentives for businesses to make investments. Even though an incremental credit would be less costly, the standard tax credit makes more sense as a permanent feature of the tax code.

Capital Gains

Of all potential investment incentives, preferential income tax treatment of capital gains is probably the most controversial. Although such a preference was part of the tax code before 1987, it was eliminated by the 1986 Tax Reform Act. The ink was barely dry on the legislation, however, before Congress was urged to bring back the capital gains tax preference. President Bush proposed reducing the tax rate on capital gains at least twice, but Congress failed to enact the proposals.

The arguments on this issue have become familiar. Proponents of the tax preference typically claim that restoring capital gains incentives would promote long-run growth by encouraging innovation and the formation of new businesses. Opponents question whether these benefits will occur. They also point out that most of the tax benefits will flow to a few very wealthy taxpayers. Such incentives are therefore inequitable.

Before turning to these issues, we need to clarify one thing. Under current tax law, gains on the holdings of assets are treated no differently from other kinds of income. But because taxes are not assessed on capital gains until gains are *realized*—that is, until the assets themselves are sold—the current tax code is already modestly favorable toward capital gains. The reason lies in the time value of money. At any positive rate of interest, other things being equal, it is always better to pay taxes later than to pay them now. Moreover, investors are permitted to time their realizations of capital gains so as to minimize tax liabilities, and they are permitted to postpone realization until death, when many capital gains will escape taxation altogether.

The principal question is whether, in addition to the benefits of deferral, the tax rate on capital gains should be lowered to some level below the rate applicable to other income. In our view, equity considerations should count in answering this question but should not be decisive. Instead, attention should be focused on whether reducing the tax rate on capital gains is the most effective way to encourage the activity that supporters claim they wish to encourage—namely, investment in long-term projects, such as innovation, that are likely to generate spillover benefits for the economy as a whole.

We believe the answer is no, for several reasons. First, if encouraging innovation is the main objective, a tax credit like the one we have supported for research and development will be far more effective. It is aimed specifically at increasing investment in R&D. In contrast, cutting the capital gains tax helps a broad class of investors, whether or not substantial spillover benefits result from their investment. Indeed, one of the central goals of eliminating the capital gains tax preference in the 1986 Tax Reform Act was to sharply reduce incentives for speculation in real estate and for the creation of wasteful tax shelters.

Second, reducing capital gains taxes to stimulate entrepreneurship would not be cost-effective. Studies have shown that three-quarters of the funds available for new firms are provided out of sources not subject to capital gains taxation, largely pension funds.[23] Even for those investors who would be subject to taxes on their capital gains, any preference is likely to have very small effects. As Charles Schultze has shown, a 30 percent capital gains exclusion would increase the after-tax proceeds on a high-risk venture by only a small amount, about 10 percent. Few entrepreneurs, who are risk-takers to begin with, are likely to be discouraged from investing by such small changes in the net return of an investment project.[24] It is questionable whether the small gains would be worth the windfalls that a capital gains preference would generate for all other classes of investors.

Supporters of a capital gains tax preference are correct in pointing out the unfairness of taxing asset holders on gains that are due to inflation and not to real appreciation in prices. At the same time, however, the inflation problem afflicts many parts of the tax code. If only capital gains were adjusted for inflation and the cost of borrowing was not similarly treated, taxpayers would be given powerful incentives to take on even more debt to purchase assets whose gains would be given preferential income tax treatment.

Public Infrastructure

Political support has grown in recent years for increased investment in public infrastructure, including such traditional items as roads, sewers, and airports as well as newer projects such as fiber optic networks and new transportation technologies. During his election campaign President Clinton promised to increase federal spending in both those areas by $80 billion over four years.

Infrastructure spending is often justified on short-run grounds as

FIGURE 6-6. *Net Public Capital Stock and Gross Investment as Percent of GNP, 1950–91*

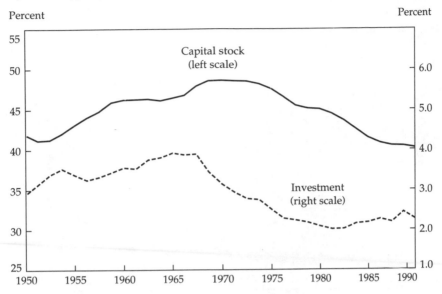

Source: Clifford Winston and Barry Bosworth, "Public Infrastructure," in Henry J. Aaron and Charles L. Schultze, eds., *Setting Domestic Priorities: What Can Government Do?* (Brookings, 1992), p. 268.

useful for generating employment. But virtually any spending program for goods and services will create jobs. The recent popularity of public infrastructure investment arises from new studies purporting to show that such spending has strong spillover benefits for the rest of the economy. In fact, the claimed payoffs to society are larger than those from most private investment. Some of these studies attribute most of the slowdown in productivity growth in the United States to the decades-long slowdown in the rate of public capital spending.[25]

We do not dispute the fact that the United States has for the past two decades devoted a steadily shrinking share of its output to infrastructure investment. Figure 6-6, taken from a study by Brookings economists Clifford Winston and Barry Bosworth, shows that gross public investment fell from a high of close to 4 percent of GNP in the mid-1960s to about 2 percent of GNP in the 1980s. The stock of public capital as a percent of GNP also fell after 1970. A large part of the decline in infrastructure investment after 1970 was concentrated in

FIGURE 6-7. *State and Local Government Investment in Core Infrastructure Projects, by Type, 1950–91*

Billions of 1990 dollars

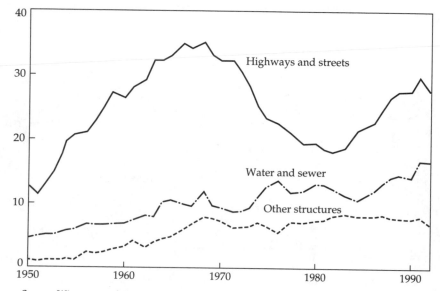

Source: Winston and Bosworth, "Public Infrastructure," p. 271.

highway construction (figure 6-7). State and local infrastructure investment stagnated beginning in the late 1960s; federal spending fell after 1980 (figure 6-8).[26]

Several factors explain why public investment in highways and buildings has stagnated or decreased. The interstate highway system has been completed, so spending has shifted from construction to maintenance. Rural residents have stopped moving to urban areas, so fewer new roads in the cities are needed. The baby boom generation has graduated from school, so local school boards have closed old schools and stopped building new ones. Because of developments in medical treatment, hospital stays have become much shorter, so that an excess of hospital beds has emerged. All levels of government have been pressed by the rising cost of income support and health programs, on the one hand, and by the demands by taxpayers for lower taxes, on the other. As a result, less money has been available to fund government investment, particularly at the state and local levels, where balanced budgets are often required by law.

FIGURE 6-8. *Federal and State and Local Government Expenditures for Core Infrastructure, 1960–90*

Billions of 1990 dollars

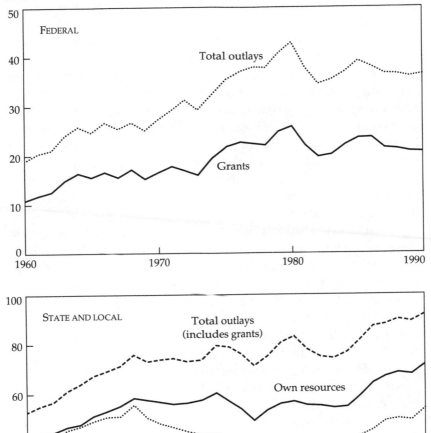

Source: Winston and Bosworth, "Public Infrastructure," p. 272.

All these factors are important. But in setting public policy toward future spending on public infrastructure, it is critical to know to what extent the reduction in public investment has been responsible for the productivity slowdown. If the adverse effects have been significant, we could infer that infrastructure spending has substantial spillovers. A major expansion of infrastructure spending would be warranted. We are skeptical, however, that the spillovers are large.

We focus on the studies by David Aschauer, since they have provided the foundation for most of the claims by enthusiasts for infrastructure spending. Aschauer's conclusions are based on a historical analysis of U.S. economic data. He finds a strong statistical relation between the level of productivity and the size of the public capital stock. He also finds a correlation between productivity growth and additions to the public capital stock. In a separate cross-country analysis, he finds that public capital spending is positively correlated with productivity growth.[27]

Aschauer's conclusions seem doubtful. For one thing, the correlation between infrastructure spending and growth in the United States is not strong. As noted in chapter 2, productivity growth slowed in the U.S. economy in the late 1960s, whereas the public capital stock as a share of GNP did not begin to decline until the early or middle 1970s. This pattern suggests that slow economic growth may have caused the decline in public spending, rather than vice versa, as federal and state and local budgets were squeezed.[28]

Second, Aschauer's hypothesis that public capital caused the slowdown in productivity growth has not been tested systematically against other reasonable hypotheses. Statistical techniques "explaining" productivity always seek out a variable that changes about the time of the break in the productivity trend. If public capital is the only candidate, it will get the prize and "explain" slow growth. When other variables are considered, such as the rise in oil prices, they reduce or eliminate the apparent causal effect of public capital.[29]

Third, the impact of public capital that Aschauer finds is implausibly large. Much public investment has only a weak relation to productivity, particularly in the short run. It seems unlikely, for example, that investments in new government office buildings have much effect on productivity. Investments in transportation infrastructure and water and sewage facilities are the main components of expenditure that are plausible sources of improved private sector productivity. To justify

Aschauer's finding, one would have to believe those investments have astronomical rates of return.[30] In any event, a study by the Congressional Budget Office reports that the correlation between productivity and investment in transportation infrastructure and water and sewage facilities weakens over time.[31]

Given these objections, we believe it is farfetched to suggest that a program of public investment will have a very large effect on productivity. The nation does not need a lot of new schools or hospitals; the education and medical care industries suffer from serious problems, but they are unlikely to be remedied by new capital construction. Even in transportation, much of the gain from any increase in investment will show up as reduced commuting time—a benefit, certainly, but not one that is counted in GNP.

One need not believe the absurd estimates of the benefits from added public investment to accept the view that there are good returns to investment in new roads, bridges, urban transit projects, and airports. It is plausible to argue that *some* public capital contributes to private sector productivity. In particular, is there a high social return to public investment in selected transportation projects?

Both the prevailing evidence and economic logic suggest caution. Studies of infrastructure projects often find fairly high rates of return—30 to 40 percent—on investments to sustain the quality of the existing infrastructure, but returns of only 10 to 20 percent for selected new projects.[32] These calculations, however, typically ignore interactions between the effects of investment in one sector on returns from investments in others. Improvements in the interstate highway system, for example, would probably make trucking more efficient and less expensive. But this improvement could cut rail traffic and reduce the productivity of the nation's railroads. Many states and localities use infrastructure projects to lure businesses to their communities. But the gain in efficiency in one community may be offset by the loss of efficiency in others that lose businesses to the expanding community. Transportation investments might nonetheless have some positive effects because companies in the same or similar industries often cluster together in the same geographic area, which implies that synergies among people and companies are important. We discuss this phenomenon in greater detail below. To the extent it exists, transportation-related infrastructure investments would presumably increase the potential for positive synergies.[33] Taken together, however, these interactions are not likely to change the overall verdict on transportation investments.

In short, the weight of the evidence suggests that additional spending to *upgrade* the existing transportation infrastructure is likely to generate larger social benefits than those generated by private sector investments. Higher investment in transportation projects therefore seems warranted. In fact, a federal program is already under way to boost transportation spending. Given the poor condition of some of the nation's infrastructure, there is a case for increasing total expenditures even for upgrading. Winston and Bosworth estimate that an additional $11 billion in annual spending would maintain the current ratio of public infrastructure capital to output.[34]

The case for going well beyond simple upgrading efforts is much weaker,[35] especially because there are often cheaper solutions for relieving congestion than building wider roads or bigger airports. Rather than construct larger facilities simply to accommodate traffic or airport landings at peak hours, it would be far more cost-effective to encourage users of roads and airports to spread use of the facilities more evenly throughout the day. That can be accomplished by charging higher prices to travelers who use highways and airports at times of peak congestion.

The principle is easiest to illustrate for airports. Because small planes now pay a much smaller fee than larger planes to take off and land at large airports, owners of private aircraft have little incentive to land at small airports. Scheduled airlines usually do not pay substantially higher landing fees during the morning and afternoon rush hours than at other times of the day. Relating landing and takeoff fees to the amount of congestion at an airfield would address these problems. If pilots of small airplanes faced steeply higher fees to land at congested airports, they would use less congested airports. If commercial airliners were compelled to pay sharply higher fees for rush-hour take-offs and landings, they would pass the additional costs along to their passengers, who would then have greater incentives to avoid flying at times of peak congestion. That would lessen the need to build new airports or expand old ones.

We recognize, of course, the significant political obstacles to introducing congestion pricing at airports. The general aviation industry would lobby strongly against a system of pricing that discourages its members from using the most convenient airports. The commercial airlines and many of their customers would be unhappy about paying higher peak-time landing fees. But raising taxes or cutting expenditure programs to finance infrastructure spending also has its political costs, especially when it can be demonstrated that some of this spending can be avoided. Efficient pricing of transportation facilities is a cheaper alternative than building new or larger facilities.

The objections to congestion pricing for road use are more than political. Timothy Hau points out several technical problems in charging directly for road use.[36] Toll plazas are expensive to operate, both in their direct costs and in the delays and congestion they impose on motorists. In the past, electronic devices that identify vehicles by remote sensor have been tried, but these technologies often turned out to be expensive or unreliable. New technologies have been developed, however, that can inexpensively identify and charge vehicles that travel on specific roads. In fact, such technology is already used in some American cities and in other countries. A simple automatic vehicle identification (AVI) system was introduced at the Crescent City Bridge in New Orleans in 1989 at a cost per transaction of about 4 cents, roughly 1 percent of the toll revenue. Similar systems are used for the Dallas North Tollway (where users pay $2 a month for the rental of a transponder) in Oklahoma, in New York City, and in several locations overseas.[37]

Also under development are more complicated systems that allow authorities to charge motorists for the use of downtown city streets. The Dutch government hopes to introduce a comprehensive road pricing system, using the so-called smart card technology, where each car is fitted with a meter. Whenever a vehicle passes a charging point along a highway, a fee will be deducted from its meter. But though the Dutch government has earmarked the proceeds of the tolls for road and tunnel construction, political opposition to the scheme continues. Another approach to the political problem is being tested in Cambridge, England, a congested town with many tourists. Residents of Cambridge are given free smart cards, but visitors are required to purchase the cards before entering the city in their cars.

Technological barriers to more rational pricing of congested urban roads will soon disappear. The principal obstacle to rational pricing schemes will be political, for it is difficult to make people pay for using roads that once were free. Yet the scheme has some clear advantages besides its likely effects on congestion. Congestion pricing is a way to raise revenue. More important, it may reduce the pressure on politicians to invest in new roads or costly improvements in existing roads.[38]

Some additional infrastructure investment may be needed, perhaps $10 billion a year, to avoid the erosion of the transportation system and to upgrade the system in areas where there is particular need—for example, the air traffic control system. Added public spending on infrastructure beyond that level would not yield exceptional returns. Nor would it greatly improve overall productivity performance. And the need for additional spending can be reduced by rational pricing of roads, airport landing rights, and other public facilities.

Targeted Investment in Designated Communities

We believe investment in particular regions of the country can also produce social benefits in excess of private returns. These kinds of regional investments should therefore be candidates for special incentives.

Michael Porter of the Harvard Business School suggests one reason to favor certain kinds of regional investment. He points out the tendency of firms in particular industries to cluster in certain countries and, more specifically, within certain regions of those countries. Why, he asks, have two world-class truck manufacturers located in Sweden? Why are American high-technology companies clustered in Silicon Valley, in Texas, and along Route 128 in Massachusetts? The answer, Porter suggests, is that these firms benefit from close proximity to other producers in the same industry, attracting infrastructure, specialized suppliers, and skilled workers.[39]

If the proposed initiatives in technology development described in chapter 4 are successful, they will create new options for industrial development. But it is not clear whether American industry will be able to take advantage of the opportunities. Technologies developed with the support of U.S. taxpayers may lead to new clusters of production overseas rather than in the United States.

The challenge is to devise and implement policies that encourage the expansion of existing production clusters or the formation of new clusters in the United States. The federal government can play a small part by providing additional incentives for investment in R&D and new equipment. Federal policy probably cannot do much more. If anything has been learned from past federal policy, it is the difficulty of targeting federal aid to specific regions of the country. Legislators and lobbyists from other regions eventually request similar assistance, whether needed or not, for their own areas. This was the experience with the Model Cities program launched by the Johnson administration. We see no reason why it would not repeated if the federal government tried to create new Silicon Valleys or to revive old ones.[40]

A far better approach is for state and local governments to create or preserve industrial clusters themselves. Typically they can do so by funding local university research and outreach programs, as well as by providing suitable infrastructure and job training. Such regional efforts do not need to be a zero-sum game. That is, the gains of one region will not necessarily be offset by losses in other regions if the regional efforts actually lead to the creation of new clusters of innovative activity.[41]

A second way in which investment might be usefully targeted is to promote new investment in low-income regions of the country, especially in low-income urban areas. There is a clear case on equity grounds for doing so.

The Los Angeles riots of 1992 reminded Americans of the practical reasons to favor investment in low-income urban areas. Urban areas that cannot offer job opportunities to local residents tend to be plagued with many other social problems, including crime, poor educational opportunities, and weak families. We do not pretend to have solutions to these social problems. But all of them will be much more difficult to resolve if communities cannot offer well-paying jobs for their residents. If investment in new businesses, in structures and equipment, can be attracted to low-income areas, the social payoff could be substantial.

In 1992, in response to the Los Angeles riots, Congress passed, but President Bush later vetoed, legislation that would have created enterprise zones in fifty U.S. cities. In return for making investments in these zones, individuals and firms would have received various tax incentives.[42] Enterprise zones might help revitalize the inner cities if they were included in a comprehensive package that provided additional resources and new approaches for addressing the problems of poor education and crime. We claim no special expertise on these subjects and thus will not expand on them here. But we suspect that even the best designed programs will not work unless they succeed in channeling more funds into private sector investment in the inner cities.

A key question is how best to increase financing for businesses that locate in inner cities. We favor two approaches. The fastest and most direct way is to directly subsidize the borrowers who will make the investments. The best way to accomplish that is for the government to support the creation of a secondary market in loans to such borrowers. The government created the secondary market in home loans when it established the federal housing finance agencies. The main problem in developing a secondary market for inner city loans is to establish underwriting standards to determine which loans might qualify for a government guarantee. Government officials must strike the right balance between strict lending criteria, which would minimize taxpayer losses, and standards liberal enough to provide meaningful access to credit by borrowers, many of whom would otherwise find it difficult to obtain a loan.

We of course recognize the danger in any program aimed at assisting only those borrowers who invest in inner-city areas. The programs can easily be expanded to include loans to other borrowers, precisely the kind of problem that undermined the Model Cities program. The risk can be minimized by limiting eligibility for financing only to establishments physically located in designated census tracts where average personal incomes are well below the statewide or national average.

It would also be desirable to create institutions that lend in low-income areas. As a candidate, President Clinton proposed federal sponsorship for creating community development banks (CDBs) around the country. These banks would both take deposits from and lend in underdeveloped areas. Clinton's proposal is modeled on the South Shore Bank of Chicago, which was capitalized by a foundation grant. The bank is run by people who have invested the time and effort to train inner-city borrowers in how to use bank loans to reap commercial success. Clinton essentially proposes to clone the South Shore Bank and establish similar institutions in hundreds of other communities. He did not suggest the direct use of federal funds. Instead, commercial banks would be required to help capitalize these specialized financial institutions. Clinton also proposed strengthening the Community Reinvestment Act, which now requires all commercial banks to make efforts to lend to local residents and businesses.

Clinton's CDB proposal has promise. The lack of financing for investment in inner cities makes it essential to create specialized lend-

ing institutions. At the same time, the community reinvestment requirements have proved to be costly and controversial. Banks criticize
the regulatory compliance costs of the reinvestment act. Local and
consumer organizations, on the other hand, criticize bank regulators
for giving almost all banks a high community reinvestment rating,
even though many have not actually made loans to local residents.
(Instead, many have compiled excellent documentation proving they
have made reasonable efforts to offer such loans.)

We question whether further strengthening the community reinvestment requirements offers much promise of improving financing
for inner-city projects. Moreover, by compelling all banks to make
efforts to lend to borrowers in areas where the banks may not have
special expertise, the community reinvestment approach discourages
the development of specialized institutions that can reap economies
by focusing specifically on those areas.

A more constructive approach, in our view, is to combine Clinton's
CDB proposal with the community reinvestment requirement. If
banks can demonstrate they have invested a certain minimum portion
of their capital, say 1 percent, in a qualified CDB, that could be deemed
to satisfy the bank's community reinvestment requirement.

We suspect that a large proportion of the nation's 12,000 banks
would leap at this opportunity because investing in CDBs would
allow them to be more certain that they were in compliance with the
requirement. More lending would be channeled to inner cities by
institutions whose sole mission is to support such investment. A
simple calculation illustrates the possibilities. At the present time the
U.S. banking system has about $250 billion in equity capital. If banks
holding half this capital took advantage of our proposal and invested
1 percent of their capital in CDBs, $1.25 billion in capital would be
provided to CDBs around the nation. Since the typical bank is able
to lend about ten times its capital base, this capital contribution could
be leveraged into $12.5 billion in inner-city lending, an amount that
would grow as the earnings of CDBs rose and commercial banks made
steadily larger capital contributions to meet their 1 percent community
reinvestment obligation.

The charters for CDBs must require sufficient targeting of loans to
the right areas without entailing excessive bureaucracy. We believe
census-tract earmarking could be used for this purpose. The CBDs
might be required to lend a specified percentage of their assets to

individuals or establishments within designated low-income tracts. But whether enough people could readily be trained in the kinds of techniques that the South Shore Bank has pioneered is uncertain. This issue is really a matter of timing. Clearly, any large CDB program could not be developed overnight. That is why we also favor federal support of a secondary market for inner-city loans that could temporarily fill the gap in inner-city financing until CBDs begin to function.

One objection to our two proposals is that they are open to abuse. Many borrowers whose loans are guaranteed might default, leaving the government with the costly obligation of redeeming its loan guarantees. And a number of CDBs might fail, leaving commercial banks to pick up the pieces. Both results are possible. But they should not prevent practical tests of our proposals; the economic and social problems of inner cities are too severe. Both our suggestions can leverage relatively small amounts of money into potentially large payoffs. In the case of CDBs, the funds come from the private sector rather than the government. As Arthur Okun noted, government programs to help the poor are similar to leaky buckets. The critical question is whether the leaks are so large that filling the bucket becomes a waste of time and energy. Given the likely size of the leaks and the magnitude of potential gains, it makes sense to start filling the bucket.

Summary

If the American economy is to grow faster, the share of total output devoted to investment must be increased. The higher level of investment should be financed by domestic saving, which for all practical purposes means that the federal budget deficit must be sharply reduced.

Government incentives to channel investment into certain types of activities can yield large social payoffs. We favor a permanent tax credit for investment in equipment and new programs to encourage private investment in inner cities. The latter effort could make an important contribution to improving the distribution of income as well as increasing growth. It would be a mistake to try to stimulate investment by reducing the tax rate on capital gains. Though we see good arguments for some increase in infrastructure investment, particularly for repairing and upgrading existing facilities, we are skeptical of the benefits of a massive new public investment effort. The nation would see better results if it moved toward congestion pricing of overcrowded roads and airports.

Seven

Foreign Trade
and Investment

FREE TRADE stimulates economic growth. In combination
with unhindered movement of foreign investment funds
into the United States, free trade can accelerate the pace of product
innovation and productivity improvement within U.S. borders.

The United States is now very much part of the world economy.
This was not always true. When the country emerged as the world's
leading power after World War II, combined U.S. imports and exports
comprised less than 7 percent of total output. By 1992 foreign trade
comprised more than 16 percent of U.S. output.[1]

A similar pattern emerged for direct foreign investment in the
United States. Investments by foreign residents in U.S. companies
and real estate totaled only $3 billion in 1950, or 0.3 percent of the
nation's total capital stock held by the private sector. By 1990 foreign
direct investment in the United States had soared to $403 billion,
representing 2.3 percent of the nation's capital stock.[2]

Ironically, as the United States has become more linked with the
global economy, the voices urging a more insular economic role have
become louder. Fears of job displacement caused by rising imports
have intensified the pressure for trade protection. Increased foreign
investment has triggered growing concern about the dangers of a
larger foreign presence.

We understand these fears and concerns. But in this chapter we
try to show why it would be wrong for the United States to react to
them by turning inward. In fact, we are confident that continued
openness—indeed, greater openness—to foreign trade and investment will promote economic growth rather than reduce it. The remedies for the dislocations and wage pressure caused by foreign trade
lie not in trade protection but in policies to improve the productivity

of U.S. workers and to insure workers against extraordinary losses from liberal trade policies.

Promoting Productivity through Freer Trade

Competition is essential not only to make certain that goods and services are available at low prices but also to spur firms to innovate, to search for lower-cost production methods, to improve products and services, and to strive for greater quality. This lesson is clear from the nation's experience with the economic deregulation of the transportation and telecommunications industries. By ridding firms in those industries of controls on prices and entry, Congress and the regulatory agencies have generally lowered prices and forced the firms to trim labor and other costs and, in the process, improve productivity.[3]

If competition is useful for encouraging productivity growth, there is no rational basis for distinguishing between the residence or nationality of the competitors. Competition from foreign firms, whether from those doing business in the United States or from those exporting their products from abroad, is as essential for encouraging productivity among businesses located here as the competition provided solely by domestic firms. We recognize that this is not the premise on which free trade has traditionally been defended. The classic rationale has been based on the mutual benefits of trade at a single point in time. According to this view, it is cheaper for a country to specialize in the production of goods and services in which it has a comparative advantage and to export them in exchange for imports of goods and services in which it does not have a comparative advantage. That is true whether or not a country is now producing or is capable of producing a particular product or service.

Some analysts have pointed out that countries such as the United States, which are nearly capable of self-sufficiency, may find that passing up the benefits of free trade is not particularly costly. Paul Krugman, for example, has calculated that a world trade war that cut the volume of trade by half would reduce world output by only 2.5 percent.[4] But this static analysis understates the value of free trade, probably by a large margin, because it ignores the *dynamic* gains—particularly the long-term productivity gains—of open trade. These benefits come in several forms.

Trade Allows Diversity of Products

Openness to trade makes it possible for consumers to enjoy a wider diversity of products and services, a benefit likely to grow as technological advances around the world multiply.[5] Even the United States obtains many products through trade with other countries that it does not produce at home. Diversity is not only important for consumers, but for producers as well. For example, certain imports, such as fax machines or laptop computer display screens, were not commercially developed in the United States, but they have become essential for producing other goods and services that U.S. firms manufacture and deliver. And imports of consumer products not made in the United States have become essential to the development of related industries (for example, video rental stores depend on VCRs).

Some critics express concern about the tendency of companies doing business in the United States to rely on foreign-manufactured components, a process often referred to as "hollowing-out." Such practices have become common in the computer industry, whose circuit boards and other components are manufactured overseas; in heavy machinery; and more recently, in the aircraft industry, as manufacturers of the next generation of civilian airplanes rely more and more heavily on foreign-made components and parts. Not coincidentally, however, many of the firms that rely on imported inputs are also among this country's leading exporters. In an increasingly global economy, only the low-cost producers are able to sell their products in world markets. At the same time, workers employed in aircraft manufacture and other U.S. export industries tend to earn higher wages than those earned by workers in import-competing industries.[6] If the United States wants to maintain the viability and encourage the expansion of many of its high-wage export industries, it cannot employ trade restrictions that drive up the prices or limit the availability of critical inputs.

Trade Stimulates Productivity Growth

As we have already suggested, trade competition enhances productivity growth in the same way that domestic competition does—by encouraging domestic firms to develop and introduce the latest and most effective production techniques and managerial practices. But while this proposition may be readily accepted as true for developing countries, where domestic markets are too small to support enough competitors to ensure a competitive market structure, some may question its relevance for the United States.[7] With the largest market in the world, why is the hot breath of foreign competition needed to keep domestic industries innovative and competitive?

In some industries, the size of the U.S. market does ensure strong competition. But the United States no longer has a comfortable technological lead in all industries.[8] The large size of the U.S. economy has not been sufficient to ensure that competition among domestic firms alone will induce American firms to produce high-quality products or to generate rapid gains in productivity. Imagine the state of the automobile industry, for example, if U.S. auto manufacturers had not faced stiff import competition during the 1980s. Would American consumers have seen such impressive quality improvements in auto showrooms? Would U.S. producers have built cars as efficiently?[9]

Figure 7-1 provides direct evidence on the effects of trade on industrial productivity performance. The figure shows average labor productivity growth and import and export shares of total shipments in four classes of American manufacturing industries. (The underlying data for the figures are shown in table 7-1.) U.S. manufacturing industries are ranked by their productivity performance during two recent economic cycles, 1973 to 1979 and 1979 to 1988. Industries in the top 25 percent of industries in terms of productivity improvement are always included in the first quartile, industries in the next 25 percent of industries ranked by productivity growth are included in the second quartile, and so on.[10] If openness to trade did not affect productivity performance, import penetration and the share of total shipments exported should be roughly constant across all four productivity quartiles.[11] Figure 7-1 shows that proposition to be approximately true for exports. Regardless of their productivity performance, industries in all four quartiles exported similar shares of their total shipments. But for imports the story is different. Industries in the top two quartiles of productivity growth—the industries that displayed the most rapid rates of productivity improvement in each of the cycles—had markedly higher import penetration ratios than the industries in the bottom two quartiles. Since it is unlikely that higher productivity in these top performing industries could have led to higher import penetration,

FIGURE 7-1. *Relationship of Trade and Productivity Performance, Selected Periods, 1973–88.*

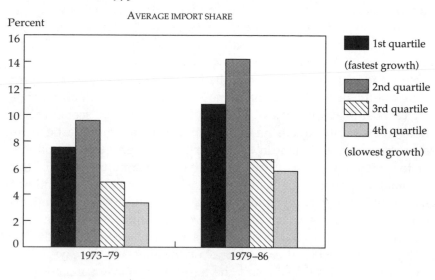

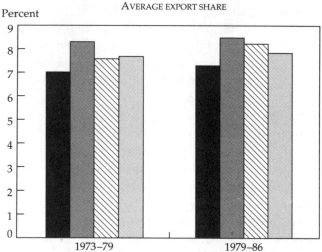

Sources: Department of Commerce, unpublished data; and Charles Ardolini and Mark Sieling, "Productivity Trends in Selected Industries," *Business Economics*, vol. 26 (October 1991), pp. 26–30.

FIGURE 7-1. *(continued)*

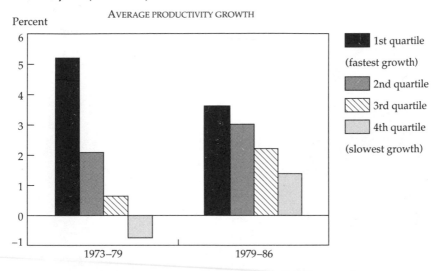

AVERAGE PRODUCTIVITY GROWTH

■ 1st quartile
(fastest growth)

▨ 2nd quartile

▧ 3rd quartile

▢ 4th quartile
(slowest growth)

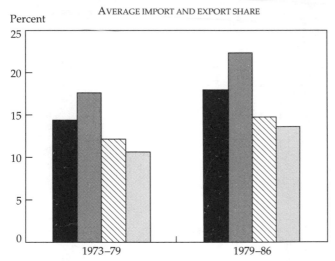

AVERAGE IMPORT AND EXPORT SHARE

the correlations between import penetration and productivity growth suggest that import competition stimulates productivity improvement, even in an economy as large as that of the United States.[12]

Import competition helps to prevent domestic markets from becoming oligopolistic and earning excessive profits that can lead to complacency. In more competitive markets, companies may be unable to reap the same rewards from each new innovation, but precisely for

TABLE 7-1. *Productivity Growth and Trade Data, Selected Periods, 1973–88*
Percent unless otherwise specified

Quartile 1973–79	Industries in group 1973–79	Range of productivity growth 1973–79	Average productivity growth		Ratio of average imports to shipments		Ratio of average exports to shipments		Ratio of average exports + imports to shipments	
			1973–79	1979–88	1973–79	1979–86	1973–79	1979–86	1973–79	1979–86
1	31	17.2–3.1	5.2	3.6	7.4	10.8	7.0	7.3	14.4	18.1
2	34	3.0–1.3	2.1	3.0	9.5	14.1	8.2	8.4	17.6	22.5
3	29	1.2–0.2	0.7	2.2	4.8	6.7	7.5	8.2	12.2	14.9
4	27	0.1–3.9	−0.7	1.4	3.2	5.8	7.6	7.8	10.8	13.6

Sources: Numbers calculated from Department of Commerce, unpublished data; and Ardolini and Sieling, "Productivity Trends in Selected Industries," pp. 26–30.

this reason, they may have incentives to develop and introduce more innovations to avoid being displaced by their rivals, domestic or foreign.[13] In a recent Brookings study, Michael Salinger found that import competition has limited the excess profits that are typically found in U.S. industries where the firms have market power.[14] This suggests that domestic competition by itself may not be enough to provide appropriate discipline.

Some economists argue that many American industries are really more competitive than their concentration levels suggest because their markets are contestable. As long as entry by other firms is possible at reasonable cost, the mere threat of potential entry by other domestic competitors should be sufficient to discipline the behavior of existing competitors.[15] If this were true, U.S. openness to international trade would not be as important as we suggest.

Although it is true that some markets are contestable, others are not. The capital costs or other costs of entering a market are often so high that they protect existing competitors against any credible threat that new entrants could compete. Capital-intensive industries, such as automobile manufacturers, are obvious examples. Limited landing slots and other entry barriers make competition less than perfectly contestable in the airline industry. Indeed, Joseph Stiglitz cast sufficient doubt on the general applicability of the contestability assumption so that, in our view, openness to trade appears to be needed to bring vigorous competition to many domestic markets.[16]

Japan's Sheltered Markets and the Idea of Protection

Japan's economic development seems inconsistent with the view that openness to import competition is good for growth. The conventional wisdom is that Japan grew rapidly by shielding its infant industries from foreign competition.

A closer look however, reveals several features of Japan's development that suggest the need for a competitive market to stimulate innovation and productivity improvement. Although imports into Japan were restricted, Japanese domestic manufacturing markets were and remain highly competitive. Equally important, even while it restricted the entry of foreign goods, Japan did not restrict—indeed it actively welcomed and solicited—the entry of foreign technology, ideas, and practices that later proved instrumental to its success in manufacturing. Thus Japanese companies obtained licenses to foreign technologies. They invited such American experts as W. Edwards Deming to help improve their production methods.

Because American technology has fallen behind in certain industries, the United States must display the same openness to foreign ideas and technology that Japan displayed in an earlier era. The most practical way to gain access to better ideas and technology is through openness to foreign direct investment. At the same time, attempts by the United States to emulate the trade restrictions that Japan employed to give its infant industries time to mature may backfire. U.S. proponents of trade restrictions are often the same people who wish to place restrictions on foreign direct investment, which, as we show later, would reduce rather than expand growth by impeding the flow of valuable new technology from abroad. As a practical matter, any movement toward trade protection is likely to be accompanied by attempts to place restrictions on foreign investment.

Japan also severely restricted foreign investment, but it compensated by encouraging many of its young students, executives, and engineers to receive schooling or work experience overseas. The United States has not pursued this strategy, nor is it likely to any time soon. Few of our highly educated citizens speak a language other than English. The United States needs to continue attracting foreign investment as a way of promoting the transfer of valuable foreign learning and technology. When Japan pursued its protectionist strategy, it was a small and relatively backward country. It was not one of the world's leading economic powers. If the United States were now to reverse several decades of commitment to open trade, it would send a powerful signal to the rest of the world that trade protection is not only acceptable but preferable. This kind of signal could unleash a beggar-thy-neighbor protectionism that would leave all countries, including the United States, worse off.

Promoting Productivity through Foreign Direct Investment

As noted in chapter 2, the United States has become dependent on foreign investment to finance its budget and trade deficits. But as long as this country continues to save too little, foreign investment will be needed to promote economic growth. Without foreign funds,

U.S. interest rates would be higher, domestic investment would be lower, and economic growth would proceed at a slower pace.

But what if the United States were to raise domestic saving significantly? Would foreign investment be any less desirable? The answer, we think, is no. Even when the United States did not "need" foreign capital, it attracted large amounts because foreigners found the rewards attractive. For example, during the 1970s—when, on average, the nation had rough a balance in its current account—foreigners invested $31 billion a year. Of this annual amount, roughly $4 billion comprised foreign direct investment in U.S. companies.[17]

Analysts distinguish two kinds of foreign investment: portfolio investments in U.S. bonds and other financial instruments and direct investments in enterprises operated by foreign companies. Of these two forms of investment, the latter will almost certainly do more to promote economic growth in the long run. The reason is simple. When foreigners make significant investments in U.S. companies, either existing enterprises or new ones, they bring the best of their technologies and managerial methods with them. U.S. companies and workers can learn from these foreign methods and improve their own best practices.

To date, the research linking foreign direct investment with growth has concentrated on the benefits such investment has brought to developing countries, who lag far behind the industrialized world in technology.[18] By the same logic, foreign direct investment in advanced countries, especially when accompanied by a transfer of successful technologies, should also promote growth.

The U.S. auto industry has benefited from this kind of technology transfer. The well-known joint venture of General Motors and Toyota at GM's failed manufacturing plant in Freemont, California, produced sizable productivity gains.[19] And although one report suggests that Chrysler's partnership with Mitsubishi Motors of Japan has been disappointing,[20] the arrangement did induce Chrysler to adopt team methods of designing new models that helped trim the company's product development cycle by a full year. New car models are now developed in three and one-half years, nearly equal to the three-year cycle typical of Japanese auto manufacturers. In addition, Chrysler has claimed annual savings of nearly $1 billion as a result of working more closely with its suppliers, an innovation adapted from successful Japanese auto companies.[21]

Chrysler's apparent success with its latest automobile designs confirms other studies on the advantages of teamwork in product design. One study found that auto companies assigning teams from different departments to design new models, under the direction of a single manager, were more likely to bring out new models at a faster pace and with lower cost than companies that gave design responsibilities to separate units divorced from other departments in the corporation.[22] Press reports say that Chrysler has taken this lesson to heart, developing a new sports car, jeep, and line of family automobiles with roughly half the number of people formerly used to develop new car models. Other American companies are now studying Chrysler, which modeled its design program after Honda's.[23]

Trade Protection as an Incentive for Foreign Direct Investment

If we are right in arguing that foreign direct investment can be an effective mechanism for transferring foreign technology to the United States, how should it be encouraged? Paradoxically, some foreign companies may be encouraged to invest in the United States as a result of restrictions on trade. Foreign producers of televisions and automobiles, for example, established major production facilities in the United States only after their exports were penalized with antidumping orders (televisions) or by other types of protection (voluntary export restraints applied to Japanese automobiles). The desire to avoid these barriers through direct investment seems to have been especially strong among Japanese companies. According to a survey, 753 Japanese companies had entered into some type of alliance with American companies in 1991, up from 477 in 1990. Both numbers greatly exceeded those from any other country.[24]

Still, it would be a mistake to adopt protectionist measures to encourage growth-enhancing foreign direct investment. First, the same political momentum that pushes legislators toward a more restrictive trade policy could push them to restrict foreign investment as well. It is hardly a coincidence that the Congress which enacted tougher trade legislation in 1988 also adopted legislation to discourage some direct foreign investment. The Exon-Florio amendment gives the president authority to block foreign acquisitions or investments in U.S. companies that threaten national security. Congress has shown continued interest in widening the standards under the amendment for blocking foreign acquisitions as well as for changing the composition of the review panel to make it more likely that foreign investments would be blocked. Even if Congress does not toughen the current law, the Exon-Florio amendment gives a president inclined to support protectionism great power to discourage or prevent foreign direct investment in the United States.

A more recent and potentially even more dangerous move against foreign investment was included in proposed trade legislation offered in 1992 by Representatives Richard Gephardt of Missouri and Daniel Rostenkowski of Illinois. This legislation would have limited the sales not only of imported goods (automobiles) but also of goods manufactured in the United States by foreign-owned enterprises unless Japan substantially reduced its bilateral trade surplus with the United States. Although the proposal was eventually dropped from trade legislation considered by Congress in 1992, the strong interest it attracted cannot be encouraging to foreign companies considering direct investment in this country. Ironically, Japanese auto companies began investing heavily in the United States in the first place in response to the "voluntary" trade restraints placed on imports of Japanese autos in 1981. If a little more than a decade later the United States punishes Japanese auto companies now that their U.S.-based enterprises have become successful, it will not encourage investment here.

The growing trend toward cross-border company alliances is a second reason it would be a mistake for the United States to adopt trade protection to attract foreign direct investment. Historically, many firms have established cross-border joint ventures to enter foreign markets more quickly and efficiently. In recent years, however, international joint ventures have also been formed to develop new products or technologies or to engage in new businesses. This is especially true in the fast-changing and highly competitive computer and semiconductor industries, in which high costs and huge risks of developing new technologies have led many of the major competitors to form alliances.[25] Companies involved in alliances with partners from abroad must be able to trade inputs and end products freely across national borders. Trade restrictions impede such trade and thus reduce the value of alliances.

Third, and most important, trade restrictions would mean that part of the positive impact of increased foreign competition would be lost.

FIGURE 7-2. *Alternative Rates of Return for the United States, 1983–90*

Percent

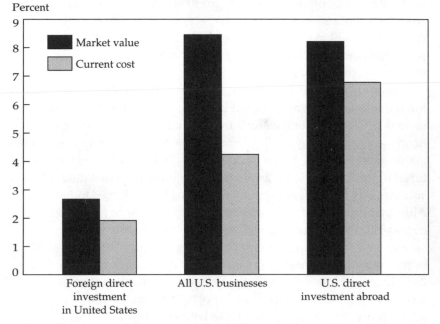

Source: Department of Commerce, *Survey of Current Business*, vol. 71 (August 1991), p. 44.

We need free trade to ensure that companies operating in the United States, whether owned by U.S. or foreign residents, always have to compete with the world's best so that they become or remain equal to the world's best.

One legitimate complaint against foreign direct investment is that foreign-owned companies operating in the United States do not appear to pay corporate taxes proportionate to their sales or true economic profits. Reported rates of return earned on foreign direct investment in the United States have been suspiciously below rates earned on U.S. business investment both in this country and overseas (figure 7-2). Although a number of factors contribute to this disparity, its magnitude provides circumstantial evidence that foreign firms use creative accounting practices to minimize their taxable profits.[26] It is difficult to evaluate the transfer prices that multinational companies use to value the costs of inputs they obtain from abroad. By assigning artificially high prices to their inputs, foreign firms can minimize their

U.S. taxes. For this reason, we support efforts to assign more realistic transfer prices, even though the resulting increase in corporate tax liabilities might discourage some foreign investment.[27]

The best policy to encourage foreign direct investment is to make it clear that the door is open to foreign investors and will remain open. Beyond that, the nation should simply follow policies that encourage efficiency and productivity in all companies operating in the United States. All companies, for example, need a well maintained public infrastructure and a well-educated work force.

Critics of Foreign Direct Investment

Foreign direct investment is not universally popular, of course. Some critics fear that it threatens U.S. national security. Foreigners doing business here might not be as willing to share their secrets with our Defense Department as U.S.-owned companies are. It was for this reason that Congress enacted the Exon-Florio amendment. In principle, foreign direct investment might one day pose this kind of threat. But only one transaction has thus far been rejected under the Exon-Florio law, suggesting that fears for national security are overblown. So far the potential danger posed by foreign investment is slight. Even though the share of U.S. corporate assets held by foreign investors has grown steadily, by 1988 that share was still only 5 percent for all nonfinancial corporations, and an even lower 2 percent for all corporations.[28]

A second criticism of foreign direct investment is that foreigners are attracted to do business here solely to exploit low-cost U.S. labor while keeping or transferring high-value jobs abroad. There is little evidence to support this claim. Foreign companies, including those from Japan, pay essentially the same compensation per worker and record essentially the same value added in the United States as do U.S.-owned companies.[29]

Some critics of foreign direct investment fear that foreign companies distort the American political process by lobbying elected U.S. leaders on matters of concern to them. This criticism neglects to consider that, at least at the federal level, foreign companies lobby largely for defensive reasons, to ensure that they receive the same treatment given to their American-owned competitors. Moreover, while some critics of foreign direct investment single out lobbying by U.S. subsidiaries of foreign firms, these same critics ignore or even rationalize the lobbying of domestic producers, who often seek trade protection and other policies costly to U.S. consumers and taxpayers.

Lester Thurow has criticized foreign firms, especially those from Japan, for imposing a glass ceiling that limits the promotion opportunities of Americans in their U.S. subsidiaries. He notes that almost 70 percent of the senior managers of Japanese affiliates in the United States are from Japan, and only 20 percent are American.[30] We are unaware of comparable statistics for U.S. affiliates owned by residents of other countries or of foreign affiliates of U.S. companies. But if Thurow is correct that Japanese-owned companies are more insular than their U.S. or European counterparts, it may indeed matter who owns the companies that do business within our borders.

We think Thurow's fears are reasonable but somewhat exaggerated. If foreign companies consistently discriminate against American citizens in hiring and promotion, they face heavy penalties under U.S. employment law. And disgruntled American employees have filed several employment discrimination lawsuits against a handful of Japanese companies, although no judgments have yet been reached. More important than the penalties of U.S. law are the long-term penalties exacted in the U.S. marketplace. If foreign companies acquire a reputation for discriminating against American nationals in promoting employees to senior management positions, they will find it increasingly difficult to attract talented American employees and managers. Some current managers, frustrated by restricted opportunities in foreign companies, will leave and take with them valuable on-the-job experience. The marketplace imposes exactly the same penalty on domestic companies that fail to promote or suitably reward their most talented employees.

Another fear of foreign direct investment is that some U.S. industries may become too dependent on vertically integrated suppliers headquartered in other countries. U.S. firms may be denied the latest technologies, which may instead be provided only to the suppliers' parent or sister firms in foreign countries. In fact, the General Accounting Office found evidence that certain Japanese firms may have engaged in this behavior, delaying delivery of advanced state-of-the-art equipment, including display screens for laptop computers and new equipment for manufacturing semiconductors.[31]

Even if such behavior exists, it is important to recognize that it does not represent an indictment of foreign investment per se. Foreign suppliers can withhold advanced technology from their competitors, whether or not these suppliers have facilities in the United States. Indeed, to the extent such behavior occurs at all, U.S. firms are better off if it occurs in the United States, for they would have better access to antitrust remedies under American law.[32] Advanced foreign technologies can also leak out to current or new U.S. competitors, possibly as a result of employee turnover, if the technologies are used within our borders. If the advanced technologies are used exclusively abroad, this kind of leakage is less likely to occur.

Another criticism leveled against Japanese manufacturers investing in the United States is that some of these firms bring with them their *kereitsu* partners from back home, including their suppliers and bankers. U.S. suppliers and financial service firms, it is argued, are shut out of an increasingly important part of the manufacturing market. Even if this were true, it is not clear why that should concern most Americans. When Japanese supply firms open factories in the United States, they raise and improve the U.S. capital stock, employ American workers, and bring new production techniques that may not be available among suppliers based in the United States. Even though the owners of domestic supply companies might wish it were otherwise, each of these additions to the U.S. economy brings tangible advantages to American workers and consumers.

In the long run, policies that have the effect of imposing local content or purchasing requirements on foreign investors raise the cost of doing business in this country. They are likely to discourage foreign companies from opening facilities in the United States. What may sound like a reasonable policy in the short run for helping a specific industry or set of firms may not make sense in the long run when applied more broadly.

Many critics view foreign direct investment with suspicion because they believe the investors will hide or restrict access to their best technologies. Of course, there is no reason to believe that U.S. owners behave any differently. Judging by the amount of U.S. litigation over intellectual property rights, domestic residents vigorously pursue their right to restrict the use of their technology or to be appropriately compensated when it is used. In any event, the superior productivity of some foreign companies, particularly Japanese auto manufacturers, appears to owe as much to their workplace management methods and relationships with suppliers as to any technological superiority.

These methods are difficult, if not impossible, to hide, especially when workers and managers leave foreign firms to work for domestically owned companies.

Whether or not the United States runs a trade deficit, encouraging foreign investment makes good economic sense. Foreign investors keep U.S. domestic interest rates lower than they would otherwise be. They are also important for transferring new technologies and management ideas to establishments within U.S. borders. When America was a major direct investor in the rest of the world, its business executives made similar arguments in trying to persuade the business and political leaders of other countries. These arguments have been enthusiastically embraced in Singapore, Argentina, Mexico, and other countries.[33] Since the early 1980s the United States has become a net debtor to the rest of the world and is increasingly the recipient of more foreign funds than it invests abroad. We should apply in our own policymaking the advice we formerly gave to other countries.

New Strategies for Gaining Access to Foreign Markets

While the long-run advantages of open markets for both goods and investment may be clear, we often hear a powerful political argument against opening our markets. Since other nations do not accord American goods or capital equitable treatment in their markets, why should we offer foreign goods and capital even-handed treatment in ours? Many advocates of reciprocity use the "level playing field" argument to mask protectionist intentions. But others use an analogy from arms control discussions, contending that it would be wrong for the United States to disarm unilaterally by dropping its barriers to foreign goods and capital without gaining increased access to foreign markets for U.S. goods and capital. This principle lies at the heart of a provision in U.S. trade law known as Section 301, which grants the president authority to threaten trade retaliation against nations that deny reasonable access for U.S. goods.

In the recent past, the United States has increasingly relied on sticks rather than carrots to open foreign markets. This strategy is clearly at odds with our proposed emphasis on maintaining the openness of our market to foreign goods and capital. In the more distant past, the United States relied on a very different strategy. It was a leading proponent of international trade negotiations, under the auspices of the General Agreement on Tariffs and Trade, as the primary vehicle for opening foreign markets. The last successful GATT round of negotiations was completed in 1979. The recent Uruguay Round has been under negotiation for six years, but as we write this chapter, the future of the negotiations appears cloudy. In recognition of the possibility that the GATT talks may fail, the United States has turned to regional free trade agreements, signing one with Canada and successfully negotiating the North American Free Trade Agreement (NAFTA) with Canada and Mexico. Meanwhile, despite some recent setbacks, the European Community seems poised to achieve a high degree of economic integration. Can the United States maintain an open policy toward trade and investment in a world that may soon be dominated by regional trading blocs?

The Case for Multilateral Trade Liberalization

Notwithstanding the rise of regional trading blocs, it is premature to abandon the multilateral negotiating process. All nations, including the United States, gain handsomely from free trade with other nations on equal terms. Regional arrangements necessarily distort trade and limit access by consumers to the cheapest and highest-quality products made in countries outside the preferred regions. As regional arrangements are expanded, they may give participants an excuse not to proceed to the next step—truly multilateral liberalization—on the ground that the regional markets are already large enough and would not benefit from broader liberalization.[34]

The United States has much to gain from improved access to markets outside the Western Hemisphere because these markets receive two-thirds of current U.S. exports. The nation is likely to find it easier to negotiate market-opening measures with both Europe and Japan in a multilateral context, in which all parties have more to gain, than to continue down the path of negotiating on a bilateral basis. Regional trade arrangements with low-wage countries such as Mexico raise fears about job migration that are less likely to arise in broader multilateral negotiations, where industrialized countries have greater weight in the negotiating process.

For all these reasons, we believe it would be in the best interests of the United States to renew its efforts at multilateral trade negotiation. The Uruguay Round has stalled in part because the United States insisted on deeper cuts in agricultural subsidies by the European Community than the EC or some of its members were willing to grant. As a result, the United States could lose all the benefits negotiated so far, including liberalization of trade in services and stronger protection of intellectual property rights. By pressing too hard for an ideal agreement, the United States may lose a good agreement.

Switching from Sticks to Carrots

Whatever course the United States adopts in the next round of trade negotiations, domestic political pressure will continue to push it toward gaining greater access to foreign markets. We think the country should try a different approach. The United States has relied heavily on the stick, threatening offending countries with trade or investment restrictions. We believe it would be better to offer a carrot, and we have a particular carrot in mind.

U.S. trade law now includes penalties against the unfair trade practices of foreign industries. In principle, the penalties are designed to discourage subsidizing or dumping foreign products sold in the United States. Foreign industries found to engage in these practices are penalized by being required to pay import duties that offset the margins of subsidy or unfair dumping.[35] Increasingly, U.S. industries have used these statutes to gain protection against foreign competition and have been successful. More than half of the 327 dumping cases filed during the 1980s resulted in penalties.[36]

The unfair trade practice laws are not as fair as they seem. They are administered in ways that defy economic logic and common sense, and they discriminate against foreign respondents.[37] The United States is not alone in this respect. The dumping procedures followed by the European Community have a similar bias.

The protectionist bias built into the administration of the unfair trade practice laws has an impact beyond the narrowly defined industries in which these cases are filed. It has the not-so-subtle effect of tending to raise the prices of foreign products that are not the subject of direct challenge. In addition, several "voluntary" restraint agreements, which have limited exports of steel, semiconductors, and lumber, were implemented to settle charges of dumping and unfair subsidization. The U.S. reaction to foreign dumping can also have perverse effects on U.S. employment. When the Commerce Department slapped antidumping duties on Japanese-made screens for laptop computers, both Apple and Compaq moved their laptop assembly operations offshore. The United States lost many more jobs in computer assembly than it gained in screen manufacturing.

The protectionist tilt of the trade laws can be turned to American advantage. Ideally, liberalization of the unfair trade rules to bring them more in line with modern economic thinking should be accomplished on a multilateral basis. But at this writing, that seems unlikely. Although reform of the antidumping laws has been on the negotiating agenda of the Uruguay Round, few of the principal defects in the administration of these laws have been addressed.

We propose that the United States consider unilateral adoption of a new two-tier system of administering the trade laws. The nation should develop a new, rational, and more liberal system for weighing unfair practices of those countries that our government deems to provide "effective market access" to foreign products. It should retain the current system of penalties for imports from all other countries. Under the new liberalized system, authorities would determine and measure dumping and subsidization in a fashion fully consistent with modern economic principles.[38] Because it would be available only to countries with open economies, the new system would provide strong incentives to all countries to be aggressive in removing not only de jure limitations on imports but de facto restrictions as well. In this respect, the proposed reform could be especially useful in opening the Japanese market, which contains relatively few formal trade barriers but which in practice limits imports through various means (for example, as a product of the *keiretsu* system).[39] By providing a more sensible mechanism for calculating dumping and countervailing duties, the two-tiered mechanism would also help discourage filing such cases against countries that are deemed open to U.S. products.

We recognize there will be some objections to this proposal. Perhaps most important, critics might argue that it abandons the most-favored-nation principle of the GATT, since it would apply different dumping standards to different countries. But it would raise no new restrictions, since countries that are not deemed to be effectively open to U.S. products would face no harsher dumping or subsidy penalties than they currently face. To the contrary, the two-tiered mechanism would promote further trade liberalization by encouraging other countries to provide effective market access to foreign imports generally (although that determination would rest with the United States).

A second criticism is that the determination of effective market access could be highly subjective and politicized. We grant this possibility. But precisely because the U.S. administration is given discretion in determining open market access, it would have significant leverage in obtaining concessions or obtaining market-opening measures from trading partners.

Ideally, we would prefer to see the dumping laws replaced with an international antitrust regime that punished predatory pricing but not arbitrarily defined dumping. As a second-best policy, it would be desirable to gain GATT approval for the two-tiered regime just outlined. But in the absence of quick GATT action on either proposal, U.S. unilateral adoption of the two-tiered policy could put pressure on the other countries to come to international agreement on the issue and also encourage them to drop some current barriers to imports from the United States and elsewhere.

Helping Displaced Workers

We recognize that a policy of openness to trade entails dislocation for workers in import-competing industries. A standard response to this problem is to compensate those who are adversely affected. In fact, the United States has maintained a system of trade adjustment assistance for the past two decades, although it was used much more intensively before 1981 than it has been since.

The problem of dislocation is not limited to workers who are affected by trade. Economic progress means economic dislocation. If the economy is functioning efficiently, workers in less productive or failing industries must move to more efficient and expanding ones. Many workers and businesses will resist these changes when the transfer of resources entails sizable economic loss. In a pure laissez faire economy, such resistance would of course be futile. Less efficient businesses and production processes would be supplanted by more efficient ones, regardless of the complaints of the workers and owners of failing businesses.

Neither the United States nor any other advanced industrialized country operates in a pure laissez faire environment, however. Workers and business owners harmed by economic change are quick to seek remedies from their representatives. These remedies are usually harmful to the wider economy. Government intervention to protect jobs and failing businesses often prevents consumers from buying goods or services from the most efficient producers. Tariffs and quotas to fend off foreign competition and defend domestic producers ordinarily injure the nation's standard of living. They reduce the pressure on domestic producers to reform production methods or abandon inefficient facilities.

Opposition to economic change can be lessened if losers are assured that their losses will be manageable. Improvements in employment services and in the general training of average workers could reduce earnings losses suffered as a result of economic change. In addition, losses can be reduced in a way that actually speeds up the reallocation of resources from declining to growing industries. When the government faces calls for protection, it should consider directly compensating losers rather than adopting measures that would halt or slow down economic change. Our proposal focuses on compensating workers for the costs of economic change. We do not propose that workers in declining industries be fully compensated for earnings losses when employment shrinks. Instead we suggest that displaced workers be offered time-limited "earnings insurance."

Under our proposal, workers would receive monthly or quarterly earnings supplements for a percentage of the earnings losses they suffer as a result of displacement. With a program that replaced 50 percent of lost earnings, for example, a displaced worker whose previous wage was $400 a week would receive a weekly insurance check of $100 if forced to accept a new job that paid only $200 a week. The percentage of earnings replacement could be tied to a worker's age and time on the job, with the supplement rising for older workers and those with longer tenure because they suffer proportionately larger and more permanent earnings losses than younger workers.

A crucial feature of the plan is that earnings supplements would not be payable until a worker became reemployed, and they would cease within a specified period after displacement occurs (say, after two years). Workers who found new jobs early in the two-year period would receive larger cumulative payments than those who delayed accepting a new job. This limitation provides workers with an incentive to accept promptly the consequences of permanent job loss. One of the main reasons that displaced workers delay serious job searches is their failure to accept the fact that their job has permanently disappeared. By encouraging workers to accept this fact right away, earnings insurance would induce workers to take constructive action to become reemployed as fast as they can.

This proposal avoids some of the existing problems in unemployment insurance and trade adjustment assistance.[40] Workers receiving unemployment benefits have an incentive to delay finding a job until their eligibility for benefits is exhausted, usually after six months. The longer they delay, the more unemployment checks they receive. This kind of incentive can be beneficial for workers who use their eligibility period to search diligently for good jobs. Economists widely agree, however, that both the availability and generosity of unemployment benefits tend to prolong joblessness. Since many workers end up accepting jobs they could have obtained soon after becoming unemployed, some of the extra idleness represents a pure economic loss. Earnings insurance avoids this problem. If workers delay finding a job for one year, they will effectively lose the right to collect earnings insurance for that year. Because the insurance benefits compensate workers for only a fraction of the difference between their current and former weekly wages, workers are encouraged to find as good a job as they can as soon as they can.

Although earnings insurance offers a superior method of compensating workers for earnings losses, at least compared with trade adjustment assistance, it is not clear what circumstances would justify compensating displaced workers for their economic losses. The traditional argument in favor of trade adjustment assistance is that workers injured by international trade are making sacrifices in the interest of the common good. To obtain workers' consent for trade liberalization, a compensation scheme is politically necessary. As a practical matter, however, it is uncertain whether political resistance to free trade was diminished as a result of trade adjustment assistance. The Labor Department paid $4 billion in readjustment allowances to trade-displaced workers between 1976 and 1985, but these outlays did not prevent the president and Congress from enacting a number of protectionist measures.[41]

Some might also question the fairness of restricting generous assistance payments to workers injured by international trade. Those who suffer displacement as a result of other kinds of structural change surely believe that their situation justifies compensation too. Employees of defense contractors probably think they deserve compensation for accepting job loss as a result of cuts in the defense budget. It is difficult to know where to draw the line in offering compensation for job losses associated with structural change. A generous plan might offer earnings insurance to all workers who lose jobs they have held for a minimum period, say, five years. (Workers who retire, quit, or are dismissed for cause would not be eligible. They are also usually ineligible for regular unemployment insurance.) Establishing such a plan would be costly, however, and would require large contributions by employers or workers to an earnings insurance fund. A more restrictive plan might provide assistance only to workers affected by a massive permanent layoff or permanent plant shutdown. Analysts who have studied the experiences of displaced workers agree that unemployment is more severe and earnings loss larger when displacement occurs in a local labor market where the unemployment rate is already high.

To economize on compensation, Congress could restrict coverage to only the most senior employees, to workers involved in a mass layoff, or to those who become unemployed in local labor markets where the unemployment rate is well above the national average. The crucial advantage of earnings insurance in comparison with other compensation schemes is that it offers clear incentives for insured workers to accelerate rather than delay their adjustment after suffering permanent job loss.

Eight

An Agenda for Growth
and Equity

THE PROBLEMS of slow growth and widening income inequality are not unsolvable. This book contains a variety
of proposals that address one or both of them.

Our proposals are summarized in table 8-1. For each proposal the
table shows an approximate annual price tag, a suggested method of
financing the cost, and our judgment about the nature, size, and
certainty of the benefits the proposal would achieve. The list is broken
down into the four categories suggested by the titles of chapters 4
through 7. We will not repeat our earlier descriptions of the proposals;
instead, we summarize some of the broad themes that link them.

Increasing and Reallocating Investment

Added investment is the key to improving growth and reversing
the trend toward greater inequality. More investment in machines,
research, and development will raise productivity, which in turn will
raise average living standards. Supplementary investment in the training of non-college-educated workers is needed to improve the earnings prospects of those at the bottom of the income distribution.

Many different methods should be used to increase the share of
the nation's total output that is invested. To increase investment in
human beings, we recommend an employer-based national training
program, coupled with more emphasis on apprenticeships for high
school graduates who do not go on to college. To boost investment
in equipment, we recommend a permanent investment tax credit.
To raise investment in new products and process technologies, we
recommend a larger and permanent research and development tax
credit. To improve both the level and the allocation of U.S. spending
on commercially useful technology, we recommend a shift in federal

R&D spending toward civilian uses, but with less emphasis on gargantuan projects such as the breeder reactor or supersonic transport, which in the past have often been the product (and the victim) of pork barrel politics. While a modest increase in public infrastructure spending is warranted, the government should devote much more attention to the efficient pricing of existing public facilities, such as user fees for roads and airports, and thus reduce the need for some infrastructure investment.

The nation should finance increased investment out of domestic resources, that is, by increasing its saving rate to match the rise in the share of output devoted to investment. In view of the persistent and large federal budget deficits, a gradual, but credible plan for eliminating the deficit is essential. Such a plan by itself could raise national saving by nearly enough to achieve the added domestic investment we recommend.

It will take more than tax incentives and added government spending to spur a better allocation of new investment in equipment and R&D and the speedy introduction of new methods of work and management. We recommend changes in corporate governance and executive compensation to encourage managers and corporate directors to pay more attention to longer-run profitability. Tying some portion of workers' compensation to company performance can also increase average productivity. The nation's borders must remain open to foreign competition and capital, both to give U.S. firms access to the latest and cheapest technology and to prevent corporate complacency. Domestic competition can and should be strengthened in certain industries where productivity growth is still held back by economic regulation. Legal and regulatory changes could help reduce the cost of capital and thus encourage innovation.

Helping Workers

Faster growth often means more job displacement. By definition, improved productivity means using fewer workers to produce the same amount of goods and services. For both social and political reasons, it is essential to minimize the economic losses and personal disruptions that displacement can entail. We urge the introduction of a new system of earnings insurance for displaced workers as well as improvement in the Employment Service, the government's main job placement program for the unemployed. The best way to minimize

TABLE 8-1. *Summary of Proposals*
Costs in billions of 1993 dollars

Proposal	Approximate annual cost	How financed	Enhances growth, equity, or both	Size of the benefit	Strength of the evidence
Innovation policies					
Strengthen basic science research					
Authorize NSF oversight of peer review	0	. . .	Growth	Small	Plausible
Reexamine allocation of current federal budget	0	. . .	Growth	Small	Plausible
Stengthen precompetitive R&D					
Funding only projects with private sector financial support	0	. . .	Growth	Small	Plausible
Fund broad diversity of projects (avoiding "big science")	0	. . .	Growth	Small	Plausible
Create a Civilian Technology Board (to provide peer review)	0	. . .	Growth	Small	Plausible
Fund precompetitive research	0	Reallocation from other federal R&D	Growth	Perhaps moderate	Reasonably strong
Promote commercial R&D by doubling the R&D tax credit	2	Offsetting increase in corporate taxes	Growth	Moderate	Strong
Lengthen business time horizons					
Encourage equity ownership by bankholding companies	0	. . .	Growth	Small	Plausible
Institute tax penalties on executive-director stock options with short exercise periods	Small revenue gain	. . .	Growth	Small	Plausible

Policy					
Institute tax penalties for paying directors in cash	Small revenue gain	...	Growth	Small	Plausible
Reduce risks of innovation					
Adopt modest "tort" reforms, accompanied by strengthened R&D and enforcement by regulatory agencies	0	...	Growth	Small	Plausible
Continue to allow joint R&D	0	...	Growth	Small	Plausible
Labor policies					
Improve skill training of schools					
Encourage schools to provide high school transcripts to prospective employers	0	...	Growth and equity	Small to moderate	Reasonably strong
Require national standardized tests	1	Reallocation of current education budgets	Growth and equity	Small	Plausible
Tie compensation and promotion of teachers and principals to performance of students on national test	0	...	Growth and equity	Small	Plausible
Improve skills of current labor force					
Establish public-private labor authority to develop tests and credentials for noncollege occupations	1	Out of training tax	Growth and equity	Small	Plausible
Institute pay-or-play training requirement for non-college-educated workers	46[a]	2 percent of employer payrolls	Growth and equity	Moderate to potentially significant	Reasonably strong
Establish national apprenticeship program for non-college-ducated workers	Part of pay-or-play training requirement	Out of training tax	Growth and equity	Moderate	Reasonably strong

TABLE 8-1. *Continued*

Proposal	Approximate annual cost	How financed	Enhances growth, equity, or both	Size of the benefit	Strength of the evidence
Establish improved R&D programs for such public training efforts as Job Corps and Job Training Partnership Act (JTPA)	1	Reprogramming existing federal funds for adult training programs	Growth and equity	Small	Plausible
Encourage firms to link worker pay with division of company-level performance	0	. . .	Growth	Moderate	Strong
Cushion economic shocks					
Upgrade national and state employment services	Less than 1	Tax for unemployment insurance	Growth and equity	Small	Plausible
Establish a non-cause-related program of earnings insurance[b]	2–16[b]	Increased federal payroll tax and general revenues[b]	Equity	Moderate	Plausible
Investment policies					
Raise investment share of total output Reduce, and ultimately eliminate, federal budget deficit	200, (3 percent of GDP)	Higher taxes, lower spending	Growth (and equity, if taxes concentrated on upper income)	Significant	Strong
Encourage particular types of investment with spillover benefits to the rest of the economy					

Policy		Offsetting	Effect	Magnitude	Strength of case
Enact a permanent 5% income tax credit for equipment investment	15	Offsetting increase in the corporate tax rate	Growth	Moderate to significant	Strong
Spending somewhat more on infrastructure, concentrated on upgrading existing facilities	10	Higher gasoline taxes and/or other tax increase or spending reduction	Growth	Modest	Reasonably strong
Encourage regional industry "clusters" by states or localities	Possibly small	. . .	Growth	Small to modest	Plausible
Allow banks to meet CRA requirement through investments in community development banks	0	. . .	Equity (and conceivably growth)	Modest to significant	Plausible
Trade and foreign investment policies					
Encourage further multilateral liberalization of trade and foreign investment	0	. . .	Growth	Modest to significant	Reasonably strong
Use liberalized (and more rational) treatment under U.S. "unfair trade practice" status as carrot to obtain better access to foreign markets	0	. . .	Growth	Small to modest	Plausible

a. Amount that would be spent by employers on training if they fully met the 2-percent-of-payroll training requirement. Most employers already spend some money training non-college-educated workers, so the net amount of extra spending, although unknown, would be substantially less than $46 billion a year. If employers spend no money on approved training, the proposed training tax would raise $23 billion in revenues annually.

b. Amount spent would depend on generosity of earnings insurance and stringency of eligibility criteria. More generous programs would require funds from general revenues as well as increases in the federal unemployment insurance tax.

worker losses from economic displacement is to maintain low unemployment rates. The challenge of ensuring full employment is one that can be met only through suitable macroeconomic policy.

It is not enough, however, for displaced workers simply to find new jobs. The United States has been conspicuously successful in creating new jobs over the past two decades. It has been far less successful in ensuring that the new jobs offer good wages and decent fringe benefits. Since the early 1970s adult men near the bottom of the earnings distribution have found that full-time, year-round jobs pay declining real wages. To replace part of the wage losses that displaced workers suffer when they accept new jobs, we recommend a novel earnings insurance program that would not only cushion the blow of displacement, but would provide incentives for unemployed workers to find new jobs more quickly. Earnings insurance would thus relieve one of the most painful side effects of economic progress while speeding up the labor market transitions that make progress possible.

The best long-run remedy for the widening earnings inequality in the United States is to improve the skills of workers now stuck at the bottom of the wage distribution. We recommend a fundamental reorientation of the current system for providing non-college-educated workers with improved general occupational skills. We suggest a much more activist government policy to encourage private companies to invest in the job skills of workers who have not received a college education. This policy must be combined with a much greater public-private effort to define and certify necessary occupational skills, preferably within the framework of an expanded apprenticeship system. Improved workplace training is mainly the responsibility of the private sector. The public sector is responsible for preparing young people in school so that they can exploit the training opportunities available to them when they enter the job market. American schools have not fulfilled this responsibility for the majority of students who do not go on to college. The performance of the nation's high schools must be improved, too.

Making Hard Choices and Implementing Change

Some of our suggestions have been advanced in one form or another by earlier analysts. Most involve short-term political or economic pain. For the nation to escape its long-standing economic malaise, however, hard choices are necessary. To eliminate the federal budget deficit, for example, will require short-run sacrifice by those who must pay higher taxes and by others who will be required to accept reductions in government services. To keep U.S. borders open to foreign competition exposes some businesses and workers to harm so that the majority of Americans can benefit. To stimulate investment in machines, workers, and new technology demands that the government abandon the ideology embraced by a large number of Americans and by the Reagan and Bush administrations. A basic tenet of this ideology is that government is part of the problem, not part of the solution. That is clearly wrong. American government can and should help frame solutions to the nation's economic problems. It can do so not by subverting the market but by reinforcing and supplementing it in the limited ways we have suggested in this book.

Economic policy debate in the United States often degenerates into a shouting match between those who do not trust market forces and those who worship markets uncritically. On one side of this debate are people who believe that wealthy Americans and giant corporations abuse their enormous economic power. On the other side are those who believe that government regulation gets in the way or that unemployed workers are encouraged to accept their joblessness because of short-sighted government redistribution policies. Robert Solow has remarked that when he hears critics of capitalism deriding the operation of competitive markets, he wonders why they cannot see the blessings it confers. And when he hears conservative defenders of capitalism extolling the virtues of the market, he wonders why they are blind to the harmful consequences of pollution, monopoly power, and inequality of economic opportunity.[1] We believe the debate over long-term economic policy should reflect an informed and open-minded analysis of options. Proposals to redirect or supplement market forces should always be viewed with healthy skepticism, but they should not be automatically ruled out of bounds.

A new direction for economic policymaking will clearly require presidential leadership. But U.S. presidents can be successful in implementing dramatic policy change only if they are backed by informed public support. The new president and his administration have an excellent opportunity to begin explaining to the American people the logic of policy change and the need to make hard choices. Adopting painful remedies would be made much more palatable if our political leaders also pointed out that the pain need not be as bad as many Americans fear. There can and should be immediate benefits as well as long-run gains.

Consider, for example, the federal budget deficit. The traditional argument for eliminating the deficit is that its reduction is essential for improving long-run economic growth. Indeed, some consider deficit reduction in moral terms, as necessary to prevent saddling the next generation with an earlier generation's debts. But it is also relevant to the present.

Even though the spending cuts and tax increases needed to reduce the deficit would clearly be painful for many, immediate gains could be forthcoming. Deficit reduction, especially if coupled with an easing of monetary policy, would bring down intermediate- and long-term interest rates and benefit a wide range of borrowers, including consumers buying new cars, corporations seeking to finance new investment, and young people hoping to buy new homes. Moreover, lower interest rates would lead to higher prices of stocks and bonds. Thus a tax increase borne by those in higher income brackets could be less painful than popularly believed, since they would disproportionately benefit from the resulting increase in wealth. Policymakers would also find it easier to obtain support for freer trade if they simultaneously implemented programs to cushion the pain of dislocation and to retrain the workers harmed by liberal trade policies. Our recommendations for displacement earnings insurance and a workplace training system provided and supported by all firms are designed to do just that.

The proposals advanced in this book are designed to accelerate change by increasing productivity growth while easing the burdens of change. Proposals to halt economic change in a misguided effort to freeze the status quo will doom the economy to continued stagnation. No economic policy package can work miracles overnight. And no magic bullet can eliminate the problems of slow growth and rising inequality, even in the long run. The experiment with dramatic tax reductions in the early 1980s, for example, worsened our long-run economic problem. It brought on a string of unprecedented peacetime government deficits that continue to cripple national saving as well as the government's capacity to deal with growing inequality.

It is time to implement a comprehensive set of policies that can speed growth and reduce inequality. But it is also time for realism.

There are no free lunches. Hard choices must be made if the nation is to achieve sustained economic improvement. Readers who reject our specific policy suggestions should consider carefully what alternative policies could attain similar effects at equal or lower cost. We do not think inaction is an acceptable policy response to the nation's difficulties. The problem of slow economic growth might be tolerable if all Americans enjoyed equal, though slow, improvement in their living standards. For the past two decades, however, slow economic improvement for middle-class Americans has been accompanied by deteriorating living standards among the less well off. To reverse this trend, the nation must achieve either faster growth or less inequality. We believe the policies recommended in this book can achieve both.

Appendix

Research from the Center for Economic Progress and Employment

Books

Blair, Margaret M. *Handbook on the Deal Decade* (Brookings, forthcoming).
Blair, Margaret M., ed. *The Deal Decade: What Takeovers and Leveraged Buyouts Mean for Corporate Governance.* 1993.
Blinder, Alan S., ed. *Paying for Productivity: A Look at the Evidence.* 1990.
Burtless, Gary, ed. *A Future of Lousy Jobs? The Changing Structure of U.S. Wages.* 1990.
Crandall, Robert W. *Manufacturing on the Move.* 1993.
Denison, Edward F. *Estimates of Productivity Change by Industry: An Evaluation and an Alternative.* 1989.
Huber, Peter W., and Robert E. Litan, eds. *The Liability Maze: The Impact of Liability Law on Safety and Innovation.* 1991.
Litan, Robert E., Robert Z. Lawrence, and Charles L. Schultze, eds. *American Living Standards: Threats and Challenges.* 1988.
Shoven, John B., and Joel Waldfogel, eds. *Debt, Taxes, and Corporate Restructuring.* 1990.

Brookings Papers on Economic Activity, Microeconomics

Baily, Martin Neil, and Clifford Winston, eds. *Brookings Papers on Economic Activity, Microeconomics,* 1988.
    Bresnahan, Timothy F., and Peter C. Reiss. "Do Entry Conditions Vary across Markets?" pp. 833–81.
    Clark, Kim B., W. Bruce Chew, and Takahiro Fujimoto. "Product Development in the World Auto Industry," pp. 729–81.
    Katz, Harry C., Thomas A. Kochan, and Jeffrey H. Keefe. "Industrial Relations and Productivity in the U.S. Automobile Industry," pp. 685–727.
    Levin, Richard C., Alvin K. Klevorick, Richard R. Nelson, and Sidney G. Winter. "Appropriating the Returns from Industrial Research and Development," pp. 783–831.

Lichtenberg, Frank R., and Donald Siegel. "Productivity and Changes in Ownership of Manufacturing Plants," pp. 643–83.

Stiglitz, Joseph E. "Technological Change, Sunk Costs, and Competition," pp. 833–947.

Baily, Martin Neil, and Clifford Winston, eds. *Brookings Papers on Economic Activity, Microeconomics*, 1989.

Griliches, Zvi. "Patents: Recent Trends and Puzzles," pp. 291–330.

Joskow, Paul L. "Regulatory Failure, Regulatory Reform, and Structural Change in the Electrical Power Industry," pp. 125–208.

Katz, Lawrence F., and Lawrence H. Summers. "Industry Rents: Evidence and Implications," pp. 209–90.

Morrison, Steven A., and Clifford Winston. "Enhancing the Performance of the Deregulated Air Transportation System," pp. 61–123.

Pakes, Ariel, and Margaret Simpson. "Patent Renewal Data," pp. 331–410.

Peltzman, Sam. "The Economic Theory of Regulation after a Decade of Deregulation," pp. 1–59.

Baily, Martin Neil, and Clifford Winston, eds. *Brookings Papers on Economic Activity, Microeconomics*, 1990.

Baily, Martin Neil, and Charles L. Schultze. "The Productivity of Capital in a Period of Slower Growth," pp. 369–420.

Bhagat, Sanjai, Andrei Shleifer, and Robert W. Vishny. "Hostile Takeovers in the 1980s: The Return to Corporate Specialization," pp. 1–84.

Hall, Bronwyn H. "The Impact of Corporate Restructuring on Industrial Research and Development," pp. 85–135.

Hart, Oliver, and Jean Tirole. "Vertical Integration and Market Foreclosure," pp. 205–86.

Katz, Michael L., and Janusz A. Ordover. "R&D Cooperation and Competition," pp. 137–203.

Romer, Paul M. "Capital, Labor, and Productivity," pp. 337–67.

Salinger, Michael. "The Concentration-Margins Relationship Reconsidered," pp. 287–335.

Baily, Martin Neil, and Clifford Winston, eds. *Brookings Papers on Economic Activity, Microeconomics*, 1991.

Caves, Richard E., Michael D. Whinston, and Mark A Hurwitz. "Patent Expiration, Entry, and Competition in the U.S. Pharmaceutical Industry," pp. 1–66.

Davis, Steve J., and John Haltiwanger. "Wage Dispersion between and within U.S. Manufacturing Plants, 1963–86," pp. 115–200.

Fisher, Franklin M. "Organizing Industrial Organization: Reflections on the *Handbook of Industrial Organization*," pp. 201–40.

Klevorick, Alvin K. "Directions and Trends in Industrial Organization: A Review Essay on the *Handbook of Industrial Organization*," pp. 241–80.

Mannering, Fred, and Clifford Winston. "Brand Loyalty and the Decline of American Automobile Firms," pp. 67–114.

Willig, Robert D. "Merger Analysis, Industrial Organization Theory, and Merge Guidelines," pp. 281–332.

Baily, Martin Neil, and Clifford Winston, eds. *Brookings Papers on Economic Activity, Microeconomics*, 1992.

Baily, Martin Neil, Charles Hulten, and David Campbell. "Productivity Dynamics in Manufacturing Plants," pp. 187–267.

Boozer, Michael A., Alan B. Krueger, and Shari Wolkon. "Race and School Quality Since *Brown* v. *Board of Education*, pp. 269–338.

Farrell, Joseph, and Carl Shapiro. "Standard Setting in High-Definition Television," pp. 1–93.

Friedlaender, Ann F., Ernst R. Berndt, and Gerard McCullough. "Governance Structure, Managerial Characteristics, and Firm Performance in the Deregulated Rail Industry," pp. 95–186.

Jorgenson, Dale W., Daniel T. Slesnick, and Peter J. Wilcoxen. "Carbon Taxes and Economic Welfare," pp. 393–454.

Lakonishok, Josef, Andrei Shleifer, and Robert W. Vishny. "The Structure and Performance of the Money Management Industry," pp. 339–91.

Related Brookings Research

Aaron, Henry J., and Charles L. Schultze, eds. *Setting Domestic Priorities: What Can Government Do?* 1992.

Aaron, Henry J., Barry P. Bosworth, and Gary T. Burtless. *Can America Afford to Grow Old? Paying for Social Security.* 1989.

Baily, Martin Neil, and Robert J. Gordon. "The Productivity Slowdown, Measurement Issues, and the Explosion of Computer Power." *Brookings Papers on Economic Activity*, 2:1988, pp. 347–431.

Boltuck, Richard, and Robert E. Litan, eds. *Down in the Dumps: Administration of the Unfair Trade Laws.* 1991.

Litan, Robert E., and Clifford Winston, eds. *Liability: Perspectives and Policy.* 1988.

Schultze, Charles L. *Memos to the President: A Guide through Macroeconomics for the Busy Policymaker.* 1992.

Small, Kenneth A., Clifford Winston, and Carol A. Evans. *Road Work: A New Highway Pricing and Investment Policy.* 1989.

Winston, Clifford, and associates. *Blind Intersection? Policy and the Automobile Industry.* 1987.

Winston, Clifford, Thomas M. Corsi, Curtis M. Grimm, and Carol A. Evans. *The Economic Effects of Surface Freight Deregulation.* 1990.

Notes

Chapter One: Introduction and Summary

1. The appendix provides a list of the publications sponsored by the center as well as related books and articles published by Brookings that contain insights and information relevant to the issues discussed here.

2. Arthur M. Okun, *Equality and Efficiency: The Big Tradeoff* (Brookings, 1975).

3. This topic is addressed in Henry J. Aaron and Charles L. Schultze, eds., *Setting Domestic Priorities: What Can Government Do?* (Brookings, 1992).

4. For an excellent guide to the debate on the productivity slowdown, see the papers by Stanley Fischer, Zvi Grilliches, Dale W. Jorgenson, Mancur Olson, and Michael J. Boskin in *Journal of Economic Perspectives*, vol. 2 (Fall 1988).

5. Charles L. Schultze, *Memos to the President: A Guide through Macroeconomics for the Busy Policymaker* (Brookings, 1992).

Chapter Two: Slow Growth and Other Economic Ills

1. William J. Baumol, Sue Anne Batey Blackman, and Edward N. Wolff, *Productivity and American Leadership: The Long View* (MIT Press, 1989).

2. Angus Maddison, "Growth and Slowdown in Advanced Capitalist Economies," *Journal of Economic Literature*, vol. 25 (June 1987), pp. 649–98; and Maddison, "Explaining the Economic Performance of Nations, 1920–1989," paper presented at a New York University conference on the International Convergence of Productivity, April 23–24, 1992.

3. Martin Neil Baily and Robert J. Gordon, "The Productivity Slowdown, Measurement Issues, and the Explosion of Computer Power," *Brookings Papers on Economic Activity*, 2:1988, pp. 347–420 (Hereafter *BPEA*).

4. The method of adjusting for inflation, for example, involves valuing the goods and services produced in the prices of a base year. This overstates growth in subsequent years by counting too heavily in total productivity growth those products and services in which growth is rapid. See ibid.

5. See Henry J. Aaron, Barry P. Bosworth, and Gary Burtless, *Can America*

Afford to Grow Old? Paying for Social Security (Brookings, 1989), especially pp. 91–98.

6. This statement is only approximate because of the existence of trade with other nations. The impact of trade on total U.S. consumption is typically modest, however.

7. U. S. Bureau of the Census, "Money Income and Poverty Status of Families and Persons in the U. S.," *Current Population Reports*, series P-60 (Department of Commerce, various years).

8. Reported in "Time for Uncle Sam to Pitch In?" *Business Week*, April 6, 1992, p. 76.

9. See Barry Bosworth, Gary Burtless, and John Sabelhaus, "The Decline in Saving: Some Microeconomic Evidence," *BPEA*, 1:1991, pp. 183–241.

10. See Barry Bosworth and Gary Burtless, "Effects of Tax Reform on Labor Supply, Investment, and Saving," *Journal of Economic Perspectives*, vol. 6 (Winter 1992).

11. The declinist literature is large and growing. Its most prominent entry is by Paul M. Kennedy, *The Rise and Fall of the Great Powers* (Random House, 1987). Lester C. Thurow's *Head to Head: The Coming Economic Battle among Japan, Europe and America* (William Morrow, 1992) is one of the most recent. For opposing views, see Joseph S. Nye, *Bound to Lead: The Changing Nature of American Power* (Basic Books, 1990); and Henry R. Nau, *The Myth of America's Decline: Leading the World Economy into the 1990's* (Oxford University Press, 1990).

12. For example, one of the aspirants for the Democratic presidential nomination, former Senator Paul S. Tsongas, entitled his election manifesto *A Call to Economic Arms: Forging a New American Mandate* (Boston: Tsongas Committee, 1992). The analogy of military competition is also used in the title of Thurow's thoughtful book on current economic issues, *Head to Head: The Coming Battle among Japan, Europe and America*. Although Thurow eschews the military analogy in favor of an athletic one, the title and some of the discussion in his book nevertheless imply that the economic challenge facing the United States has elements of international confrontation rather than cooperation.

13. Alice Rivlin, *Reviving the American Dream: The Economy, the States, and the Federal Government* (Brookings, 1992), chap. 2.

14. Robert Reich, "Do We Want U.S. to Be Rich or Japan Poor?" *Wall Street Journal*, June 18, 1990, p. A10.

15. Some economists have attempted to place market values on certain nontraded activities and factors, but there is no conventionally accepted single measure of overall welfare or standard living that has been consistently quantified over an extended period of time. For selected references, see William D. Nordhaus and James Tobin, "Is Growth Obsolete?" in Milton Moss, ed., *The Measurement of Economic and Social Performance* (National Bureau of Economic Research, 1973), pp. 509–31.

16. See, for example, Robert Repetto, "Environmental Productivity and Why It Is So Important," *Challenge*, vol. 33 (September–October 1990), pp. 33–38.

17. *1988 Annual Report of the Board of Trustees of the Old-Age and Survivors Insurance and Disability Insurance Trust Funds* (Baltimore: Social Security Administration, 1988), p. 79.

18. *1986 Green Book*, Committee Print, House Committee on Ways and Means, 99 Cong. 2 sess. (Government Printing Office, 1986), pp. 82, 84; and *1991 Green Book*, 102 Cong. 1 sess. (GPO, 1991), p. 1343.

19. Most important, Denison removed capital depreciation from his measure of output and adjusted for the effects of the business cycle. Edward F. Denison, *Trends in American Economic Growth, 1929–82* (Brookings, 1985).

20. Dale W. Jorgenson, Frank M. Gollop, and Barbara M. Fraumeni, *Productivity and U.S. Economic Growth* (Harvard University Press, 1987).

21. See Charles Murray and R.J. Herrnstein, "What's Really Behind the SAT Score Decline?" *Public Interest*, vol. 106 (Winter 1992), pp. 32–56; and John H. Bishop, "Is the Test Score Decline Responsible for the Productivity Growth Decline?" *American Economic Review*, vol. 79 (March 1989), pp. 178–97.

22. Bishop, "Is the Test Score Decline Responsible?"

23. These studies are reviewed and cited in Baily and Gordon, "Productivity Slowdown."

24. David Aschauer "Is Public Expenditure Productive?" *Journal of Monetary Economics*, vol. 23 (March 1989), pp. 177–200.

25. F. M. Scherer, "Lagging Productivity Growth: Measurement, Technology, and Shock Effects," Harvard University, Kennedy School of Government, September 1992.

26. Martin Neil Baily and Alok K. Chakrabarti, *Innovation and the Productivity Crisis* (Brookings, 1988).

27. Robert H. Hayes and William J. Abernathy, "Managing Our Way to Economic Decline," *Harvard Business Review*, vol. 58 (July–August 1980), pp. 67–77.

28. Ibid.

29. Michael L. Dertouzos and others, *Made in America: Regaining the Productive Edge* (MIT Press, 1989).

30. For a discussion of ideas similar to these see Mancur Olson, "The Productivity Slowdown, the Oil Shocks, and the Real Cycle," *Journal of Economic Perspectives*, vol. 2 (Fall 1988), pp. 43–71.

31. The real exchange rate of the United States measures the value of the dollar in terms of the level of goods and services the dollar can buy in foreign countries at current exchange rates. If inflation rates are the same in both the United States and its trading partners, a decline in the real dollar exchange rate occurs if one dollar buys fewer units of foreign currency, that is, fewer marks or pounds or yen.

32. Hendrik Houthakker and Stephen P. Magee, "Income and Price Elasticities in World Trade," *Review of Economics and Statistics* vol. 51 (May 1969), pp. 111–25.

33. Robert Z. Lawrence, "The International Dimension," in Robert E. Litan, Robert Z. Lawrence, and Charles L. Schultze, eds., *American Living Standards: Threats and Challenges* (Brookings, 1988), pp. 41–49. For a survey of

similar estimates, see Robert A. Blecker, "Structural Roots of U.S. Trade Problems: Income Elasticities, Secular Trends, and Hysteresis," *Journal of Post-Keynesian Economics*, vol. 14 (Spring 1992), pp. 321–46.

34. Stephen S. Cohen and John Zysman, *Manufacturing Matters: The Myth of the Post-Industrial Economy* (Basic Books, 1987).

35. Tsongas, *Call to Economic Arms*.

36. When manufacturing output is measured in inflation-adjusted dollars, the share of manufacturing in total output appears to be relatively flat over the past several decades. See Robert Z. Lawrence, *Can America Compete?* (Brookings, 1984). Lawrence R. Mishel has made some valid, technical criticisms of this finding, but they do not, in our view, fundamentally change the conclusion. See *Manufacturing Numbers: How Inaccurate Statistics Conceal U.S. Industrial Decline* (Washington: Economic Policy Institute, 1988). When manufacturing output and total output are measured in current dollars, however, the share of manufacturing has been declining.

37. Dale Russakoff, "Lives Once Solid as Steel Shatter in Changed World," *Washington Post*, April 13, 1992, p. A14.

Chapter Three: Inequality

1. These wage developments were examined in detail in the essays in Gary Burtless, ed., *A Future of Lousy Jobs? The Changing Structure of U.S. Wages* (Brookings, 1990).

2. Joseph A. Pechman, "The Future of the Income Tax," *American Economic Review*, vol. 80 (March 1990), pp. 2–3.

3. Chinhui Juhn, Kevin M. Murphy, and Robert H. Topel, "Why Has the Natural Rate of Unemployment Increased over Time?" *Brookings Papers on Economic Activity*, 2:1991, p. 78. (Hereafter *BPEA*.)

4. U.S. Bureau of The Census, "Poverty in the United States, 1991," *Current Population Reports, Consumer Income*, series P-60, no. 181 (Department of Commerce, 1992), p. 4.

5. Gary Burtless, "Earnings Inequality over the Business and Demographic Cycles," in Burtless, ed., *A Future of Lousy Jobs?* pp. 77–117; Robert A. Moffitt, "The Distribution of Earning and the Welfare State," in ibid., pp. 201–30; and Lynn A. Karoly, *The Trend in Inequality among Families and Workers in the United States: A Twenty-Five-Year Perspective* (Santa Monica, Calif.: Rand, 1992).

6. Hourly *compensation* rather than hourly money wages represents a better approximation to the pure price of labor. Unfortunately, the Census Bureau cannot collect reliable information about the compensation paid to individual workers because few know how much their employers pay for health and social insurance and private pension contributions. To measure labor market inequality, analysts are therefore forced to rely on information on money wages rather than compensation.

7. *Economic Report of the President, February 1992*, p. 344.

8. Chinhui Juhn, Kevin M. Murphy, and Brooks Pearce, "Wage Inequality

and the Rise in the Returns to Skill," University of Chicago, Department of Economics, October 1989, pp. 25–27.

9. Juhn, Murphy, and Pearce estimate that almost 90 percent of the growth in inequality of male wages since 1979 is due to the growth of inequality within each of the major industries. Ibid.

10. *Economic Report of the President, February 1992*, p. 340.

11. Burtless, "Earnings Inequality."

12. McKinley L. Blackburn, David E. Bloom, and Richard B. Freeman, "The Declining Economic Position of Less Skilled American Men," in Burtless, ed., *A Future of Lousy Jobs?* pp. 31–76; and Lawrence F. Katz and Kevin M. Murphy, "Changes in Relative Wages, 1963–1987: Supply and Demand Factors," NBER working paper 3927 (Cambridge, Mass.: National Bureau of Economic Research, December 1991).

13. *The Universal Almanac, 1992*, p. 216. The rate jumped from an average annual rate of about 1.6 per 1,000 residents in the 1950s and 1960s to 2.9 per 1,000 in the 1980s.

14. Richard B. Freeman and Harry Holzer, "The Deterioration of Employment and Earnings Opportunities for Less Educated Young Americans: A Review of Evidence," NBER, August 18, 1991, p. 9.

15. George J. Borjas, Richard B. Freeman, and Lawrence F. Katz, "On the Labor Market Effects of Immigration and Trade," NBER working paper 3761 (June 1991).

16. Katz and Murphy, "Changes in Relative Wages," pp. 20–23.

17. William B. Johnston and others, *Workforce 2000: Work and Workers for the 21st Century* (Indianapolis: Hudson Institute, 1987).

18. Ann P. Bartel and Frank R. Lichtenberg, "The Comparative Advantage of Educated Workers in Implementing New Technology," *Review of Economics and Statistics*, vol. 69 (February 1987), pp. 1–11.

19. Alan B. Krueger, "How Computers Have Changed the Wage Structure: Evidence from Microdata, 1984–89," Princeton University Economics Department, August 1991.

20. Juhn, Murphy, and Pearce, "Wage Inequality"; Burtless, ed., *A Future of Lousy Jobs?*; and Katz and Murphy, "Changes in Relative Wages."

21. Freeman and Holzer, "Deterioration of Employment," p. 15.

22. Blackburn, Bloom, and Freeman, "Declining Economic Position," pp. 31–76; and Richard B. Freeman, "Employment and Earnings of Disadvantaged Young Men in a Labor Shortage Economy," in Christopher Jencks and Paul E. Peterson, eds., *The Urban Underclass* (Brookings, 1991), pp. 103–21. One of the reasons that unionization declined is that industries with high unionization rates have declined. However, the estimates of these authors are supposed to reflect the effect of declining unionization rates within U.S. industries.

23. John A. Byrne, "What, Me Overpaid? CEO's Fight Back," *Business Week*, May 4, 1992, p. 143.

24. Lester C. Thurow, *Generating Inequality: Mechanisms of Distribution in the U.S. Economy*, (Basic Books, 1975), p. 6.

25. Census statistics on family income reflect the experiences of American

families but not unrelated individuals. A family, as defined by the Census Bureau, is group of two or more persons related by blood, marriage, or adoption who share living quarters.

26. Congressional Budget Office, "Measuring the Distribution of Income Gains," staff memorandum, March 1992, p. 3.

27. *1991 Green Book*, Committee Print, House Committee on Ways and Means, 102 Cong. 1 sess. (GPO, May 1991), pp. 1226–27.

28. To correct for differences in family size, CBO calculates individual families' incomes in terms of multiples of the poverty threshold for family units of different sizes. In 1989, for example, the poverty line was equal to $6,311 for an unrelated individual, $8,076 for a family of two, $9,885 for a family of three, and so on (*Universal Almanac, 1992*, p. 225). To translate multiples of the poverty threshold into understandable income amounts, we assume each family unit has 2.4 members—the average in 1989—and calculate the poverty threshold for the average family as $9,161. If the average family in a quintile has an income equal to twice the poverty threshold, the table would show its income as $18,322 (two times $9,161). Readers should remember that the figures shown in the table reflect approximate family *living standards* rather than exact income levels reported by families and unrelated individuals in each quintile.

29. Barry Bosworth and Gary Burtless, "Effects of Tax Reform on Labor Supply, Investment, and Saving," *Journal of Economic Perspectives*, vol. 6 (Winter 1992), pp. 11–14.

30. Rebecca M. Blank, "Why Were Poverty Rates So High in the 1980s?" NBER working paper 3878 (October 1991).

31. See Timothy M. Smeeding, Michael O'Higgins, and Lee Rainwater, eds., *Poverty, Inequality, and Income Distribution in Comparative Perspective: The Luxembourg Income Study (LIS)* (Washington: Urban Institute Press, 1990), especially pp. 33–49.

32. Barry Bosworth, Gary Burtless, and John Sebelhaus, "The Decline in Saving: Some Microeconomic Evidence," *BPEA, 1:1991*, pp. 183–241.

33. Greg J. Duncan and James N. Morgan, eds., *Five Thousand American Families—Patterns of Economic Progress*, vol. 4: *Family Composition Change* (Ann Arbor, Mich.: Institute for Social Research, 1976), p. 339.

34. Peter Gottschalk, Sarah McLanahan, and Gary Sandefur, "The Dynamics and Intergenerational Transmission of Poverty and Welfare Participation," Institute for Research on Poverty, October 1992. Joan R. Rodgers and John L. Rodgers, using very different methods, found that the persistence of American poverty worsened in the 1980s compared with the 1970s. See "Chronic Poverty in the United States," *Journal of Human Resources*, forthcoming.

35. Gary Burtless, "Inequality in America; Where Do We Stand?" *Brookings Review*, vol. 5 (Summer 1987), p. 14.

Chapter Four: Increasing the Pace of Innovation

1. Robert M. Solow, "Technical Change and the Aggregate Production Function," *Review of Economics and Statistics*, vol. 39 (August 1957), pp. 312–20;

Edward F. Denison, *Trends in American Economic Growth, 1929–82* (Brookings 1985); and Dale W. Jorgenson, Frank W. Gollop, and Barbara M. Fraumeni, *Productivity and U.S. Economic Growth* (Harvard University Press, 1987).

2. Linda R. Cohen and Roger Noll, with Jeffrey S. Banks, Susan A. Edelman, and William M. Pegman, *The Technology Pork Barrel* (Brookings, 1991).

3. Edwin Mansfield, "Academic Research and Industrial Innovation," *Research Policy*, vol. 20 (1991), pp. 1–12.

4. Richard R. Nelson, Merton J. Peck, and Edward D. Kalachek, *Technology, Economic Growth and Public Policy* (Brookings, 1967).

5. Kenneth Flamm, *Creating the Computer: Government, Industry, and High Technology* (Brookings, 1988).

6. Richard R. Nelson, "U.S. Technological Leadership: Where Did It Come from and Where Did It Go?" in F. M. Scherer and Mark Perlman, eds., *Entrepreneurship, Technological Innovation, and Economic Growth: Studies in the Schumpeterian Tradition* (University of Michigan, 1992), pp. 25–50.

7. Ibid.

8. In the shuttle project, adequate consideration was not given to radically different designs for the shuttle. And the initial project evaluation ignored the alternative of improving unmanned launch vehicles. In the breeder project, only very-high-conversion targets were considered, targets that turned out to be costly and difficult to meet. The focus of the synfuels project was on using eastern coal, even though western coal is much easier to convert into gas or liquid fuel.

9. Panel on the Government Role in Civilian Technology, *The Government Role in Civilian Technology: Building a New Alliance* (Washington: National Academy Press, 1992).

10. Carnegie Commission on Science Technology and Government, *Technology and Economic Performance: Organizing the Executive Branch for a Stronger National Technology Base* (New York, September 1991).

11. Linda R. Cohen and Roger G. Noll, "The Applications Technology Satellite Program" in Cohen and Noll, *Technology Pork Barrel*, pp. 173–77.

12. Joseph Farrell and Carl Shapiro, "Standard Setting in High-Definition Television," *Brookings Papers on Economic Activity, Microeconomics, 1992*, pp. 1–77. (Hereafter *BPEA, Micro*.)

13. Bruce L. R. Smith, "Critical Technologies," *Brookings Review*, vol. 10 (Winter 1992), p. 54.

14. For a discussion of the puzzle of slow productivity growth in the service sector, see Martin Neil Baily "Productivity and the Electronics Revolution," *Bell Atlantic Quarterly*, vol. 3 (Summer 1986); and Stephen S. Roach "Policy Challenges in an Era of Restructuring," Special Economic Study, Morgan Stanley, New York, January 8, 1992.

15. See for example, Martin Neil Baily and Robert Z. Lawrence, "Tax Policies for Innovation and Competitiveness," April 3, 1987, and "Tax Incentives for R&D: What Do the Data Tell Us?" Studies prepared for the Council on Research and Technology, Washington, January 28, 1992.

16. Edwin Mansfield "Microeconomics of Technological Innovation," in Ralph Landau and Nathan Rosenberg, eds., *The Positive Sum Strategy: Har-*

nessing Technology for Economic Growth (Washington: National Academy Press, 1986), pp. 307–25.

17. Robert Eisner, testimony, August 2 and 3, 1984, in *Research and Experimentation Tax Credit*, Hearing before the Subcommittee on Oversight of the House Committee on Ways and Means, 98 Cong. 2 sess. (GPO, 1985), pp. 64–82.

18. Two analytical approaches were used to obtain these estimates. First, dummy variables were introduced covering the main subperiods where the incentives varied. The second approach specified a numerical variable giving the percentage tax incentive for commercial R&D in each year.

19. James R. Hines, Jr., "On the Sensitivity of R&D to Delicate Tax Changes: The Behavior of U.S. Multinationals in the 1980s," Harvard University, November 1991.

20. Because the cost of R&D goes *down* when there is a tax credit, these estimates are equivalent to finding elasticities of 1.5 or 1.6 with respect to the incentives provided by the credit, substantially larger than the ones reported by Baily and Lawrence. Differences in results were to be expected, however, because Hines's empirical strategy was very different from the earlier one. Baily and Lawrence looked at R&D spending over time and determined whether it was increased by the availability and generosity of the credit. The variation of R&D over time is a natural way to test for the credit's effectiveness, but it can yield an overestimate or underestimate of the impact of the credit if other changes in the investment climate occur at the same time. Hines looked instead at a cross-section of companies and determined whether R&D grew more slowly in companies that were subject to 861-8 than it did in companies with deficit foreign tax credits. His approach seems better in principle at eliminating the effects of extraneous factors, although the elasticities that he estimates are surprisingly high.

21. Michael L. Dertouzos, Richard K. Lester, and Robert M. Solow, *Made In America: Regaining the Productive Edge* (MIT Press, 1989).

22. Martin Neil Baily and Alok K. Chakrabarti, *Innovation and the Productivity Crisis* (Brookings 1988).

23. For a persuasive demonstration along these lines, see Council on Competitiveness, *Capital Choices: Changing the Way America Invests in Industry* (Washington, 1992).

24. Ibid.

25. Adolf A. Berle and Gardiner C. Means, *The Modern Corporation and Private Property* (New York: Commerce Clearing House, 1932).

26. Economists have since relabeled the problem identified by Berle and Means as the "principal-agent" problem, which arises when the interests of managers (as agents) do not coincide with those of their shareholders (as principals). See Michael C. Jensen, "Agency Costs of Free Cash Flow, Corporate Finance, and Takeovers," *American Economic Review*, vol. 76 (May 1986, *Papers and Proceedings, 1985*), pp. 323–29.

27. In 1950, households held over 90 percent of all corporate equities, but their share in 1991 was a little more than 50 percent. See Margaret M. Blair, *Handbook on the Deal Decade* (Brookings, forthcoming).

28. William F. Long and David J. Ravenscraft, "Decade of Debt: Lessons from LBOs in the 1980s," in Margaret M. Blair, ed., *The Deal Decade: What Takeovers and Leveraged Buyouts Mean for Corporate Governance* (Brookings, forthcoming).

29. Frank Lichtenberg and Donald Siegel, "Productivity and Changes in Ownership of Manufacturing Plants," *BPEA, Micro, 1987*, pp. 643–73.

30. See Sanjai Bhagat, Andrei Shleifer, and Robert W. Vishny, "Hostile Takeovers in the 1980s: The Return to Corporate Specialization," *BPEA, Micro, 1990*, pp. 1–72.

31. Frank Lichtenberg, "Industrial Dediversification and its Consequences for Productivity," NBER working paper 3231 (Cambridge, Mass.: National Bureau of Economic Research, January 1990).

32. See, for example, Bronwyn H. Hall, "The Impact of Corporate Restructuring on Industrial Research and Development," *BPEA, Micro, 1990*, pp. 85–124, for findings on R&D, and Long and Ravenscraft, "Decade of Debt," for findings on investment.

33. Margaret M. Blair and Martha Schary, "Industry Level Pressures to Restructure," in Blair, *Deal Decade*.

34. See Barrie A. Wigmore, "The Decline in Credit Quality of New Issue Junk Bonds, 1980–88," *Financial Analysts Journal*, vol. 46 (September–October, 1990), pp. 53–62. In 1991 *Fortune* followed the performance of forty-one companies identified in previous years as "deals of the year" and found that only nineteen were financially stronger; fourteen were financially weaker and seven had either defaulted on their bonds, entered chapter 11, been restructured, or liquidated. See Edmund Faltermayer, "The Deal Decade: Verdict on the 80's," *Fortune*, August 26, 1991, pp. 58–74.

35. John Pound, "Beyond Takeovers: Politics Comes to Corporate Control," *Harvard Business Review*, vol. 70 (March–April 1992), p. 83.

36. For discussions of these developments, see Pound, "Beyond Takeovers," and John Pound, "After Takeovers, Quiet Diplomacy," *Wall Street Journal*, June 8, 1992, p. A10.

37. The SEC also requested comment on a proposal by Edward Regan, the comptroller of the state of New York, to allow large shareholders to enclose a brief critique of their companies' performance with the annual proxy statement, providing reasons, if any, why they would not support the nominees to the board of directors.

38. It may also be desirable to change or remove current rules of the Federal Trade Commission that require notification if a shareholder takes certain actions deemed "inconsistent with an investment-only intent" (including nominations of directors, proposing corporate action requiring shareholder approval, and soliciting proxies). See Michael T. Jacobs, *Short-Term America: The Causes and Cures of Our Business Myopia* (Harvard Business School Press, 1991), pp. 47–50.

39. Robert N. McCauley and Steven A. Zimmer, "Explaining International Differences in the Cost of Capital," *Federal Reserve Bank of New York Quarterly Review*, vol. 14 (Summer 1989), p. 22.

40. See Takeo Hoshi, Anil Kashyap, and David Scharfstein, "The Role of

Banks in Reducing the Costs of Financial Distress in Japan," *Journal of Financial Economics*, vol. 27 (September 1990), p. 70.

41. In fact, there is strong evidence that banks seek to maintain capital-to-asset ratios above the regulatory minimum, so even a higher capital standard for banks invested in corporate equities would not prevent those that suffered an erosion in their capital due to declining equity values from constraining their growth to keep their capital ratios above the higher minimum. See Herbert Baer and John McElravey, "Capital Adequacy and the Growth of U.S. Banks," working papers series, Federal Reserve Bank of Chicago, June 1992.

42. Michael E. Porter, "Capital Disadvantage: America's Failing Capital Investment System," *Harvard Business Review*, vol. 70 (September–October 1992), pp. 65–82.

43. In fact, Michael Jacobs cites Labor Department data indicating that annual turnover of pension portfolios is more than 50 percent. Jacobs, *Short-Term America*, p. 42.

44. Ibid., pp. 51–52.

45. Josef Lakonishok, Andrei Shleifer, and Robert Vishny, "The Structure and Performance of the Money Management Industry," *BPEA, Micro, 1992*, pp. 339–91.

46. About 30 percent of the variation in compensation was due to company size, but more than 60 percent of the variation was unexplained. See Graef S. Crystal, "Executive Compensation in Corporate America 1991," United Shareholders Association, Washington, 1991. For similar findings that the relationship between executive compensation and company performance is tenuous, see Michael C. Jensen and Kevin J. Murphy, "Performance Pay and Top Management Incentives," *Journal of Political Economy*, vol. 98, (April 1990), pp. 225–64.

47. See Blinder, "More Like Them?" p. 58.

48. Michael T. Jacobs argues that stock options may create perverse incentives on the part of the managers who receive them, encouraging them to have their companies retain profits and reinvest them in projects with potentially lackluster returns. See *Short-Term America*, p. 205. But managers already have other incentives not to retain profits in an effort to build up the size of the company, namely the desire to work at larger companies that typically provide their managers higher salaries and corporate perquisites. To the extent they view their stock options as investments, however, they would not want profits reinvested in projects with potentially subpar returns.

49. Porter, "Capital Disadvantage."

50. The penalty might even apply for executives or directors who leave their companies, on the grounds that one important function for which they should be held responsible is picking their successors.

51. Tillinghast Company, "Tort Cost Trends: An International Perspective," Philadelphia, 1989.

52. See papers by John Graham and Andrew Craig in Peter W. Huber and Robert E. Litan, eds., *The Liability Maze: The Impact of Liability Law on Safety and Innovation* (Brookings, 1991).

53. Industries that were particularly affected by high tort costs included general aviation, rubber products, some fabricated metal products and metal-working machinery, electrical equipment apparatus, and scientific instruments. See W. Kip Viscusi and Michael J. Moore, "An Industrial Profile of the Links between Product Liability and Innovation," in Huber and Litan, *Liability Maze*, pp. 81–119; see also W. Kip Viscusi, *Product Liability* (Harvard University Press, 1991), and testimony of Kip Viscusi in *Product Liability Laws and Their Impact on Small Business Innovation and Competitiveness*, Hearing before the Senate Committee on Small Business, 102 Cong. 2 sess. (GPO, 1992), pp. 9–54.

54. Some investigators have found corroborating anecdotal evidence of this effect in other industries, notably in automobiles, medical devices, and pharmaceuticals. See the papers by Murray Mackay, Laurence Tancredi and Dorothy Nelkin, and Louis Lasagna, in Huber and Litan, *Liability Maze*.

55. Contrary to the pronouncements of critics of some of these proposals, there is empirical evidence that several—notably, modification of the "joint and several" liability doctrine and limiting noneconomic and punitive damages—have indeed lowered insurance costs and premiums. See Glenn Blackmon and Richard Zeckhauser, "State Tort Reform Legislation: Assessing Our Control of Risks," in Peter Schuck, ed., *Tort Law and the Public Interest: Competition, Innovation, and Consumer Welfare* (Norton and American Assembly Press, 1991), pp. 272–300.

56. We emphasize that we do not mean that these federal agencies should mandate even tougher design and product standards. For the well-known reasons outlined by Charles Schultze, such "command and control" regulation is generally ineffective when compared to incentive-based regulatory tools, including taxes and tradable permits. However, even the incentive systems require vigilant enforcement, and this is the activity that we recommend strengthening. See Charles L. Schultze, *The Public Use of Private Interest* (Brookings, 1977).

57. Under the National Cooperative Research Act of 1984, firms that notify the Federal Trade Commission and the Department of Justice of their intent to enter a joint R&D arrangement will have their activities judged under a "rule of reason" rather than a per se standard of illegality under the antitrust laws. In addition, even if such arrangements are found to be unreasonable restraints of trade, the parties are subject only to single damages, not the ordinary treble damages applicable for other antitrust violations.

58. Michael L. Katz and Janusz A. Ordover, "R&D Cooperation and Competition," *BPEA, Micro, 1990*, p. 171.

59. See John Carey and Otis Port, "One Stepper forward for Sematech," *Business Week*, June 8, 1992, pp. 110–12. This article also suggests that Sematech has aided the development of advanced-circuit printing tools.

60. See, for example, the general discussion of the Katz and Ordover paper, *BPEA, Micro, 1990*, pp. 197–98.

61. Charles Schultze delivered one of the earliest and most effective attacks on industrial policy. See "Industrial Policy: A Dissent," *Brookings Review*, vol. 2 (Fall 1983), pp. 3–12. For a more recent attack, see Pietro Nivola, "More

Like Them? The Political Feasibility of Trade Policy," *Brookings Review*, vol. 9 (Spring 1991), pp. 14–21.

62. Charles L. Schultze, *Memos to the President: A Guide through Macroeconomics for the Busy Policymaker* (Brookings, 1992), p. 321.

Chapter Five: Improving the Labor Market

1. John E. Chubb and Eric A. Hanushek, "Reforming Educational Reform," in Henry J. Aaron, ed., *Setting National Priorities: Policy for the Nineties* (Brookings, 1990), p. 215.

2. Carnegie Commission on Science, Technology, and Government, *In the National Interest: The Federal Government in the Reform of K-12 Math and Science Education* (New York: Carnegie Corporation, 1991), p. 18.

3. *National Assessment of Educational Progress*, various issues, cited in Robert B. Reich, *The Work of Nations: Preparing Ourselves for 21st Century Capitalism* (Vintage Books, 1992), p. 227.

4. Richard J. Murnane and Frank Levy, "Education and Training," in Henry J. Aaron and Charles L. Schultze, eds., *Setting Domestic Priorities: What Can Government Do?* (Brookings, 1992), p. 190.

5. General Accounting Office, *Training Strategies: Preparing Noncollege Youth for Employment in the U.S. and Foreign Countries*, GAO/HRD-90-88 (May 1990), pp. 12, 16–17, 36–37; and Michael L. Dertouzos and others, *Made in America: Regaining the Productive Edge* (MIT Press, 1989), p. 87.

6. Dertouzos and others, *Made in America*, pp. 87–88. See also General Accounting Office, *Training Strategies*, pp. 17–18, 37–38.

7. General Accounting Office, *Training Strategies*, p. 18.

8. Lee A. Lillard and Hong W. Tan, *Private Sector Training: Who Gets It and What Are Its Effects?* (Santa Monica, Calif.: Rand, March 1986), pp. 11–17.

9. Robert I. Lerman and Hillard Pouncy, "The Compelling Case for Youth Apprenticeships," *Public Interest*, no. 101 (Fall 1990), p. 69.

10. Lillard and Tan, *Private Sector Training*, p. vi.

11. Departments of Labor, Education, and Commerce, *Building a Quality Workforce* (1988), cited in General Accounting Office, *Training Strategies*, p. 10.

12. Sar A. Levitan and Frank Gallo, "Got to Learn to Earn: Preparing Americans for Work," occasional paper 1991-3, Center for Social Policy Studies, George Washington University, September 1991, p. 38.

13. See, for example, Heizo Takenaka, *Contemporary Japanese Economy and Economic Policy* (University of Michigan Press, 1991), pp. 160–65; Masanori Hashimoto, "Employment and Wage Systems in Japan and Their Implications for Productivity," in Alan S. Blinder, ed., *Paying for Productivity: A Look at the Evidence* (Brookings, 1990), pp. 247–51; and Alan S. Blinder, "Maintaining Competitiveness with High Wages," occasional paper 26, International Center for Economic Growth, San Francisco, 1992, p. 25.

14. Ellen Graham, "High Tech Training: Companies Turn to Technology

to Try to Bring Their Employees Up to Speed," *Wall Street Journal*, February 9, 1990, p. R16.

15. "Odd Jobs," *Washington Post*, June 28, 1992, p. H2; and *Economic Report of the President, February 1992*, p. 334.

16. See Thomas E. Faison and others, *Ahead of the Curve: Basic Skills Programs in Four Exceptional Firms* (Washington: Southport Institute for Policy Analysis, 1992), especially pp. 7–17.

17. See Lisa M. Lynch, "Private-Sector Training and the Earnings of Young Workers," *American Economic Review*, vol. 82 (March 1992), pp. 299–312; and Lynch, "Differential Effects of Post-School Training on Early Career Mobility," NBER working paper 4034 (Cambridge, Mass: National Bureau of Economic Research, 1992).

18. For recent discussions of school reform, see John E. Chubb and Terry M. Moe, *Politics, Markets, and America's Schools* (Brookings, 1990); and Chubb and Hanushek, "Reforming Educational Reform."

19. This discussion is based on John Bishop, "Incentives for Learning: Why American High School Students Compare So Poorly to Their Counterparts Overseas," in Commission on Workforce Quality and Labor Market Efficiency, *Investing in People: A Strategy to Address America's Workforce Crisis*, background papers, vol. 1 (Washington: Department of Labor, 1989), pp. 1–84; James E. Rosenbaum, "What If Good Jobs Depended on Good Grades?" *American Educator*, vol. 13 (Winter 1989), pp. 10–15, 40–42; and Albert Shanker, "A Proposal for Using Incentives to Restructure our Public Schools," *Aspen Institute Quarterly*, vol. 3 (Spring 1991), pp. 72–108.

20. Laura Sharpe and others, *Vouchered Training: Past Experiences and Their Implications for Future Manpower Programs* (Washington: Bureau of Social Science Research, April 1982).

21. Lerman and Pouncy, "Compelling Case for Youth Apprenticeship," p. 65.

22. Joint prepared statement of Marc Bendick, Jr., and Mary Lou Egan, "Promoting Employer-Provided Worker Reskilling: Lessons from a Tax Credit System in France," in *Competitiveness and the Quality of the American Work force*, Hearings before the Subcommittee on Education and Health of the Joint Economic Committee, 100 Cong. 1 sess. (GPO, 1988), pp. 70–72.

23. If no employers provided qualified training, a 1 percent payroll tax would raise about $23 billion. It might be desirable to impose the same tax and training obligation on government employers, but constitutional scholars doubt that the federal government can impose payroll taxes on state governments.

24. See, for example, Lerman and Pouncy, "Compelling Case for Youth Apprenticeships."

25. General Accounting Office, *Training Strategies*, p. 32; and General Accounting Office, *Transition from School to Work: Linking Education and Worksite Training*, GAO/HRD-91-105 (August 1991), p. 2.

26. Lerman and Pouncy, "Compelling Case for Youth Apprenticeships," p. 69.

27. General Accounting Office, *Apprenticeship Training: Administration, Use and Equal Opportunity*, GAO/HRD-92-43 (March 1992), p. 20.

28. See General Accounting Office, *Training Strategies*, p. 17.

29. Burt S. Barnow, "The Impact of CETA Programs on Earnings: A Review of the Literature," *Journal of Human Resources*, vol. 22 (Spring 1987), pp. 157–93.

30. Howard S. Bloom and others, "The National JTPA Study: Title II-A Impacts on Earnings and Employment at 18 Months—Executive Summary," Abt Associates, Bethesda, Md., 1992, p. 4. In comparison with typical evaluation results, these findings are unusually credible. The estimates were obtained in a controlled, random-assignment experiment rather than by using more questionable statistical methods.

31. See Bloom and others, "National JTPA Study," p. 4.

32. See especially Martin L. Weitzman, *The Share Economy: Conquering Stagflation* (Harvard University Press, 1984).

33. Alan S. Blinder, ed., *Paying for Productivity: A Look at the Evidence* (Brookings, 1990).

34. See Ronald Ehrenberg, "Comment," in ibid., p. 89.

35. Daniel J. B. Mitchell, David Lewin, and Edward E. Lawler III, "Alternative Pay Systems, Firm Performance, and Productivity," in ibid., pp. 15–88.

36. Martin L. Weitzman and Daniel L. Kruse, "Profit Sharing and Productivity," in ibid., pp. 95–140.

37. See David I. Levine and Laura D'Andrea Tyson, "Participation, Productivity, and the Firm's Environment," in ibid., pp. 183–237.

Chapter Six: Promoting Investment

1. See Andrew Dean and others, "Saving Trends and Behaviour in OECD Countries," *OECD Economic Studies*, no. 14 (Spring 1990), pp. 7–58.

2. Charles Schultze, *Memos to the President: A Guide through Macroeconomics for the Busy Policymaker* (Brookings, 1992), p. 50.

3. Barry Bosworth, Gary Burtless, and John Sabelhaus, "The Decline in Saving: Some Microeconomic Evidence," *Brookings Papers on Economic Activity* 1991: 1, pp. 183–256.

4. Another piece of evidence suggests that demographic changes have had very little effect on the overall personal saving rate. The saving rate from the end of World War II through 1980 was remarkably stable, hovering at or near 8 percent of disposable income, even though the age composition of the population changed greatly during this period. See ibid., pp. 195–206.

5. See Daniel Feenberg and Jonathan Skinner, "Sources of IRA Saving," in Lawrence Summers, ed., *Tax Policy and the Economy 3* (MIT Press, 1989), pp. 25–46; William G. Gale and John Karl Scholz, "IRAs and Household Saving," University of Wisconsin, Madison, July 1990; Harvey Galper and Charles Byce, "Individual Retirement Accounts: Facts and Issues," *Tax Notes*, vol. 31 (June 2, 1986), pp. 917–21; Jane G. Gravelle, "Do Individual Retirement Accounts Increase Savings?" *Journal of Economic Perspectives*, vol. 5 (Spring

1991), pp. 133–48; Steven F. Venti and David A. Wise, "Tax-Deferred Accounts, Constrained Choice, and Estimation of Individual Saving," *Review of Economic Studies*, vol. 53 (August 1986), pp. 579–601; and Venti and Wise, "Have IRAs Increased U.S. Saving? Evidence from Consumer Expenditures Surveys," NBER working paper 2217 (Cambridge, Mass., National Bureau of Economic Research, April 1987.)

6. For a detailed presentation, see H. Ross Perot, *United We Stand: How We Can Take Back Our Country* (Hyperion, 1992).

7. *The CSIS Strengthening of America Commission* (Washington: Center for Strategic and International Studies, 1992).

8. Charles L. Schultze, "Paying The Bills," in Henry Aaron and Charles L. Schultze, eds., *Setting Domestic Priorities: What Can Government Do?* (Brookings, 1992), pp. 295–318.

9. Schultze, *Memos to the President*, pp. 240–41.

10. Few economists believe, however, that a sustained rise in the nation's rate of saving and investment could boost the growth rate indefinitely. In the very long run, say, over a period longer than fifty years, the rate of growth depends on the rate of improvement in the technical efficiency of production. But over the next three or four decades, a sustained rise in the investment rate will produce faster economic growth.

11. Robert Eisner, *How Real Is The Federal Deficit?* (Free Press, 1986).

12. Allan H. Meltzer, "Worry about Under-Investment, Not Deficits," *Wall Street Journal*, March 17, 1992, p. A14.

13. As a share of GDP, interest on the federal debt rose from 2 percent in fiscal year 1980 to 3.5 percent in fiscal year 1991, an increase of 1.4 percentage points. By comparison, the total deficit as a share of GDP increased during the same period from 2.8 percent to 4.8 percent, a rise of 2 percentage points.

14. This argument was advanced in Robert J. Barro, "Are Government Bonds Net Wealth?" *Journal of Political Economy*, vol. 82 (November–December 1974), pp. 1095–1117. Martin J. Bailey made the same argument a decade earlier in *National Income and the Price Level: A Study in Macrotheory* (McGraw-Hill, 1962), pp. 154–77.

15. *Budget of the United States Government, Fiscal Year 1993*, part three-35–three-38.

16. Fred Block and Robert L. Heilbroner, "The Myth of a Savings Shortage," *American Prospect*, no. 9 (Spring 1992), pp. 101–06.

17. Capital gains can create some real resources for investment if the appreciated assets are sold to foreign residents. This consideration does not appear to be important in the 1980s, however. Net investment in the United States declined as a percentage of national income, even including the investment that was financed with the resources of foreigners.

18. See J. Bradford De Long and Lawrence H. Summers "Equipment Investment and Economic Growth," *Quarterly Journal of Economics*, vol. 106 (May 1991), pp. 445–502, and their more recent paper "Equipment Investment and Economic Growth: How Strong Is the Nexus?" *Brookings Papers on Economic Activity*, 1992:2.

19. At the very end of its 1992 session, Congress passed a bill, later vetoed by President Bush, introducing new tax incentives for investors in commercial real estate. Some of these incentives had been removed by the 1986 Tax Reform Act. We oppose this kind of costly tax preference for commercial real estate investment.

20. Robert E. Hall and Dale W. Jorgenson, "Application of the Theory of Optimum Capital Accumulation," in Gary Fromm, ed., *Tax Incentives and Capital Spending* (Brookings, 1971), p. 59. The Long Amendment, effective during 1962 and 1963, eliminated the credit from the cost basis of an asset for purposes of depreciation and thus reduced the effective rate of the credit by approximately 1 percentage point. These provisions were repealed in 1964.

21. Joseph A. Pechman, *Federal Tax Policy*, 4th ed. (Brookings, 1983), p 154. Pechman does qualify the statement, however, by adding that the sizable incentive applies on the assumption that the corporate income tax is not shifted through higher prices.

22. In 1991, $416 billion was spent on producers' durable equipment. If all producers paid income tax, a 5 percent credit would therefore translate into a cost of $20.8 billion. Our estimated cost of $15 billion reflects an assumption that some portion of equipment investment is made by firms that pay no corporate taxes. Meanwhile, total corporate income tax receipts for fiscal 1991 were $96 billion, which suggests that the average corporate income tax would have to be increased by approximately 5 percentage points (or by 15 percent) to offset any revenue loss from the ITC.

23. See James M. Poterba, "Capital Gains Tax Policy toward Entrepreneurship," *National Tax Journal*, vol. 42 (September 1989), pp. 375–89.

24. Schultze, *Memos to the President*, p. 281.

25. David Alan Aschauer, "Is Public Expenditure Productive?" *Journal of Monetary Economics*, vol. 23 (March 1989), pp. 177–200; Aschauer, "Infrastructure, Productivity, and Economic Growth: Fair Dinkum?" Bates College, June 1992; and Alicia H. Munnell, "Why Has Productivity Growth Declined? Productivity and Public Investment," *New England Economic Review* (Federal Reserve Bank of Boston, January–February 1990), pp. 3–22.

26. The largest component of public capital consists of highways and streets, making up almost one-third of the total in 1990, and the stock of this component fell from 18.2 percent of GNP in 1970 to 13.3 percent in 1990. The next largest component of public capital consists of buildings, making up almost 29 percent of the total in 1990, and this component fell from 15 percent of GNP in 1970 to 12 percent in 1990. The remaining components of public capital consist of sewer systems, water supply facilities, mass transit systems, airports, electric and gas facilities, and conservation and development facilities and equipment. None of these components is particularly large in itself, but together they comprised 38 percent of total public capital in 1990. However, this part of the public capital stock has fallen only slightly, from 15.8 percent of GNP in 1970 to 15.5 percent in 1990. See Winston and Bosworth, "Public Infrastructure," p. 269.

27. David A. Aschauer, "Public Investment and Productivity Growth in the Group of Seven," *Economic Perspectives*, vol. 13 (Federal Reserve Bank of Chicago, September–October 1989), pp. 17–25.

28. Some evidence of "reverse causality" in the relation between public capital and productivity is given in Douglas Holtz-Eakin, "Private Output, Government Capital and the Infrastructure Crisis," discussion paper 394, Columbia University, 1988. Moreover, Charles R. Hulten and Robert M. Schwab find only a weak correlation between public investment and regional manufacturing productivity. See "Public Capital Formation and the Growth of Regional Manufacturing Industries," *National Tax Journal*, vol. 4 (December 1991), pp. 121–34.

29. See Henry J. Aaron, "Discussion," in Alicia H. Munnell, ed., *Is There a Shortfall in Public Capital Investment?* (Federal Reserve Bank of Boston, 1990), pp. 51–63; and Charles R. Hulten and Robert M. Schwab, "Is There Too Little Public Capital?" paper prepared for the American Enterprise Institute conference, Infrastructure Needs and Policy Options for the 1990s, February 1991.

30. W. David Montgomery, Michael D. Deich, and Elizabeth A. Pinkston, "Lessons from the Past, Opportunities for the Future: The Changing Role of Public Investment in Economic Growth," paper prepared for the Colloquium on the Nation's Infrastructure Policy, Washington, D.C., November 17, 1989.

31. Congressional Budget Office, *How Federal Spending for Infrastructure and Other Public Investments Affects the Economy*, (1991).

32. See Winston and Bosworth, "Public Infrastructure."

33. This argument needs to confront countervailing forces however. New auto plants by both Japanese and U.S. auto companies have been built in Ohio or Tennessee, away from the traditional auto cluster in Michigan. The development of electronic communications and overnight delivery has greatly speeded up the ability of people to work together even when they are not located close to one another.

34. Winston and Bosworth, "Public Infrastructure," pp. 279–80.

35. For example, President Clinton promised during the course of his campaign to have the federal government support the development of high-speed "Maglev" trains and other related transportation projects. But in 1983 the Office of Technology Assessment looked at Maglev trains and other passenger rail technologies and concluded that there were only a very few high-density routes within the United States that should even be considered for such transportation systems. See Office of Technology Assessment, *U.S. Passenger Rail Technologies* (1983). Accordingly, while modest spending for such technologies may be appropriate, a substantial effort does not appear to be worth the cost.

36. Timothy D. Hau, "Congestion Charging Mechanisms: An Evaluation of Current Practice," World Bank, Washington, March 23, 1992.

37. In a typical AVI system, a transponder placed in a vehicle transmits its identification to a roadside antenna. It is possible also to have a light by

the roadway that flashes green if the vehicle has paid up its account. Motorists are thus charged for the use of the road, either when they receive a monthly bill or when they pay in advance.

38. The advantages of the smart-card technology seem particularly compelling in our own metropolitan area, Washington D.C. Tens of thousands of commuters from Maryland and Virginia come into the city each day, even though a modern, underused public transportation system is available. The District of Columbia would be delighted to find a way of obtaining extra revenue from the commuters who use its streets.

39. See Michael E. Porter, *The Competitive Advantage of Nations* (Free Press, 1990).

40. Originally designed to assist only a few distressed urban areas, the Model Cities program gradually expanded to cover 150 cities, each receiving only a fraction of the funding that would have been truly helpful. See Charles L. Schultze, "Industrial Policy: A Dissent," *Brookings Review*, vol. 2 (Fall 1983), pp. 9–10.

41. For a comprehensive survey of new industrial clusters around the United States, see Kevin Kelly and others, "Hot Spots: New Growth Regions Are Blossoming despite the Slump," *Business Week*, October 19, 1992, pp. 80–88.

42. The legislation would have excluded from taxation 50 percent of capital gains on assets held in a zone for at least five years. In addition, it would have provided a $20,000 deduction in the first year of operations for newly purchased equipment; an annual deduction of up to $25,000 for purchases of stock in businesses investing in the zones (up to $250,000 for each person); and a 15 percent credit to employers for wages paid to residents living in the zone, up to an annual maximum of $3,000 per worker. President Bush vetoed the legislation because it included certain tax increases that he opposed.

Chapter Seven: Foreign Trade and Investment

1. Figures from *International Financial Statistics* (August 1992), pp. 56–57; and *Economic Report of the President, February 1992*, table B-100.

2. Figures are from Robert E. Lipsey, "Foreign Direct Investment in the U.S.: Changes over Three Decades: Appendices," NBER working paper 4124A (Cambridge, Mass.: National Bureau of Economic Research, 1992); and *Survey of Current Business*, vol. 72 (January 1992), p. 108, and vol. 72 (August 1992), p. 38.

3. For a survey documenting these results, see Clifford Winston, "Economic Deregulation: Days of Reckoning for Microeconomists," *Journal of Economic Literature* (forthcoming). For evidence of the beneficial effects of deregulation in the trucking and railroad industries in particular, see Clifford M. Winston, *The Economic Effects of Surface Freight Deregulation* (Brookings, 1990). For evidence relating to the productivity benefits of airline deregulation, see Douglas W. Caves and others, "An Assessment of the Efficiency Effects of

U.S. Airline Deregulation via an International Comparison," in Elizabeth E. Bailey, *Public Regulation: New Perspectives on Institutions and Policies* (MIT Press, 1987), pp. 285–320. And for evidence of the benefits from telecommunications deregulation, see Robert W. Crandall, *After the Breakup: U.S. Telecommunications in a More Competitive Era* (Brookings, 1991).

4. Paul R. Krugman, *The Age of Diminished Expectations: U.S. Economic Policy in the 1990s* (MIT Press, 1990), p. 105.

5. Among the leading academic exponents of the view that trade promotes growth are Gene M. Grossman of Princeton and Elhanan Helpman of Tel Aviv University. See their *Innovation and Growth in the Global Economy* (MIT Press, 1991).

6. Lawrence F. Katz and Lawrence H. Summers, "Industry Rents: Evidence and Implications," *Brookings Papers on Economic Activity, Microeconomics, 1989*, pp. 209–75. (Hereafter *BPEA, Micro*.)

7. See World Bank, *World Development Report 1991* (Oxford University Press, 1991), pp. 98–99; Sebastian Edwards, "Trade Orientation, Distortions and Growth in Developing Countries," NBER working paper 3716 (May 1991); and James R. Tybout, "Linking Trade and Productivity: New Research Directions," *World Bank Economic Review*, vol. 6 (May 1992), pp. 189–212.

8. Michael Dertouzous and others, *Made in America: Regaining the Productive Edge* (MIT Press 1989).

9. Even with these improvements, American automobile manufacturers have not been able to prevent a steady erosion of brand loyalty on the part of American consumers. See Fred Mannering and Clifford Winston, "Brand Loyalty and the Decline of American Automobile Firms," *BPEA, Micro, 1991*, pp. 67–103.

10. A total of 118 industries, classified at the four-digit SIC level, comprise the sample. The productivity data for these industries were drawm from Charles Ardolini and Mark Sieling, "Productivity Trends in Selected Industries," *Business Economics*, October 1991, pp. 26–30. The data for export and import penetration, which run only through 1986, are taken from unpublished data of the Bureau of the Census.

11. The import and export shares are calculated only through 1986, the latest year for which some data were available.

12. The growth-promoting effects of import competition were much more powerful in a statistical sense in the second period than the first. Thus whereas the correlation between the import penetration ratio and productivity growth during the 1973–79 period was 0.13, the correlation coefficient for the 1979–88 period was 0.44. The second correlation coefficient was statistically significant.

13. For a theoretical demonstration of this proposition, see Richard E. Baldwin, "On The Growth Effects of Import Competition," NBER working paper 4045 (April 1992).

14. Michael Salinger, "The Concentration-Margins Relationship Reconsidered," *BPEA, Micro, 1990*, pp. 287–321.

15. Contributors to the contestability literature include Elizabeth E. Bailey, "Contestability and the Design of Regulatory and Antitrust Policy," *American*

Economic Review, vol. 71, (May 1981, *Papers and Proceedings, 1980*), pp. 178–83; and William J. Baumol, John C. Panzar, and Robert D. Willig, *Contestable Markets and the Theory of Industry Structure* (Harcourt Brace, 1982).

16. Joseph E. Stiglitz, "Technological Change, Sunk Costs, and Competition," *BPEA, Micro, 1987*, pp. 883–937.

17. Under the International Investment and Trade in Services Survey Act, foreign direct investment is defined as the ownership by a foreign person or business of at least 10 percent of the voting equity of a firm located in the United States. Before 1974 the minimum equity threshold was 25 percent. Bureau of the Census, *Statistical Abstract of the United States, 1984* (1984), pp. 818–19.

18. For example, a recent study has documented the growth-promoting effects of U.S. investment in Mexico. Magnus Blomstrom and Edward N. Wolff, "Multinational Corporations and Productivity Convergence in Mexico," NBER working paper 3141 (October 1989).

19. This plant has been recognized by *Industry Week* as one of the twelve most outstanding manufacturing facilities—in productivity and quality—in the United States. See John H. Sheridan, "America's Best Plants," *Industry Week*, October 15, 1990, p. 40.

20. James B. Treece, "The Partners," *Business Week*, February 10, 1992, p. 102.

21. David Woodruff, "Chrysler May Actually Be Turning the Corner," *Business Week*, February 10, 1992, p. 32.

22. Kim B. Clark, W. Bruce Chew and Takahiro Fujimoto, "Product Development in the World Auto Industry," *BPEA, Micro, 1987*, pp. 729–771.

23. See Bradley A. Stertz, "Driving Back: Chrysler Is Making Solid Progress despite Turmoil over Who Will Succeed Iaococa," *Wall Street Journal*, March 3, 1992, pp. A1, A7.

24. "The Marriage of True Minds," *Economist*, September 19, 1992, p. 79.

25. Indeed, in 1992 alone, joint ventures were formed by three major consortia—IBM/Siemens/Toshiba, Advanced Micro Devices/Fujitsu and Intel/Sharp—to develop and manufacture advanced-memory computer chips. Similarly, U.S. companies have engaged in numerous joint ventures with foreign steel companies, principally those from Japan, to gain access to both capital and state-of-the-art steelmaking technology.

26. Among the other factors that account for the low reported rates of return by foreign-based multinationals are the relative newness of their investments here and the willingness to accept subpar returns to gain access to the U.S. market, to protect against exchange rate risk, and to ensure access to the U.S. market in the event imports are restricted. See *Survey of Current Business*, vol. 71 (August 1991), pp. 44–45.

27. However, it would almost certainly be counterproductive to base the taxes of foreign companies on average profits earned by U.S. companies. This tax treatment would violate U.S. obligations in international tax treaties that guard against discrimination. Moreover, such efforts would be likely to provoke foreign retaliation against U.S. companies that operate abroad.

28. Lipsey, "Foreign Direct Investment," p. 13.

29. Edward M. Graham and Paul R. Krugman, *Foreign Direct Investment in the United States*, 2d ed. (Washington: Institute for International Economics, 1991).

30. Lester C. Thurow, *Head to Head: The Coming Economic Battle among Japan, Europe, and America* (Morrow, 1992), pp. 200–01.

31. General Accounting Office, *U.S. Business Access to Certain Foreign State-of-the-Art Technology: A Report to the Honorable Lloyd Bentsen, U.S. Senate*, GAO/NSIAD-91-278 (September 1991).

32. The Justice Department has nevertheless announced a more aggressive policy of pursuing antitrust actions against foreign companies whose practices may harm competition in this country.

33. Raymond Vernon, "Are Foreign-owned Subsidiaries Good for the United States?" Group of Thirty occasional papers 37, Washington, 1992, p. 9.

34. See Jagdish Bhagwati, "Regionalism and Multilateralism: An Overview," discussion paper 603 (Columbia University, 1992).

35. Technically, subsidies are subject to penalties only if they are provided for exporting or have the effect of assisting exports. Dumping duties are imposed where foreign goods are sold in the United States at prices below those sold in the home or third markets (or where such prices are not usable, below the cost of production).

36. I. M. Destler, *American Trade Politics*, 2d ed. (Washington: Institute for International Economics, 1992), pp. 166–68.

37. See Richard Boltuck and Robert E. Litan, eds., *Down in the Dumps: Administration of the Unfair Trade Laws* (Brookings, 1991). Among other things, the dumping calculations made by the Department of Commerce fail to average sale prices in both the home country and domestic markets (even though it has the legislative authority to do so) and to consider as unlawful sales below average cost but above marginal cost, a perfectly rational practice followed by domestic competitors but outlawed for foreign competitors. In addition, the calculations ignore the fact that certain subsidies may only provide a windfall to owners of foreign companies without influencing their production or pricing decisions and thus without having any effect on the U.S. market.

38. Thus, for example, the system for dumping could permit, among other things, averaging of both foreign and domestic sales prices and sales below average cost (but not below marginal cost); for subsidies, the system would penalize foreign imports only to the extent any subsidies they received actually harmed U.S.-made competing products. In addition, in deciding whether any dumping or subsidization causes "material injury" to U.S. producers, the International Trade Commission could be directed to weigh any losses to consumers that imposition of dumping or countervailing duties would cause.

39. For evidence of the extent of the practical restrictiveness of the Japanese market, see Robert Z. Lawrence, "Efficient or Exclusionist? The Import Behavior of Japanese Corporate Groups," *BPEA, Micro, 1991*, pp. 311–30.

40. Unemployment insurance in the United States provides laid-off work-

ers with compensation payments for up to twenty-six weeks while they search for new jobs. Weekly benefits are typically about half of weekly wages on the worker's last job, except in the case of highly paid workers, whose benefits are limited to a maximum weekly payment, which varies across states. Trade adjustment assistance (or TAA) is special compensation provided to workers who have lost their jobs as a result of increased imports. The program provides weekly cash allowances, training benefits, and job search and relocation allowances. The weekly cash payments are an extension of regular unemployment insurance benefits, payable upon exhaustion of unemployment insurance for up to seventy-eight weeks of unemployment insurance and TAA benefits combined. Weekly TAA allowances are paid conditional upon a worker's continued participation in an approved training program. In the 1970s and early 1980s, benefits could be received even by workers who were not participating in a training program. Moreover, the weekly allowances were higher than regular unemployment insurance benefits.

41. Robert Z. Lawrence and Robert E. Litan, *Saving Free Trade: A Pragmatic Approach* (Brookings, 1986), p. 56.

Chapter Eight: An Agenda for Growth and Equity

1. Robert M. Solow, "On Theories of Unemployment," *American Economic Review*, vol. 70 (March 1980), p. 2.

Index